DISPLACED

A RURAL LIFE

JOHN KINSELLA

DISPLACED

A RURAL LIFE

JOHN KINSELLA

MELBOURNE, AUSTRALIA
www.transitlounge.com.au

First published 2020
Transit Lounge Publishing

Cover image: Wendy Kinsella
Cover and book design: Peter Lo
Author image: Chris Williams

Printed in Australia by McPherson's Printing Group

A cataloguing-entry is available from the
National Library of Australia: trove.nla.gov.au

ISBN: 978-1-925760-47-7

To Tracy, Tim, and family across time and place,
in all its variations ...

I wish to acknowledge the traditional custodians and owners of country I write – the only 'ownership' of land I recognise.

It's too easy to begin with photographs taken before you were aware of what was happening. You're just there, with people who you'll gradually fit into a family jigsaw puzzle, some much sooner than others, cradled in your mother's arms, a homestead, bare paddocks that in a black-and-white photo look beige and sepia and sunwashed. Emptied.

But let's not begin with a photo. Later it will be relevant to your sense of place, but that'll be much later. When it comes to those times you want to retrieve, to make sense of something you're part of but also outside. And that photo won't make sense, because people – your auntie and uncle and cousins – fill dry places in the corners of the image, with lawn and lemon trees and mandarin trees and apricot trees all watered with a bloody discharge pumped from an earth-walled dam, one of maybe ten across the farm they called Wheatlands. Time messes with technologies; the photo fades into something beyond deceptions of 'colour', beyond specificities. It is an act.

Our fifteen-year-old son, Tim, is home from his distant school and unwell and calling out that there's a red-capped robin attacking a much larger fan-tailed cuckoo, which is strange because red-capped robins make cup nests and fan-tailed cuckoos invade the domed nests of other birds, usually. But he and I have learnt after so many years living at Jam Tree Gully that nothing is precisely as the nature guides say. There is a different science at work here, a science specific to *here*. Science is blurred and figurative as much as it is precise and utilitarian. There's a lot of wonder, there are many irregularities of growth, behaviour and loss. As the weather patterns change there are weird adjustments, increasing confrontation with what's normal and abnormal.

But the fan-tailed cuckoo, which only arrived yesterday, *is* watching the robins' mating rituals, watching and waiting for signs of nesting. It is being repelled, for the time being. Does it know they make the 'wrong' nests? It is a young bird. But an old head on young shoulders? No doubt it knows something we don't.

So, the fan-tailed cuckoo is a nest invader, a parasitic nester, especially favouring the nests of splendid blue wrens and yellow-rumped thornbills, wise little birds that make false chambers in their structures to lure such invaders into *nowhere*, into false spaces to lay an egg that will go cold, and sit unwanted next to the chamber of birth and growth and fledging. Parallel worlds. But when the cuckoo succeeds in unravelling the deception, the egg stays and the cuckoo chick will kick out any other nestlings and be raised by the little songbirds, quickly outgrowing its adoptive parents.

With this going on, and being spoken of – chatted about, exclaimed over, weighed up – and with the end of a rainless autumn almost upon us, and the hope of 'big weather' late in the week, in the final days of a European sense of season that doesn't match the *actual* seasons of this stolen country, our water supply wallows down to 7000 litres … with a hope, a vestige of hope, that the dry will end.

And a hope that farmers who have either dry-seeded (the nurturing of dust) or excessively burnt off because they know not what else to do when it's not raining, or because their fathers did so before them, or to 'add trace elements' (to add to the industrial fertiliser program), or because they are preparing for new seed programs, or because the spectre of GM crops has entwined with the flames and a phoenix of patented growth will be conjured … the metaphors are mixed. See the plumes of smoke, the carbon pillars holding up a disturbed blue-ish sky. Indelible. In medias res, this moment tacked on to the prospect of a seasonal disaster – the prospect of drought, which forecasters say won't happen in the west, though it is catastrophic in the east. Maybe the storms *will* come here, bringing trees down, but a green tinge of crops is breaking through the early knockdown herbicides, the only 'rain' the bare ground has had for so very many months.

As we reject photos of a past that made this, too, we think of the destruction of remnant bushland by stealth (with fencing, or burning that just happens to 'get away'). All the contemporary tricks of ongoing colonialism. But the cuckoo is a native bird and doesn't work as a pastoral allegory. Neither do the introduced foxes and rabbits and cats, the 'feral' – *destroyers* of this ancient land. It's so easy to blame them. That's what you learn in the paradox of non-Indigenous presence: the allegories just don't work. And so we'll leave the photos – never quite working, not really, especially the old ones. And all too easy.

~

From the north-east corner of the block where we live, which we call Jam Tree Gully, or JTG, you look out across the valley, over the creasings of hills and paddocks, across the stands of wandoo on high ground, and the remnants of York gum and jam tree bushland. A few houses come into view, but not many, and there's the odd farm shed and windmill, but what overwhelms is the curve of sky as it intersects with hills, valley and planar surfaces. Behind you, as you stand looking west, are the Victoria Plains, but they're over the top of the hill Jam Tree Gully sits on, and you can't see them until you climb to the crest. But looking west, I literally draw a breath and reach my arms out and take it all in – not to possess it, not to draw it into myself, but to be absorbed by it, to fall into it. I can never be fully part of this land, stolen as it is – as part of Noongar Boodja – but I can stand in awe of its resilience, and the hope and spiritual strength of the land. It is not mine, but land is never to be owned and will accept or reject you in ways you're not even aware of. I feel a connection though I know I unbelong. But I also feel fused with the entire planet, and that is part of who I am, as there's nothing else I can be. Respect, acknowledgement, and letting the land have the say, not the exploiters. Up there, I *am*.

~

I often try to think of how Jam Tree Gully would have fared if I had been the same child but growing up here instead. I was specifically influenced by two women growing up – two very different women – so I would still have had a kind of sensitivity to a different approach to life and dwelling. And I would have liked nothing more than wandering and seeing the birds, and the plants, and the kangaroos and goannas, and writing about it all. But the hilly aspect, and the violence of other kids in the district, would have made me defensive and introverted. I would have fortified myself, dug in, which would have made things so much worse. Even among other kids, I always felt isolated. I was close to my younger brother, Stephen, but lived in my own world – a world I constructed, in which I would be in control, would be able to determine my own fate.

Which brings me to the impact my childhood had on the environments of the places I lived, in Western Australia. A small life with big consequences, so often the tale – one of separation of cause and effect. Not a case of ill will towards nature – never that – but taking a long while to understand that the world I constructed often detrimentally affected the real world, the natural world.

I loved animals, but I hunted and fished. I 'respected' nature and wandered around reciting poems to trees and birds. And yet I also tore down branches and dug out undergrowth to make cubbies, and rode trail bikes through scrub, and committed other acts of thoughtless damage. Tim is very different – he is careful, respectful, and would never damage to entertain himself. He has been thoughtful about these things since he was a very young child. And he has more knowledge than I had. I wonder about these differences, given that I loved the bush no less at his age. One difference is that I was caught up in a fantasy of noble warfare.

I was extremely bullied as a child. The hospitalisation, the medical treatments, the psychological scarring were and remain realities. Being nicknamed 'Dictionary' was no compliment. I tried to extricate myself from this tangled web of abuse, with the help of my mother, but it was almost impossible. One of the consequences, I believe, looking back now, was a fascination for all things military. Not to attack my attackers, but to strategically and tactically out-think them. I was interested in theory, in plans, in methods. And fused with my love of the bush, of the farm, a strange kind of colonialised displacement occurred. Out in the bush I would roam with my rifle, 'surviving' – avoiding enemies, 'living off the land', prepping. It was encoding itself. And that encoding meant 'collateral damage'. I see how the same kind of fusion might default into violence towards others, but it never did for me. In fact, as I grew older and wrestled with my own aggressive tendencies, my own growing political anger at injustice, I slowly shed my aggressive impulses, or at least controlled them. And I'd never seen attack as the best form of defence – I had always been about removing myself, protecting my ground. Except that it wasn't my ground. I was realising that I was part of a colonial invasion force, and I belonged nowhere. What could I do about it? I wandered, displaced as an addict, and as someone trying to undo my own identity.

~

There is a vanity of ethics which comes out of a satisfaction that one is making the correct ethical choices, that one is moving in the best possible direction towards repair. Ethics is an array of variables that suits both essential values and a zeitgeist acceptance of what is pertinent or relevant to the wellbeing of others, the self, and the world around them. It is imperfect and it is contingent on those controlling the discussion around values. Of course, we are all part of that discussion and we all overlap in what we do and don't consider 'important' in issues of respect and justice. But I strongly feel humans know the right and wrong of things, however many degrees circumstances shift the 'pre' and 'post', the above and below. However we calibrate our behaviours, there are certain absolutes we work from – murder is wrong, theft is wrong, deception is wrong and so on. Circumstances will always offer people ways of shifting the grounds to 'permit' exceptions, but such exceptions constantly need to be defended because they rely on a wrong.

I personally didn't feel the need to turn to religion or philosophy or any other system to know this right and wrong, but I accept that some people require such assurances and certainties. And I come out of a social structure (and indeed religion) that has had such sureties as its basis, so I cannot say I have ever really stood outside the society I critique. But at Jam Tree Gully I feel enough distance from social structures to at least reflect and consider what might constitute an ethics. And though I 'unbelong', and though it is 'home' but not 'mine' (which it's not and I do not want it to be), it is a space of consideration and conservation. A place to speak out from but also, with an open door, to welcome other ways of talking, seeing and experiencing.

I love animals, and I love people, and I respect all life. But it is not mine to tell people how to live, nor how to conduct their relationships with animal or human. But I do know the biosphere is collapsing, and have known this since I was a teenager, and I have committed my writing life and my lived life to showing a different way of interacting with the environment, and being respectful of difference and 'tradition', is possible. Stephen has his way, too. His wife, Dzu, has hers. My mother has hers. Guru has his. Tracy has hers. Tim has his. You have yours. I have mine.

My sense of wrong and right is unlikely to shift. That I do know. I just heard that my brother got bogged on a gravel road early this morning and had to rely on a farmer to pull his car free with a tractor. Stephen offered the guy fifty bucks for helping out, but the guy refused. No doubt he and my brother are very different people, but need in the circumstances – it was a very isolated place – brought the best kind of ethics into play. An ethics without vanity, an ethics that works for no material or even psychological reward beyond knowing it was the right thing to do.

~

What I write here and now will be like nothing I've written before. It can't be – experience is cumulative but also fast and decisive. I see *different* as a constant. I see change as a constant, but one I so often want to undo. But I don't want to change back into damaging ways, I want to change out of them. Shifts into gears that gearboxes can't have. To understand the machine of occupation and dispossession so as to think outside it, to reject it.

Outside, the sounds of the valley are birds and distant machinery, machinery that might come closer. And I see a mouse that might actually be a rare western hopping mouse taking shelter in rocks around the base of a York gum near the house. I *walk* – it's my body's inclination, its desiring of place. Machinery edges in. I stand in front of bulldozers, I yell at them. I never whisper to them – I don't have that skill. But I know tractors inside and out, and I use that knowledge.

Ploughing. That was one of my angles into machinery. And the generator for electricity for the house. And the pumps to bring water from the dam, and from bores we no longer use because of damage to the aquifer. But these are different ruralities feeding into one rural life, a rural life across immensely different geographies.

And trucks – big machines. My father was a truck mechanic born in the bush at Gleneagle (place of the wedge-tailed eagles; an overwriting of a Noongar naming, but only part of a story of colonisation – on state forestry maps the entire district is still named Kinsella). *His* father was a state forester, his mother a woman born in the Hills, who gave birth to a daughter and a son in the Darling Range under the jarrah canopy, where the eagles nest. Before I philosophically and ideologically rejected earthmoving and other heavy machinery as an essential part of life, I was fascinated by it. The same will apply to computers. I was a very early user of computers, and designed my own in the seventies. But I eventually rejected most if not all digital technology for many years. I lived in shacks, on a commune, on the edge of a forest on a large farm called Happy Valley. Throughout my childhood, my father oscillated between the mines in the Pilbara, the saltworks near Carnarvon and Karratha, the mines of Kalgoorlie, and a massive farm near Mullewa, managing 30,000 acres and servicing the giant Steiger Panther, John Deere and Case tractors. On the verge of my teenage years and living with my mother near the Swan River, I would journey with my brother to see him. It's a complex picture of connection and disconnection. Wheat grew on Wheatlands farm and the mines kept working.

I learnt to plough on Wheatlands, and to seed, and I worked the wheatbins at harvest. All of these experiences would eventually feed a radical rurality. I separated off … from what?

~

Salinity. It keeps ghosting my words, my days. It is the dominant element of my life. I started a literary journal called *Salt*, which became a publisher called Salt. It is the most recurrent image in my writing – its catastrophic beauty, its necessity to life and the damage to life it does, its being a natural part of the environment, but which when damage is done to existing vegetation can rise up and consume all. It is the loss of livelihoods but so often provoked by the making of those livelihoods. It is a paradox. Salt crystals coat my thinking, my seeing.

As a child, I went out onto the salt to be on Mars, or really on Mercury. To be exposed to the dangerous burn of the sun reflecting off the salt crystal formations, to let my imagination flee my body. Who I might be was projected into the crystals and prismed out into spider's webs between bleached deadwood, or picked by plovers lancing through the crunch. I wanted to be alone. I like people, and enjoy talking and sharing, but (like Tracy, like Tim) I also like my aloneness. Walking outdoors, merging with the non-human, and in doing so discovering more about humanity. It's nothing original or stunning but it's part of who I am, and the desolation of salinity is warped into this seeing and unseeing, this belonging-unbelonging.

There was an occasion when, as a child, I got sunstroke on the salt; I could have died. The house that had been eaten away by salinity was hallucinated back into life, and I saw 'salty trinkets' connect to their carriers, their 'owners', and I also saw what I shouldn't have seen – the torment of the people whose land it was. I never fully recount my childhood visions – they are terrifying to me even now. When we lived in the old colonial mansion opposite the prison in Geraldton where Mum was teaching (the one that had been the nurses' quarters but became teachers' housing), I watched that shadow bolt down the long corridor, as if shrinking from who I was or might be ... and that terrified me about myself, my being there. But on the salt, I also saw visions of what had been without torment, and what could be repaired. I loved helping my uncle and cousins to plant trees, working in from those edges.

Aloneness is part of me, but back at JTG on my own yesterday it just didn't work. Tracy and Tim are so entirely part of the healing of that place, the interim moment of repair before belonging is restored across JTG and all the land (how long will it take?), that I felt lacking, inadequate to the task of ensuring all was well. Aloneness cannot heal land and community – but together we can. Such platitudes are easy to make, and utter, but this is something visceral to me.

As a kid, I would often cut myself on sharp pieces of deadwood down on the salt. The sun, the salt itself, the winds rolling across the bare scalds, would whittle wood to needle points. That wood from maybe fifty years earlier, when lower, wetter and marshy areas of the farm were vegetated and fuming with animal and bird life. Cleared to crop, and then waterlogged, and then uncroppable as the salt rose. The farmer, distraught at the labouring and the hope and the brief profit, then total loss. Alone with family, then neighbours, then the bank wanting loans for seed to be repaid. It's a tragic story. But working together, the land replanted, and hopes rising. And then the dangerous question – how can reclaimed land be used? How can it be made profitable? Some land just has to be left alone, left to be what *it* can be alone.

Tracy and I got back from a trip to the city late last night. We were down at the Crow bookshop for the launch of a young poet's first full-length book. I gave the launch speech, and we caught up with friends we hadn't seen for a while. When going down to the city (it is a couple of hours' drive south of Jam Tree Gully), we usually stay overnight in a motel. As Tim is away for a week staying with his uncle and auntie up in Geraldton, a coastal-rural town about 450 k's north, where Stephen and I went to high school, we thought we'd drive back home. It was raining, and the trucks starting out on their thunderous journey across the continent were thick on the road though it was 10 p.m. With a moon rising thickly indigo through rainclouds, it was a 'roo night'. We drove slowly, and carefully. We have been in many dangerous driving situations over the years and such nights bring them all back in a rush.

I do not like cars – I do not like their role in the biosphere's destruction, in capitalist consumerism, in the damage they do to people and animals. Insects die in their tens of thousands with every long rural journey. Kangaroos are hit, as deer were hit during the five years we lived in central Ohio. I do not like the cult of death that cars are. There is no public transport where we are, and loathe cars as I do, we keep a small one as we have no other choice ... not an excuse, but an acknowledgement of fact.

About a year ago we were in a serious car accident coming down to the city from JTG. Going through the Hills town of Mundaring on the Great Eastern Highway, a massive Western Star prime mover suddenly switched lanes and drove into us. I used a technique my father had told me as a child: turn against the pivot point and you'll likely survive. As 8 foot of bull bar and front end sliced through the car, I turned the steering wheel towards the truck and we spun across in front of it and out of the way. I was injured, we were all in shock, and the car was written off. *Written off* – even in moments of catastrophe a financial consumer descriptor of loss, a euphemism, almost, for the near-death experience of the car's contents: people.

Another incident that led to a write-off (and I wrote a poem, 'Written Off', about it), was when I hit a kangaroo after the Lakes, heading towards the town of York, where we were living just after returning from Ohio. I saw spotlights in the forest to the left, and the instant I realised that hunters were hurtling along a bush track in their utility vehicles festooned with *spotties*, likely pursuing a mob of roos, a boomer jumped onto the road in front of the car. The bonnet was entirely staved in, but I managed to angle the car off the road and it ground to a halt. My daughter was in the back. It was dark and I told her to lie down on the back seat while I got out to see if I could help the roo, and to inspect the damage. The boomer was gone, hurled off the road. There was only the light of the moon; spotlighters hunt on moonlit nights because the roos are especially active. And I told my daughter to hide because I feared the hunters and our isolation. So often alcohol is part of these expeditions in the forest for illegal shooting. I feared their behaviour because I know who they are. I *know* their behaviour. I detest guns and campaign against them, but I have known guns and gun culture – I grew up close to it, or never far from it. And that's part of this story, and why no guns and no residues of that culture are part of JTG, though we often hear shooting around the area, and often see and feel its effects.

Guns in one form or another – and they have had many forms – will appear in this story again and again. That I would never have to mention them would be a joy to me, but it's a joy I – we – can't have … not yet, anyway. Gun culture is not the sole preserve of America; it is endemic to varying degrees around the world, as I have traversed and experienced it. I am a pacifist because I have seen what guns can do, and what the consequences of violence are. Fortunately, my descent into alcoholism and addiction did not coincide with my interest in guns. In fact, as I became more immersed in the hell of addiction, I turned more and more *against* guns. So my angers and my irresponsibilities did not connect with weapons. I have been sober for almost a quarter of a century now, and that sobriety brings insights into the realities of a rural world in which 'living on the land' or having the land taken away is so often fused with depression and trauma. For a farmer to lose land to a bank after bad seasons can lead to suicide; the dispossession of land from an entire people can be cataclysmic.

But one of the main learning experiences of my life has been witnessing the resilience and strength of Indigenous cultures in maintaining their connection to country, and working to gain their cultural and material rights in relation to their land, their stolen land.

This *is* Ballardong Noongar land. It is stolen land and it needs to be returned. And then a discussion has to take place on how coexistence might work. I feel a deep belonging, but also an unbelonging because of this injustice. The question asked by many who care about the consequences of colonisation is, Where else can we go? But rather, the question is, How can we coexist justly and fairly? It is possible. Migration and respect for Aboriginal land rights are not contradictory – it's just that the discussion has to begin with Aboriginal people as to how the land might be respected.

My family and I have been lucky to have lived all around the world for long stretches, and we consider we have many homes. I still consider Gambier and Mount Vernon in Ohio homes, and certainly Cambridge, England, and Schull in Ireland. The rural aspects, the tensions over 'property', are familiar to me wherever we have lived. I know how to talk with farmers, even when I frequently and sometimes profoundly disagree with their approaches to agriculture – I oppose clearing of vegetation, I oppose the use of chemicals, I oppose monocultures, I oppose guns, I oppose private property, and, most challengingly, I oppose the exploitation of animals. It would seem we'd have little ground in common.

But, actually, we do, and it is with farmers and rural communities that I feel most kinship. I do not wish to violently change their ways – I wish to talk, to write about it, to speak poetry about it. I wish to converse. That's my kind of radicalism.

I am the anarchist you can live next door to and get on with. I will help out when need be, and I will suggest other ways things can be done. And I will listen, no matter how strong our differences.

And this is why it so upsets me that someone 'skunked' my office at Kenyon College (using a pungent chemical similar to skunk spray) because of my opposition to the second Gulf War. I still consider Kenyon College in Gambier, Ohio, home, and though I was immediately aware the contamination had been carried out by someone from outside the college – and I try to understand the yellow-ribbon pain, the view of 'protecting home and country', even indirectly – it really damaged my sense of how far the notion of free speech really extends. I am against all war – I am a pacifist. I don't validate one war over another. Among the books that were damaged in this anonymous protest was *The Norton Anthology of Poetry* – maybe it was open on my desk at the poems of W. S. Merwin, and I guess the irony speaks for itself. I think of Merwin trying to repair land and biosphere on a patch of land in Hawaii, and of positions of conscience. My door is never closed to differences of opinion, never closed to conversations. Poems are conversations. We could have swapped poems or yarns or opinions instead of it getting to this, surely? I like to talk, I like to hear what people have to say and why they hold the opinions they do. I am enriched by listening, and I have things to share, too.

Another telling incident of *unbelonging* in a place we call(ed) home, which speaks across the globe – another incident or situation that kept us distant from 'settling in', of feeling *comfort* in belonging – happened just over a year before the office poisoning. Across our time in central Ohio, we lived in four separate houses; this incident took place in the third of those houses, which was located near the centre of Gambier village.

A guy was doing some work in the house and we got chatting. No, this demands the present tense, as it will always be in the here and now for me. We are chatting about farming, about GM crops. We actually agree, and I am astonished. Or am I slipping here, back into the past, and remodelling it in the here and now – wish fulfilment? I am opposing genetic modification, and he is politely listening, not giving an opinion. Weird. But I am talking with this guy and the conversation turns from seeding methods to survivalism to bunkers. Bunkers, seriously. I recall a translator I knew who told me her husband had kept her imprisoned in a bunker out in an American rural community before she escaped. And he asks me, Do you know how to handle a gun? I roll *handle* around in my head with disgust, as I know all the inflections, and I say, Well, I used to. And he brightens up and says, Well, it's like riding a bike, you never forget. And I say, That's true, you never forget. And I am about to say how much I deplore my knowledge of them when he bursts in with, You should come out to our place one weekend – we have a small farm, you know, a couple of hundred acres, but it has hills and woods and is among farms of like-minded folk … I have a bunker and it's stocked, and I mean stocked, if you know what I mean. We are getting ready, preparing, we know it's going to come down to us or them. And I do know what he means. I know not to trigger things with a '*Who is* us*?* And he rolls on, And we do training every weekend, and neighbours and friends come in and we do target shooting and training for when the time comes. *When the time comes.* I know what that means, too. I don't want to hear more, I want it to stop, but he is so polite and one of the things Tracy and I love about the place is how polite the people are, whatever agendas are working away in the background (or not). People who would shoot you if they considered you the enemy, but would help you no matter what if you're an ally. And most central Ohioans, whatever their background, seem to have a vague idea that as Australians we are 'allies'. And the white military types among them, clinging to their whiteness and their defence of 'values' attached to it, seem to know of bonds forged in the Second World War, and even Vietnam, and riff on that. It's unsettling, but there. But we don't relate to this and I want to extricate myself from the conversation when the guy says, Come out to my vehicle, I want to show you something. I go, I follow. From his glove box he takes a Glock and hands it to me. I don't want to touch it. He says, Go on, go on ... I just acquired it ... beautifully balanced piece. *Piece.* And then he adds, as the piece can't find my wavering hand, The cop says it's a beautiful piece – come on, try it. No, we will never feel 'comfortable', and maybe we shouldn't. Strangely, it shares many things in common with aspects of where we come from. But they are just aspects of complex sociocultural and environmental pictures. And nothing is as simple as a 'picture'.

And the past is lost to the future and in the here and now I sit planning a campaign against the Australian government's desire to become a top-ten arms exporter. And I sit thinking about a Perth academic's defence of games like *Fortnite Battle Royale* and their family 'benefits', and the complete normalisation of violence. What this citified academic doesn't get is that out here in 'the bush' there are kids with dirt bikes, guns and hormonal aggression, encouraged by adults with aggression problems or unresolved childhood aspirations or traumas, who in tuning in to violent games transfer the dynamics to their own 'slice of God's own country', their own 'property' (and beyond), and live out their 'last person standing' fantasies. Maybe you have to have been shot at (I have, once at JTG and once over in York under Walwalinj), beaten up, had death threats, had your child driven from school, and had your water poisoned (as we did when living on the 'commune' in the shack just outside Bridgetown when I was in my early twenties) to comprehend this. When I went into Graves' disease toxicosis and my heart went out of control, it was a 47-degree day and I was trying to stop teenagers and their bikie father from hacking through long, dry grass on dirt bikes in the valley below. I was threatened with a beating that day as well, but my heart got in first.

This is not a fantasy of the other, but of being othered. And as the Dalek City–style towers go up around the district to service the National Broadband Network, erasing remaining patches of bush on high places (sacred to Noongar people), and high-speed broadband means more access to violent games and increased coordination between far-right hate groups, so they manifest outdoors, in real time. It's hard to get, isn't it? Hard to believe? The racist undertones, the xenophobic conditioning that fits with 'family values', this 'us' or 'them', win-at-all-costs, last MAN standing … What the city academic forgets is that for all the awareness that might come via #metoo and other technology-triggered awarenesses that reach out for the few to the many is that the same technology is part of a prepping – an analogue for the 'post-human' configuring of a desolate planet. Zombie stories are plethora for a reason, and even out here we see the desire to zombify all those people who fear, oppose, object to and hate. For many of the tree-haters around here, we are zombies. And not a few families, however disrupted or stressed or united or hard-up or well-off, are in training. We are outside class, suspected by the rich and the poor alike. The rich will always come out best here, owning the means and manipulating the discourse – but the rich want foot soldiers. They want armies. They want consumers. They want power. The poor – and there is poverty around here –

want to survive, and want not to be exploited. Sometimes, they also want or need zombies.

A couple of years ago, at the front gate of one of the big farms of the district, there appeared a bear shaped out of round hay bales. It was huge, and it had been painted with a red hammer and sickle. There was no obvious reason for its appearance other than the well-known fact that the owners of the property were campaigners for a conservative political party. Was the bear irony or had it been built to act as some kind of prophetic warning? It watched the main road constantly, with a bright smile – uncanny, eerie. In the same way that skulls and crossbones, Eureka flags, Southern Cross flags and Australian flags pop up here and there as declarations, so did the bear. It stayed sentinel from harvest right through summer, well into the following year. A silent but vocal form of communication out in the country, where messages are passed in unusual and often indirect ways, while new machinery uses GPS to seed crops, and satellite dishes pick up pay television stations.

As an aside, I think of when our daughter first went to elementary school in Gambier, other children in her class emphatically refused to believe that there was radio in Australia, especially in rural Western Australia. What does this say regarding countries of the mind, what we accept as reality, and what technology represents in terms of 'achievement' and a sense of security that makes one's own community special, and safe?

~

We arrive home late from our excursion to the city, to Perth. Perth. Perth likes to think of itself as the most isolated capital in the world. There are reasons for this. We will be back in Perth regularly. Maybe the picture will become a little clearer? We'll see.

It is late and cold and wet as Tracy opens the top gate and I drive through. I wait for her to close the gate. We have been discussing the planet Venus, and as she gets back in I am searching for Venus to the north-east, out the back window. Venus – independently our favourite heavenly body. Both of us remember nights staring at the stars, and following Venus from earliest evening. Those clouds of sulphuric acid, superheated. I say to Tracy, as we roll down the long curving driveway under the York gum limbs that sometimes act as perches for nighthawks – tawny frogmouths – whose eyes divulge the trauma of headlights, mouths agape, their presence a reminder of what being on this land means … I say to Tracy, We should get more rain tomorrow. Venus and rain. On Monday we had 48.5 millimetres – a deluge. The tank is restored; we got through the long dry. A couple of weeks back we had 30 millimetres. As it translates into capture and storage in the Great Tank, we use about 1 millimetre, as measured by the rain gauge, per day. We have a couple of months of water up our sleeve.

We pull over next to the house, turn off the lights. I say to Tracy, Wait … as I see a car's headlights across the valley, moving fast, 'doing the loop'. We live on a valley loop, closed in, and this is the angst of fire season as there are only the two ends of the horseshoe for escape. *Horseshoe*. We are vegans and have been for many decades and don't keep animals. This was once a horse property, as they call them, and there were sheep here as well. When we came here we had to remove sheep carcasses – sheep that had died after being left here to 'keep the grass down', left here during the dry months and then to rot in the wet as water cascaded down the valley walls. There were skulls mounted on the gate and the property was then called Sleepy Hollow. There were other signs of possession around the place that we removed, those reflections and emanations of colonial property-ising. Of 'ownership'. We do not call JTG a *property*, or *ours*. We are watching over the land, we are opening it to the creatures that live in the vicinity, we are trying to keep out the hunters. It's not a big allotment, but it's bush and granites, and abuts a reserve of 160 acres, which we try to look over as well. Animals know it as a safe haven; there's not a twist of barbed wire, and the electric fences were removed as soon as we arrived. The car working the loop late at night, and fast, means threat. Out here, things happen. Violence. Invasiveness. The ongoing colonialism, the cattle and sheep wars and the opportunism. The car passes above us, and I say, Okay, and we head inside, the clouds having broken apart and the moon working through strong on the wet red-beige earth, on the laterite gravel of the driveway, on the corrugated-iron roof of the house. So far from big industry, but not as far from ideas of America as you'd think, out here, a kind of bizarre Hawthorne effect.

We go inside the house feeling we are no longer under the threat of surveillance, of being observed by the car rounding the loop. Darkness has fallen. About 30 k's from here is Bindoon Army Training Area, and some nights we hear the explosions of artillery shells. The Australian military is always in sync with its American 'cousin'. It is not reassuring, any more than the trainer jets from Pearce Airbase flying low over the valley as if it's empty space. The terra nullius legal deletion of Aboriginal rights of presence, possession, and *language of land* has many ongoing manifestations. Tracy and I shudder at the training jets, at the explosions, and think of the massive advances that Aboriginal cultures made in arts, spirituality and science of place (from the stars to what's deep below the surface) across tens of thousands of years, and we think of how uncivilised Western culture is in the face of the cultures it tried to delete, but failed. Noongar people and other Aboriginal peoples of Australia are strong, resilient, and inspired in their resistance, and all the ongoing exploitations and thefts of cultural heritage won't suppress them. And this resistance is what matters most, here.

The house seems empty without Tim. This will be the longest he's been away from us. He was homeschooled for a few years after heavy bullying by the children of neo-Nazis at the local school, and has spent much time in schools in Ireland, England and Germany, where we have lived over the last decade. But JTG is his home, and he knows every particle, and his love of birds means that he has insights into place that are rare and deeply sincere. He makes lists, he converses, he observes in an active and protective way. Protective without being intrusive. Birds are the heartbeat of *here*. If we don't listen, so much will be lost. Some people in the district shoot and poison birds in vast numbers. Some people burn habitat under the guise of 'burning-off' old stubble, and 'Oops, it got away' as an excuse. Some people install new fencing to clear bushland. Sometimes hundreds of acres vanish and a fine is paid (sometimes), and that's it for habitat. Some people.

We miss Tim. We work together to restore the health of the land. But Tim loves his time with Uncle Stephen.

Stephen, younger than me by two and a half years, is a shearer. His life is rural. His life is inland and coast. He surfs and loves big waves. He met Dzu in Malaysia when he was there on one of his long surfing visits. They spend time in her homeplace of Cherating, and in Geraldton. Stephen loves animals and music, and has since he was a small child. On Wheatlands farm he would always be off with our cousin Ian, studying birds – as an adult, Ian would be one of a team that helped save the noisy scrub-bird from extinction. Ian and Stephen would be watching birds, while cousin Ken and I were camping out at Hathaways bush, checking traps for rabbits at dawn, hunting. We had paired off, and sometimes we would clash over our relationships with the bush, the land, nature. Dynamics would alter as we grew older, but they were formative and embedded in our identities.

When he gets home from the usually distant shearing shed late in the evening, Stephen will play the drums. Tim is a drummer as well. He learns.

It is raining again and it is very late. The wind is picking up a little. I am reading (re-reading, re-reading, re-reading) Blake's 'Auguries of Innocence' and discussing my issues with some of the couplets. Tracy finds another way in to them. This, too, is Jam Tree Gully.

~

The bins. That is, the wheatbins, the bulk silos, the storage granaries for a region. Working on them at twenty-one, twenty-two years of age. Working on the giant bins up at Mingenew in the northern-central wheatbelt. *Rite de passage?* Ha! Horror and complacency – always an explosive mixture.

The wheatbin down the bottom of the north outlet of the loop, down on the road to Bindi Bindi, not far from Dewars Pool, where kingfishers and hawks and black-shouldered kites keep an eye out for prey, is defunct now. Semi-decommissioned, if such a thing is possible. Occasionally stolen cars taken for country joy rides are abandoned there, sometimes burnt out – and we always hope not in summer, as such an act would take out the whole district with fire. We live with the threat of fire like an ongoing state of war waiting to erupt from attrition into full-scale conflict. It doesn't need to be like this, but a cigarette butt thrown out of a car window, or sparks from an angle grinder, or a motorbike exhaust in long grass, or some idiot lighting a fire on a warning day, will send fire sprinting up through the valley and over the hills through paddocks of dry grass and scrub and woodland alike.

About eight years ago south of the town of Toodyay, about 15 k's from JTG, forty-two houses were lost to bushfire. A few months ago, a fire threatened the hill I am writing on, started just down the loop. A few weeks ago on the foolish night of the bonfires, weather warnings in place for high winds, the one that got away uphill. We live with this. We write about it. I once wrote on the manual typewriter, clacking away, as flames approached from only a few kilometres away. Recording my end, but also getting ready to abandon the place.

The wheatbin is often surrounded by roadworking materials: blue metal, gravel, sand. The railway line still runs past in weird mockery, grain trains passing through in the night, laden with wheat from bins further north. But it's more economical for farmers here to truck their grain to the massive receival point in Northam with its tall towers painted with stretching steampunk murals without irony as the Avon Valley is whittled away into an eroded future of exhaustion. Or down to the port grain terminal at Kwinana – a long drive, placing more trucks on the road, trucks that join the proliferating quarry trucks and their heavy loads.

But the bins are at the core of who I am, and this is likely the case for many others who worked them in their youth, even if they only vaguely remember the experience. Students, especially – often going on to their middle-class lives as doctors and engineers. But all walks of life. I shared a room in the Hut (a fibro demountable) with a guy who was joining the army and was in the army reserve, and with a roo shooter (or the son of a roo shooter). 'Quick and good money' for students during the break, but a serious part of the jigsaw puzzle for itinerant labourers. But in itself, *the season*. All who worked as samplers or weighbridge officers had to pass 'the examination' to get a job on the sampling stand, or on the weighbridge. Or working as a labourer on other parts of the bin, to survive the scrutiny of the bin foreman, the hardest process of all. The world of the bin is all, with an attendant foreboding of isolation, vulnerability, and trial by masculinity.

That was back in the early eighties – has it changed much since then? I'd surely hope so. My tale is at least a cautionary one. And really, it's not so much what happened, which was often traumatic and even life-threatening, but what was thought about and discussed in the environment of the hut, in the grounds of the bins, and in excursions outside working hours, and how the experience/s altered the way I thought about the rural, my safe haven, my grounding, my space of creativity.

I'd always known there were many *rurals*, and that ongoing colonisation was expressed in land titles, surveying, farming, and mining leases. I even experienced the *vicariousness* of white farmers employing Aboriginal stookers on land that had been taken from their ancestors – their own land, Noongar land – and the evidence of (some) acknowledgement and respect from some farmers, and put-downs and exploitation by other farmers, and the dignity of the stookers and the pride in their work, and the elders ensuring ongoing connection to country for the young. As a child, I felt something change in me when I handed a water bottle to another kid, the child of stookers, and shyly said a word or two, and had a shy word or two said back. No 'race epiphany', or being lifted out of the colonial machine I was extending, but something without theory – without reality, even – happened. I knew then, and from then on there was no excuse for not being aware.

And the wheatbins clarified this. Maybe it takes hearing a white South African truck driver celebrating shooting 'blacks with an AK-47 as they came down to the waterhole to collect water back in Safrica', and his hooking up with local white racists to burn down a bloke's shack on the edge of town to drive the 'Abos' out, to get things into perspective. And that same white South African driver, who was working for a racist local farmer in Mingenew, 'in cahoots' (their words) with locals to beat me up as I drank beer in the pub, to drive me from the hut later at night, into the bush, forcing me to hide in fear for my life till I could hitch a lift 400 k's to the city to escape them. *Maybe.*

But that's a fragment of a story and only a glimpse of the thinking and talk and consequences that came out of the bins. In writing this account of rural life, such 'stories' will seep in – they just *have to*. We will come back, again and again, but hopefully not too often as it's corrosive material, it's rust in the wheat, it's contamination of the sample.

For I was a protein sampler on the bins – I tested wheat for how much protein it contained and declared it either hard or soft. Hard wheat makes good pasta. That in itself was enough to set off a pattern of sexual abuse and harassment – just the fact I worked with the terms 'hard' and 'soft'. Blunt, basic and disturbed. And guns and shooting were hooked into the matrix, as were my growing alcoholism and participation in anything that allowed me to get high enough to obfuscate the conditions of my surroundings, of the situation I was in. A vicious circle. The fertility of wheat, the treatment of stacks and piles in the bins – fumigation. To keep the pests out. The *pests*. Seeding and harvest would long be the markers I measured the year by. They still are. In odd sorts of ways. Here, on the edge of the Victoria Plains, even now in such a different mental and social and ecological space.

~

Tracy has just come back from the small independent supermarket down in town. She says that outside the front doors, on the rack usually reserved for local newspapers, there was a stack of desk-topped newsletters with the headline 'Islamists Moving In – Look Carefully Before Moving Here', or something along those lines. She wanted to bin them immediately, but they are positioned under the shop security camera, which says something about their placement and continued presence. When we go through town tomorrow I will check it out and (by mutual agreement) remove them. Let their security cameras catch me in the process. Right-wing hate cells dot the district and are the source of much low-level terror, which is ignored by the status quo. Tim had to contend with Nazi salutes, swastikas, praise of the Holocaust, and printed leaflets featuring extracts from *Mein Kampf* being handed out at primary school. These kids of far-right households knew their stuff. Tim was physically harassed for caring about the rights of all people to their own cultural heritage, to their own religious beliefs, and to gender difference. Coming back from a month in La Réunion he was attacked and jostled for 'bringing back African Bum Disease'. He had no idea what they were on about, but knew it was racist. He was a marked child. The local newspaper highlights the odd 'leftie' with crafty skills living around the hills of the town, but the truth is far grimmer. The area is also a bastion for thirties-style fascism. I have come across levels of hate and xenophobia backed with weapons and other ordnance, very like the right-wing American preppers they so admire. Whiteness here is a value and a commodity.

Maybe it is telling that Tim, after speaking out so forcefully against anti-Semitism at one of his schools, is *assumed* to be Jewish – as if it is impossible to fully envisage that bigotry is an intrinsic wrong in itself; that surely one must have a vested interest to be so concerned, to make such intense statements refusing to accept anti-Semitism in its invidious and subtle forms. It was also considered by many of his peers, and even some teachers, 'unusual' that he *chose* to hear a Holocaust survivor speak, when he didn't have to do so as part of his studies. And yet Tim considers this experience one of the most important of his life. Tim's resistance to fascism has its roots in witness – he has seen enough of hatred and bigotry in the world around him to know tyranny.

And Tim's advocacy for the natural environment has its roots in witness – or maybe it's that he notices the bulldozers, notices the vanishing birds, notices the shifting seasons more than other kids (or as much as some)? We have a saying at Jam Tree Gully – *Wrong is wrong*. This doesn't mean there are no nuances to wrong and right – of course there are – but when you know something is wrong you don't try to talk your way out of it. Confront it, sort it the best way you can. Be held accountable.

So, our anarchist vegan pacifist feminist family perched on the side of a hill surrounded by trees many would love to delete (there are actually bumper stickers that say: 'Ruin a Greenie's Day: Chop Down a Tree' … unsurprisingly, we see them around here) is something of an anomaly. There are other 'alternative lifers' around the district, of course, but the thrust of damage and clearing and mining and invasive agriculture and business means that 'control' is well and truly in the hands of political conservatives and the patriotic right. It's almost strange to use the word 'patriotic', as patriotism is something many of us here would have once associated with American nationalism, something that bound the pro-feds with the anti-feds, intense localism with a concept of a united America either isolated from the rest of the world or seeking to control the world. It's a simplistic model, but in the era of American television and movies, of American consumerist values scaffolding the nation after the Second World War, it has become an easy and available one for Australians, especially white-heritage rural Australians. The nuances of America weren't generally discussed in the broader community, but such Australians felt they knew – positively or negatively – what 'America' stood for. Australians were mates, countrymen, Aussies, ANZACs, and many other morphing collective nationalisms. Not so much patriots. But the rise of the far right over recent decades has brought the word into local parlance, with its subtext of Australian nationalists yoked to American projections of cultural and material power.

I trace one origin of this in Western Australia to the Australian Nationalist Movement and their campaigns in the eighties to 'drive Asians out'. Angered by arrivals of 'boat people' from Cambodia and Vietnam in particular after the wars there, but really annexing themselves to the anti-Chinese and anti-Muslim sentiment and violence of European-originated gold miners in the 1890s, and the resentment towards the 'Afghan' cameleers who in the nineteenth-century were one of the main sources of supply transport in outback Western Australia. Racism in this place has been diverse, but it has usually reduced itself to a white colonial hatred of competition or cultural difference. It is both a nuanced and brutally 'direct' picture. In the end, like all racisms, the fears come of a desire for control and power. The

ANM brought terror to Perth with their bombings of Chinese restaurants, their bashings, their hate propaganda campaigns, and the eventual murder of one of their own foot soldiers. It is relevant for me to bring up here because I was one of those who overtly resisted them, and had my life threatened on many occasions. I witnessed their brutality, I tore down their posters, and I defined my life as one of peace against their violent hate. I was considered a threat and was targeted by the racists. I have known violence, too, and my aggression as a hanging-out addict was inexcusable. But I knew aggression was wrong and wanted to channel my energy into stopping violence, racism and bigotry by peacefully protesting, removing their literature and speaking out against them at every opportunity.

~

On Monday we had 48.5 millimetres of rain, and on Tuesday another 21.5 millimetres. We are replete with water, with flow. The ground is softening, the greening is gaining depth. But there's no pastoral romance – the farmers (not all, but many) are out there with their spray rigs pouring herbicides down on the unwanted greenery, or using early knockdown herbicides to prevent it raising its head. Roadside vegetation is dying from extra-strong doses to keep the weeds at bay. It's chemical warfare. But not at Jam Tree Gully – there are no toxic sprays here, other than what drifts in from neighbouring properties.

An incident from a few years ago, up on the hill above us, a hill I've come to call Mount Toxic. The neighbours, when they first came in and built a house to look over their 15 acres, sprayed the entire block. The contractor fed numerous hoses out from his spray tank to saturate the weeds. Within a week the hilltop was orange. Bright orange. Winter sun setting on the orange hill was a weird melancholy that got to the very root of colonial invasiveness. But there was an intervention, ineffective at the time – over the years they do this less and less, so maybe I got through to them? – but certainly an intervention. I yelled and vociferated from below about the drift, the residues, about the proven harms of Roundup, never mind the deadlier chemicals. It didn't stop. However, the next year during a high wind, a sign blew down the hill and landed in the north-eastern hill paddock of JTG (being replanted with York gum saplings). It read: *Don't spray here as some people claim it affects them*; this was written in large looping handwriting and followed by a smiley face. Sarcastic, but also an instruction not to spray directly across the road from us. Progress can be measured in many different ways.

Is Mount Toxic being restored slowly to health? Can the state of siege be lifted? I believe it can, but most difficult to deal with, aside from guns and poisons, are the all-powerful earthmovers. And one of our neighbours down the valley owns bobcats, trucks, tractors and a tracked bulldozer. He says that bulldozing and bobcatting relieve his tension, give him focus. Sometimes he finds it hard to focus. His machinery's sounds are imitated by magpies, which have had to constantly adjust the way they negotiate their territory in accordance with the terraforming carried out by these machines. But this is a guy who would help a neighbour no matter what – he can be a scary guy, and he has in the past threatened to bury me where no one would find me (I bought him a bottle of Jacks to 'appease' him), but he ultimately wants to service a neighbourhood he can feel part of. I bother him, but he's curious. He's a hard-living bloke and he knows I was one once also. Very hard-living. We see that in each other – different politics but the same driving compulsions. Under the destruction there's a language, and I find that profoundly disturbing and I have no doubt he does, too. Only recently, he parked his bulldozer under trees below the southern limits of Jam Tree Gully. The horror machine brooded and sent me nuts. I knew that when it finally ventured forth again, puffing into the valley, choking itself, more parrot hollows, more ancient trees, more roosting places for dozens of bird species, the homes of the few remaining marsupials would fall somewhere not far away. I went down day after day to stare over the rivers of the firebreaks and examine it. I didn't touch it, didn't really go near it, I didn't sabotage it, but I studied it. I tried to find its living soul, the whole time possessed by the thought of the worst movie of all time (according to many), *Killdozer*. There's life in that machine, there's agency, there's a combination of entrapment and servitude, but surely choice as well. I took lots of photos. I wrote poems. I typed the poems on my manual typewriter. The dozer stayed in its hollow for weeks. Caterpillar. Holt and Best and Caterpillar, which have bulldozed the world to the shiny curves of a marble. Red devils. Tombowlers. Playing *keepsies*. Realpolitik. Emptiness.

~

I have to get a couple of wheelbarrow loads of wood down from the shed when we get in this evening. The red shed has power through to it, but I refuse to turn the switch on unless there's an emergency and we need to pump from the bores. The bores aren't used if we can avoid it – the aquifer is being killed, and we don't want to contribute to its death. Up there in half-light, or by moonlight. It's riskiest being in there in the half-light in summer, when dugites, mulga snakes and tiger snakes are active and hunting for mice. But I don't need to go up there for wood in summer, and in winter I try to do all the collecting from the woodpile in there while it's still daylight. The wood is sourced from storm-felled trees before they have melded into habitat. We try to leave most storm-felled limbs where they fall, so they can become part of the ecosystem, a refuge for many creatures.

Yesterday I was collecting some wood from a limb that had been cut away from over the driveway when the tanker came in to suck out our bloated septic tanks, and I noticed kangaroo scats on the gravel. We haven't seen roos for a while, but each day I see more and more signs that there's a mob actively grazing here, or passing through overnight. I also noticed a kookaburra flying fast and low down the block. Kookaburras were introduced to the south-west from the eastern states in the thirties – they have naturalised themselves. With their razor-sharp, long beaks they eat nestlings of other bird species as well as reptiles and small mammals, and rule a large territory. But it's when butcher birds come into the area that the nests of songbirds are systematically invaded. Birds of prey are also often above the nesting trees. But it's magpies that dominate the territory, and they keep it under constant surveillance.

Tim, who wants to be an ornithologist, is, like me, upset as red-capped robins, silvereyes, fairy wrens and other birds lose their nestlings to a couple of butcherbirds that have ventured into the area, but we also accept that this is the way it is. We never interfere. And if left be, the fact of the presence of these species in the first place, means that they have found ways of persisting, of surviving the dramatic shifts in climate and through the severe loss of habitat. Even the interloper kookaburra hasn't led to species loss like colonial activity has.

~

Jam Tree Gully is about coexistence. From the crack in the great water tank, the brown honeyeaters tap water, as do the kangaroo mob that live in the vicinity, when it's extremely hot and dry. We have seen few roos lately, which means the shooters have been killing them off. In a house of books collected from around the world and brought 'home' so we can read and speak back out to difference in so many different inflections – and I reiterate, books are really the only thing we 'own', though years of lending and distributing mean that 'ownership' is a technicality, not a desire – a roof overhead is as much about keeping them dry and functional as it is for our own bodies. It's a *sealed* house now, to keep out the mice, but spiders and occasionally scorpions will find their way in. Scorpions usually come in on firewood or, being so flat, under the flywire door, and the spiders are blown in as spiderlings, even through the minute grid of the flywire. Wasps make their nests on outside walls, and geckos roam those same walls at night, searching out the numerous insect species that settle on them. Over the last year we have made two sightings of extremely rare and unusual insects. We keep records. So, coexistence is about managing as humans, but allowing other creatures to manage their lives as well, and about letting vegetation appear where it needs to, other than when it's up against the house, which is an extreme fire risk, or when it threatens to undermine the house pad.

Every detail of our presence is inflected not only in my poems but also those of Tracy and Tim. It's not just a matter of recording, but of translating the consequences and actualities of presence into a matrix of understanding our own lives and, to use the relevant cliché, the world at large. I have often been interested in how one writes the macro and the micro – the great world and the (innumerable) world(s) up close. Jam Tree Gully is a process of presence and consequence. One example of observation that has wider personal resonances concerns those ring-necked parrots, often hybrids between twenty-eights and Port Lincolns, but generally referred to by locals as 'twenty-eights'. There are specific ways of telling – red above beak, yellow belly and so on – but if they make the same noise, look roughly the same shape and colour (though twenty-eights are actually slightly smaller than Port Lincolns, and we are at the northernmost point of their range, which is gradually shifting further north), then regardless they are called twenty-eights. I have a deeply enravelled history with these birds in many ways. I once shot them and kept them, I once killed them and strangely nurtured them, but for thirty-five years I have fought to protect them and their habitat. I have written innumerable poems about them and about my relationship to them, and I have written essays on them. They are also a code running through this memoir. I do not claim a totemic relationship, as within the language of country and traditional presence that is not mine to claim. An easy translation (for me, not in reality) would be along such lines, but that would be a calque and would be untrue. But I deeply care for them and respect them and learn from them, and they brighten my life as I work to sustain theirs.

One incident from last year's winter nesting season comes to mind. Tim called me to watch a female twenty-eight using its hooked grain-cracking beak to pick at the opening of a small hollow in a large York gum on the tier above the house, next to the red shed. It was systematically working its way around the circumference, trying to widen it slightly so it might be used as a nesting hollow. It was persistent over a couple of days but couldn't make it work. We expect it will probably return this year as the hollow is likely to have altered in other ways as well. However, though they are protected birds unless people have a(n obscene) licence to kill, they are picked off in vast numbers by .22 rifles, shotguns and poisoned grain. The great flocks of my childhood have largely gone. This year, we are watching out for its return – and we will know the bird, as one knows a human. There are ways of understanding, even slightly.

In getting a focus on presence, I often listen out for the night birds, especially the owlet-nightjars and the tawny frogmouths, but also the barn owls. They are more prevalent in the hot months, and not now when some mornings have ice cracking across the windows. This does not mean they are not present, but they are less vocal – no doubt to do with the mating and hunting processes. During grass-cutting time, when one is filthy, itchy and disturbed with disturbing the habitat that comes up in the cycle of annual grasses, even introduced ones like the rampant wild oats we get across the block, the disturbing of insects through slashing sets birdlife into a frenzy. Even at night, after the fallen grass has settled, and creatures have reset themselves to the fallen 'regime', the insects are more stirred up than usual and the night birds swoop in under moonlight and collect them by the beakful. It's that strange rising up out of destruction, a cost and a growth, in a similar way to the devastation of salt, which offers islands of survival for some creatures and vegetation because farmers no longer bother with it and 'don't go there'.

Nature does not abhor a vacuum (vacuums are part of nature, also) – it abhors senseless destruction. When away from Jam Tree Gully, I often find myself mentally back there for two basic reasons. One, because some natural phenomenon I experience creates an equivalence with something I've experienced at JTG (the wind howling around Sheppard Flats in Cambridge taking me back to fierce winds tearing through the valley, say), or two, because something destructive I witness (the removal of old trees in Melbourne, or the needless burning or at least over-burning of furze in West Cork) reminds me of the senseless destruction on the properties and public lands around JTG. Writing a specific place necessarily calls on the experiences of many other places, just through the use of a 'globalised' and certainly colonial language like English. Specificity, naming that is specific to one place, has to be introduced into the language so it can actually work in and for that locale. That's why I often hear from American readers that all my Australian-specific namings would benefit from a glossary. I feel quite differently about this – one can find out if one wishes, and in doing so it draws the reader into the fabric of difference. We best understand the place we are in by understanding the places it is not. In making poems of JTG, I am also making poems of language which is both specific and 'international'. This view of a world in which regionality is respected and 'valued' and contextualised within the experience and specificities of all the greater world is part of what I call 'international regionalism'.

Many small land owners on the fringes of the wheatbelt come and go. A small parcel of land is bought and people put their dream of a rural life into action. Some think they want to grow olives and tear out native vegetation to plant trees; others want to grow trees for wood-turning and illegally poison kangaroos because they 'eat the seedlings'. In both cases, what they desire is diminished by their way of getting it. In both cases intrinsic and even diabolical wrongs are committed, and in not nurturing the flora and fauna of the place they farm against the very grain of the land. We have olive trees planted among native trees – it works. And as for kangaroos eating seedlings, it's important to place protections around the seedlings, and with native flora the roos will eat the top off and then usually leave the plant alone, allowing a mallee-style growth of a plant with more than one trunk. Adaptation needs to happen in all directions and can't work without a good dose of mutual aid. But we see absurd approaches to creating romantic rural enclaves all the time – people planting trees in high summer rather than with the first rains, or burning off when it's still dry and losing control of the fire, which destroys not only native bushland but their own plantings, or constantly spraying herbicides till their soil is so bare it blows away with the summer easterlies. The list is endless. Learning is always a steep curve, but unless one works with what a place actually is, you'll always be working against 'nature' and not with it.

A photo is and isn't to be trusted. It is a moment, but it is a distilled and separated moment. Great photographers can suggest otherwise, but a photograph can only tell part of a truth of a place which in its continuance is constantly vulnerable. When away from JTG, we communicate with Mum and Guru, who visit constantly, 'keeping an eye on it', and they report back in words and photos. I often ask for specific things to be photographed, so I can see where they're at. But without the words to go around the conditions of taking the photos, some truth is not told. The eye is not the only sense. We have a lemon tree Guru planted five years ago that has remained stunted and actually switched from being a lemon to a lemon-orange cross. This is no doubt to do with the graft, and what survived in the rootstock, but while we're away we get photos and reports about it. The photos tell the same sad tale, but the reports tell of its resilience.

As I write this paragraph in a tower in Midland below the Scarp, planning on my return to JTG tomorrow, I look out at the small swimming pool below and see Tracy swimming, in the cold. She hasn't swum for ages, though she loves it more than anything else. She says it gives her a bodily and mental freedom in a way few other things do. From high above, her breast-stroke across the pool, frog-scissoring legs, is a kind of perfection. She is wearing bathers bought in La Réunion, where swimming is confined to certain safe places, and, in fact, a surfer was taken by a great white shark while we were there in 2011. Swimming is dangerous there. But alone in the pool, swimming is a freedom for Tracy, and I feel that connection we have always felt. I get that sense of things when walking, especially out on JTG. Guru whipper-snippered a path through wild oats on the west side of the block last spring so Tim could walk through the trees to the granites without the risk of suddenly coming upon a snake and not seeing it. Fire and snakes are constant in the hot weather. Tim finds the same freedom of self and mind walking the hill, the granites, noting the lichens and animal tracks. But Tracy also feels privileged swimming because water is lacking where we live, and it's something we treat with reverence, if not awe. To swim is a gift.

~

We've been over to York to pick Tim up after his return from Geraldton. On the way over, in the paddock on the corner of Toodyay Road and Clackline Road, we saw one of the horror visions produced by the makers of the machine world: a Cat D10 dozer. A monster of a machine whose only purpose is utter destruction, demolishing and carving out. Some weeks ago we noticed that an entire ridge hill area above a paddock had been cleared of powderbark wandoos, those trees that set off a mysticism in the surprised visitor with their eerie and compelling glow at sunset, that carry such significance. But not all around here feel moved by the presence of these trees. A greed for gravel, the laterite road-making material beneath these trees, and a hunger for more grazing or cropping land frequently means illegal clearing. I am checking records, shire minutes, and local chatter regarding the status of this latest tree deletion. The damage done, the D10 is parked in the paddock, standing three storeys high, gloating dead-faced, 'fully loaded', waiting for a truck to haul it to its next job. It will take a massive truck and trailer – a big Kenworth, maybe (my father was a Kenworth specialist and for him the United States was the unrealised holy land of the 'world's greatest truck') – to retrieve it. Every bit lost means we must concentrate our efforts more to protect what is. It's a second-by-second issue. Tragic and unutterable, but a way has to be found.

I have just been in the small silver shed – a shed of pressed steel whose origin, by which I mean where the ore was dug from, is likely the Pilbara. Tens of thousands of hectares of scrub cleared, sacred places violated, whole iron mountains removed. The deletions are endless. In the small silver shed I see the exoskeleton – the dried sack of a redback spider's body, hanging on long hooked legs from its scraggly web, which has lasted longer than it. Next to the corpse are three spent egg sacks, beige weavings of planets, hollow earths, which have burst out, spiderlings seething all over, desperate to disperse. But that would have been months ago in the warm weather. In the silver tin shed it gets almost boiling hot: when it gets up to 47 degrees outside, inside it bursts thermometers. But spiders and geckos work the heat, and other insects venture in, breed, and are trapped, consumed. It is like Venus in there, sans the sulphuric clouds, chemical cocktails. We keep no chemicals for gardening, no synthetic chemicals for cleaning; we use natural oils, lemon, vinegar and bicarb. But there are rakes and shovels with plastic heads and handles, and the heat breaks them down, so the air inside the shed would still be volatile with toxins. We need to consider our impact on the biosphere on every level. Nothing is straightforward, and every acquisition we make has consequences. It's an equation most people push aside, but there's no time left for that. For me, the glass remains half full but we're on the edge. Now is the time. About a decade ago I left the digital world completely for a couple of years because of its environmental impact, and I will do so again.

I know the poison of the redback spider. I have been bitten at least once by a large female on the verge of egg-laying, and wrote a poem as the neurotoxin came on – a way of recording the onset but also to understand the figurative nature of invasive forces. It was extremely painful, so painful it induced hallucinations, throwing me for the first time in decades back into flashback mode. It became a terrifying and agonising experience as I awaited medical attention. The poem was written, but what kind of poem is it, can it be?

Graphology 640: While awaiting the phantasma effects of a redback spider bite … written for Tracy to give to the Dr should I pass out …

It's weird typing this with one hand
and a couple of fingers, thumb out of action,
a redback having perched momentarily on the print
and a sharp, deep pain indicating a bite. It takes
some time before redback poison really gets hold –
I do feel nauseous and giddy and there's fire
flooding my palm, now extending to my wrist,
my full left hand, and pyrexia and paralysis
seem truisms. I have the flu anyway
so flashbacks – hallucinations –

are only a few memories away, and the swirl
I am caught up in promises the full *son-et-lumière;*
maybe I'll get the colour back into my visions.
Latrodectus. Do I imagine my lymph nodes
swelling? Ah, the glories of neurotoxins!
It is horrendously spiritual, this working up
a sweat I don't want to spill – glister
that might poison anything I touch.
I was clearing redbacks from Tim's playground.
I was searching out the comb-footed.
Catching the trip wires in bright daylight,
huddled up under shade cloth, nurtured
in window frames, collating exoskeletons,
strung out in the hot day where the hosts
won't go. My left hand aches
too much to type. The poem
is the order I try to impose
on my body. Proteins,
transmitters: excruciating
chemistry, electrics, déjà vu,
to flow through victim livestock
as blood product, as antivenene,
reaction against agony to stop the poem
in its tracks, muscling in on my apostasy,
its mismanagement of 2, 4, 6-trihydroxy purine,
its inevitability: the bite you have to have
to sign off on morbid fascination,
straight for a decade to slam dunk
an ultimate high: inosine, adenosine,
guanosine, all lit up as exit signs,
so fantastic seeing inside havoc

as exquisite as conscience,
dashing off lines without pause
when the body and its guidance systems
are being overloaded with syntax.

The redback, like the American black widow, has become a colonial mythical creature – a creature of outhouse dunnies and woodpiles, tripwires in darkness. Isolation from medical attention has been closely linked to death, and though death from a bite is not common these days with antivenom readily available, it *might* happen if a bite is left untreated. And death from the bite of one of the many toxic snakes around here was not uncommon, pre anti-venom. Even now, isolation can lead to death, as can a strong injection of venom or a severe reaction. I am acquainted with five people who have been bitten by the dugite snake, and two died. To place such loss within the mythos of 'the bush' or of an 'untamed Australia' is offensive not only to Aboriginal people in its apportioning a fear of death and vulnerability to spaces outside or beyond the reach of colonial centres, but to the victims of snakebite whatever their heritage. Becoming part of the myth is not a relief to their loved ones. Snakes and spiders are to be respected, left alone, and allowed to live their lives.

Over the last eighteen months we have seen one dugite on the drive just outside the house, and one up on the bitumen road, sadly killed by a car; our friend and relative the Guru – my mother's partner, John – who is often over here helping with things, has seen a tiger snake and a mulga snake near the red shed. And Tim and I have seen numerous snake tracks around the house. *Natural toxins*, toxins of the ecology – in and out of balance because of clearing, agriculture, mining and indifference, but still present. The potential for an animal to inject poison into a human is the basis for appropriate caution, even fear, but it's also considered by some to be an excuse to exploit the chemistry of those toxins – sometimes for medical benefits to humans, sometimes for anti-human purposes. I have encountered cone shells and blue-ringed octopuses – my brother has had one of these deadly creatures crawl over his hand. But neither of us has ever wanted to damage or investigate the toxicity of these creatures beyond the figurative. To understand the psyche of Jam Tree Gully is to understand and revere the *naturally* toxic, whether the poisonous creatures of this locale or in places we might visit, say, on the coast.

The experience of poisons and toxins would provide the metaphors for me to work through understanding. Once, as a teenager living in Geraldton, I trod on a cobbler or possibly a stonefish. The pain as I dragged myself home was beyond the redback's by many times. I wanted to shoot my foot off with my rifle. *Guns*. Poison fought with a weapon. In hospital, they gave me codeine injections and antibiotics. And as with the radiation exposure I would receive from working in mineral sand analysis labs outside Geraldton, my inability to accept the connectedness and causality of pain delayed my turning away from weapons, the military, capitalism and *the machine*. A decade later I would be protesting in forests and elsewhere to stop mineral sand mining. Pain, toxins, destruction, deletion – the body responding to invasiveness, the mind responding with a language of resistance.

My strange, contradictory childhood 'love of nature' – which was tied to outdoorsman activities and the attendant crisis of masculinity, and a contiguous understanding that the toxins of nature and the toxins manufactured by humans were *not* one and the same, and could be thought about separately (even if their effects were equally fatal) – produced a melange of metaphysical explanations for who and what I was in the world. I hadn't worked out the subtleties of irony and hypocrisy, but I knew something didn't add up between the way I felt about the world and the way I acted in it. There were differences in even the most extreme bodily scenarios of exposure and experience. And now, in mid-life, the issues of toxicity and clarity of purpose are bound together – right down to a choice of clay paints, when extending this house from the small kit home that was here when we arrived, over industrial paints with their legacy of toxicity, contamination, exploitation. Every choice we make has consequences. So often we are forced into situations we have little control over, but when we can make a choice, it becomes an expression of our respect or contempt for the biosphere. We were painstaking in our choice of insulation and building materials – often the choice with less impact is the less costly choice in all senses of the economic. It's not a case of Morgellons, those likely imaginary hairs irritating under the skin, but rather a case of understanding that manufacturing is ultimately about profit margins, and profit margins increase with increased toxicity.

And we do not believe people with limited financial means should be sold the dummy that toxic processes make manufacturing more 'affordable'. Toxicity is affordable to none and it is an abuse of human rights and the rights of the biosphere. Economics based on privilege and a right to choice dictated by how much money a person has is obscene. People spray and poison creatures whose own poisons threaten them, and in doing so poison themselves and the earth, air and water. And I think this, looking at the dead female redback with a pale glint of its once furiously red stripe out in the silver shed where I went to collect the wheelbarrow, homemade from scraps: scraps of manufacture, of production, of toxic residues, however many degrees of physical and mental separation.

Processional caterpillars move faster than you might think. Peeling out of their niche alongside the house where they'd rolled into a ball against the cold, the lead caterpillar bristles and flexes and senses the future, peeling off to lay a silken thread, blaze the trail out of the frost, as the sun hardens the orange-tamped rim of the eastern hill. Then another connects to its tail, then another and so on till there's a line inching its way towards what the collective has decided and the lead caterpillar enacts. It's not that long after they set out that they begin their climb up the rough bark of the jam tree, so named by colonials for its raspberry-jam-like odour when cut, sap spilling; it's called mungart by Ballardong Noongar people and prized for its seed, which is ground to a flour. These fast-growing tree shrubs live at most about fourteen years, and bush out like a triangle but can actually get much taller than descriptions allow.

The processional caterpillars have finished their climb and are balling up again – I wonder if this is to be the chosen place, in a cleft between trunk and branches, the place for transition. Later, looking without intruding (I hope), I note – I *will* note – that they have moved on. Restless. Like flying ants and bees on nuptial day, when with the coming of the warm weather and effusions of pollen, the old queens emerge and take a swarm with them, to embed about three-quarters of the colony elsewhere and nest. But we are talking about introduced European bees here, which, outside analogy – for pastoral conceits and pathetic fallacy have no place in the serious business of theft and deletion – drive off increasingly rare native bees, which we also find around here, glorious with their blueness, making their tunnels and laying their eggs in mud cells underground, one next to another, communing yet also strangers to each other. And I think of the rainbow birds in the sandy creek bank up behind where my mother and Guru live, under the purple shadows of the mountain-hill of Walwalinj, the rainbow birds digging their summer nests and burrowing and trying to survive the attacks of feral cats. The interconnectedness, the separations.

~

The *difference* between listening to machine-conveyed music rather than making music. Though Tim will be drumming to recorded music down 'his end' of the house. A confluence. But here, as I type, looking out over the valley and the golden midwinter light through the jam tree and the York gum, silvereyes buzzing out from roosts slightly unsettled, I am listening to Crass, the anarchist communal band from London and countryside (inheritance of Penny Rimbaud translated into a rambling house and grounds for camping and commune and big soup pots and his meeting Steve Ignorant and drumming and making sounds against Thatcherite fascism), which will reach me in late 1980 via a radio DJ in Geraldton, a bloke who is friends with my friend who is alone and removed from the school's cool social groups because he is gay and angry and fighting with God in a coastal town of racist and homophobic violence, and I hear Crass for the first time and say, I want to find them, I do not want to keep playing strategy games and I do not want to hang out with the forty-year-old bloke who has an SS-issue Mauser he uses to shoot outback telegraph posts. And I connect with my best friend who is in the process of leaving me for a cooler set of friends ... *my* friend, who is from the only Jewish family I know of in Geraldton, who opens doors to new music and cultural insights into mysticism but sways away from it intermittently as part of his process of working out who he is where he is (his parents out, he cooks bacon and mocks their strictness, but I know too that this is because he feels different and under cultural siege and I want to connect with him, but not through bacon). I want to (literally) convert to be with him so he's not alone but he doesn't want me, he wants the head girl he wants popularity he wants to eat bacon. We drink together and I slide into alcoholism further and further … These two friends of mine who have nothing to do with each other: a gay friend who is angry and says he hates homosexuality and hates people who don't believe in God, and my friend who is angry with his 'difference' and yet proud of it too, and I get that. These two friends who have nothing to do with each other at all – nothing 'in common'. And yet music is there, between them – from Crass to Pink Floyd and Country Joe. Music, with my mum teaching some of the neighbours' kids piano in the background. And I feel I need to find my way out of the isolation the violence and witnessing the race riots down on Front Beach, though later I know I will have to confront this reality of where I have grown up.

But as a seventeen-year-old I needed mental refuge to work things out. In the late seventies in Geraldton, gangs of white youth hung out at the Sail Inn hoping to fight with Yamaji guys – on the two or three occasions I (we – my brother and I) tried to object, I was beaten by some of those white guys at the Leisure Centre pinball parlour across the road on Marine Terrace, just near the sea, the harbour. I could not envisage a Jam Tree Gully, not yet, but I had just encountered Thoreau and I was wondering about what it would be like to step out, to completely remove myself from the society that claimed me but I felt in no way part of. And feeling bad about wandering outside the cultural implosion that remains my guilt, my unbelonging, my being beaten to a pulp at the Geraldton drive-in (the Gero Drives) in the late seventies by a white kid, with an Aboriginal kid stopping the bloodbath and the cops wanting me to name the Yamaji guy and me refusing. If I had 'named his name', as he told me decades later, his whole family would have suffered, would have been persecuted by the cops for the crimes of the white boy. Australia is the land of deaths in custody, where Aboriginal people are killed in custody on a regular basis. This is a fact.

It's uncomfortable talking about 'black' and 'white', isn't it? And in a racist town like Geraldton (and Carnarvon, where my father was then living) 'colour' was quite openly discussed, with gradations and nuances of permission and permissiveness. It was obscene. It was damaging. It was indelible. It was intended to be.

That night I was beaten up at the Gero Drives – when my brother and I and a friend climbed the wire fence of the waves of bitumen humps and speakers and the projector room and the confectionary shop with its screen of introduced pine trees holding the big screen in place, suppressing unpaid-for viewings from outside – my life changed from being bullied at school, and going to and from school, to being hunted down in a public place and destroyed. We took our positions at the front, just under the screen, drinking green ginger wine and watching the *Tommy* rock opera movie by The Who. I have recounted this again and again, and I am sorry if it's a refrain, but I offer it here with a different emphasis, one that has become apparent over the last decade.

The kids who found me and beat me to a pulp while my little brother tried to stop them and was held back, and my friend (whose mother was a horse trainer and whose father was in prison and who connected to me because I liked horses and didn't care that his old man was in prison) watched on in horror doing nothing and just trying to survive, did so with a purpose – to destroy not only me but also the 'learning' of a book sort that was a threat. 'Dictionary' was going to have all those shitty words beaten out of him. The kid who did most of the damage would have used and heard the word 'lippy' many times. That's what women who had an opinion were called in the domestic-violent world of Australia in the seventies. Lippy women deserved everything they got, we heard. I was like a lippy woman, according to the leader of the pack. Approaching, asking to share green ginger wine, starting small-scale harassment like mocking 'big words', which he himself could use effectively and knowingly and wanted me to feel the sting of this, schoolteacher's son that I was … and then shoving then punching then 'speak now, you lippy bastard', my head on the ground and held down by a bunch of less vocal boys, others holding back brother and friend who wanted out, and the cars angled up to the big screen and those crazy flipper fingers and Elton John in giant boots … and the fist coming down so hard again and again until the Yamaji guy says, Leave him alone … there's too much blood, and the white guy smashing again so my nose splinters. Lippy bastard I was. Dictionary trying to be cool, trying to be street. My fate was sealed. My alcoholism had begun.

The teenager beating the shit out of me was knowledgeable but hated 'school knowledge'. He felt his was street knowledge; getting off his face and avoiding beatings by his old man were his mission. It was sex and drugs and power. Book knowledge was unpredictable, slippery, and troubling to him. Irony is, I *got it*, and though I loved my books I didn't see them as the be all and end all. I just saw them as a means of augmenting knowledge, of mixing them with real experience to help make sense of a 'world turned upside down' (as I would latch onto when I read seventeenth-century English civil war history). I saw things in terms of the persecuted and the persecutors, and I wanted to know how to short-circuit this dynamic. School was torment for me too, if for different reasons. Maybe some overlapping reasons. I always felt *someone like me* could work with guys *like him* to sort out the mess, but he and his mates thought otherwise. Or did one of them not think like this? His condition of presence was fundamentally different. The Yamaji kid respected words, and he didn't call me 'lippy'. Fact. And, what's more, even with the white kid who was doing the smashing, I respected *his* knowledge, his version of word-making, his survival. He, himself, was lippy – a snarling irony of survival. A maleness made brutal that would turn on women, then men, and likely, finally, himself.

~

Garden. A word that in the singular or plural resonates for me. When we moved to Jam Tree Gully, I had plans for a two-acre vegie garden. I have always grown organic – actually, *veganic* (no animal manures etc) – vegetables. It is most important for me as a gardener not to damage in order to grow. I work around plants and trees that are already there, and work out issues of sun, shade and soil in accordance with the locale. If a soil is too acidic, I will gradually work it up with sand extracted from the least damaging place in the vicinity, and add ash from our slow-combustion heater, ash from storm-felled branches. I will prepare beds over a long time with use, especially where I am using raw green compost, working in straw and turning the soil regularly. I make compost heaps that grow over a long period, with layers of wet and dry. But when we first came to JTG I was confronted with something I had not really experienced before – and I had grown vegetables in Yarloop, Bridgetown, Perth, Geraldton, York and other places. A total lack of water.

We had our house water supplies, which could not be 'wasted' on a garden, and we have two bores, which I refuse to use because of the risk of damaging the strained and vulnerable aquifer. At first, I planted a large crop of heirloom broad beans – a crop that would serve us fresh and stored dry for a year or longer. I relied on winter rains which were sketchy that year due to ongoing drought, so the final crop was poor, with low seed yield and no reusable seed stock. I planted greens such as Swiss chard and spinach, but lost them too. And so on. Everywhere I had gardened previously, I had access to water. And then we went overseas to Cambridge and later Ireland for a few years – wet places.

Over the last half-dozen years, we've concentrated on revegetation here – mainly native trees, but also lucerne trees along the firebreaks. They are an introduced species, but grow fast and are fire-retardant, and are much loved by songbirds. But recently I have been developing a vegetable garden plan using raised beds and a couple of separate rainwater tanks, making use of a section of roof catchment that has largely gone to waste till now. Next year, I will put in a fence to keep the kangaroos from eating it all and build a number of very raised beds, for moisture retention. In these I will put in crops of tomatoes, chillies, peppers, bush beans, zucchinis, lettuces and so on, followed by a winter crop of legumes to revitalise the soil.

Soil here is another issue – it is clay-based, low in fertility, very rocky, and bakes like concrete in summer. It would be easy to truck more amenable soils in from elsewhere, but that strikes me as a bizarre way of respecting an ecology and aiming for self-sufficiency – to damage elsewhere in order to thrive here. Things are further complicated by the gravel ants – they quickly extend their colonies from gravel edges and tough ground into softer soil, and are keen on fresh vegetable matter, especially compost. We never intentionally kill or hurt any animal, so it's a matter of learning how to deter with the least possible impact on their right to exist. Over the years, I have developed many such methods for many different creatures. Probably the most significant success we've had in this capacity was during the mouse plague of four summers ago.

It was an extreme mouse plague, complementing an extreme locust plague the year before. Nothing is in balance here. We get native hopping mice around, and also the introduced house and field mice. During mouse plagues on the farm when I was a child, there'd literally be hundreds of mice bursting out in all directions if you lifted a piece of corrugated iron lying near the farm grain silos. Back then, totally immersed in the 'killing is part of farmlife' mode, I'd come up on weekends and join with my cousins in slaughtering thousands of mice. We'd pour water down their holes, and strike them with lengths of polythene pipe as they emerged; we'd shoot them in the sheds using .22 shells loaded with 'rat shot'. It was grotesque and haunts me to this day. As a child I so loved mice that I used to sing to them when I wasn't on the farm, and would be traumatised if a house mouse was caught in a trap. I still remember the names of all the mice under my care. When my animal rights sensibilities began to formulate during my late teens it was because of the use of laboratory mice.

So when the plague struck the region and JTG, I resolved to do everything I could to prevent any damage being done to the mice. As with all plagues, the mouse population would eventually peak and diminish, and I wasn't going to harm any on the way. First, we painstakingly sealed every possible entry point to the house. This took a long while, as the mice found entry points we didn't know could possibly exist. The last one we sealed was the size of a silver coin in the top corner of Tim's built-in wardrobe – he'd hear them drop through at night, and then they'd be stuck inside his room, climbing curtains and wanting out. We'd hear 'Mum … Dad! A mouse has got in!' and I'd go and let it into the main part of the house, where it would eventually be caught in one of the humane traps I had set.

Outside, we'd see dozens of them running along verandah rails, along walls, laying trails over the ground. I sealed that last hole in Tim's room with scrunched-up wire and plaster – the wire to stop them chewing through. And they ate into electrics, and the electrician told us there was no way we'd 'win'. 'They'll eat through the walls.' But we used humane traps – self-triggered when the mice went in after peanut butter – and I would carry the traps far away from the house (and other human habitation) and released the mice in different places, so they didn't concentrate and cause overwhelming problems for the habitat. That way I managed to keep them at bay. Over a period of two months I removed hundreds of mice. I often walked the block and reserve by moonlight, clutching traps holding three or four mice each, while listening to the night birds. When I released the mice it was usually into granite rock crevices, to give them a chance. That year, the birds of prey thrived.

As in all things, my way of coping was to document in poetry. But it was, as always, more than documentation; it was a communing. I do not have an anthropomorphic view of nature per se, but am necessarily and inevitably anthropomorphic when I seek to empathise with an animal. I think one has to accept the fact of being human among other animals. That's how I translate a reality of tension in our coexistence, and do so with minimal and hopefully *no* damage. Poetry is my conduit to other possible ways of expressing existence that are not just my own. People talk of the self with regard to confession, but for me the most intense poetry of the self is witnessing.

~

Though we live away from JTG for lengthy periods of time, we are lucky to have John 'the Guru' to look over it for us. He loves it here, and actually built the addition to the original house. He respects our way of living, and he and Mum are both in tune with what we're trying to achieve, what we're trying to show can be done. We are all people who like to live without adornment. Other than books, papers, and music, there is little accumulation of objects. We believe in non-ownership, sharing, and even collectivity in terms of like minds. For all our time elsewhere, the house bears little material sign of it. This is not a repository for artefacts from the rest of the world.

Growing up, my brother and I were quite different that way, though we came together in the way we see and interpret the material world as we (gradually) left our childhood behind. As a kid, I was far more concerned about 'my things' – Stephen was all for one and one for all, and didn't really consider things to be 'owned'. I see that now, and have done for forty years, but it took time. My chemistry equipment was never to be touched; his insect books were read by everyone. He shared his stamps; I hoarded mine and built an investment portfolio of rare specimens.

Stephen has always had a warm attitude to life itself, and a live-and-let-live view of things. In Malaysia, where his wife's family lives, he is liked and respected, though he is clearly 'different' from locals, and most other people in general. He has lived a very different life deep in the wheatbelt – often alone for long periods of time, making his own clothes, growing vegetables … he even lived for six months in a forest. One time when he and his wife were in Cherating, they were asked to be extras in a major Malaysian film production there. It was a sci-fi invasion disaster film set by the break where Stephen often surfs – a break where he was driven out as an interloper when he first went there, but where he is now accepted as a local. Though most of their lines were cut in the final edit, there's still a scene of them sitting on the beach, with alien mayhem and human panic all around them, and my brother smiling and saying, 'I love Malay people!' He says it in English; it is translated into Malay subtitles below.

~

The world sometimes intrudes into JTG in the most direct and dramatic way. ('Intrudes' – wrong word. I don't have the right to decide on the nature of intrusion.) Be it an escaped fire from someone's burning regime, or a neighbour's toxic spraying, or a new quarry or mine opening in the district, we are embedded in the eye of destruction.

But on this fragment of one of the region's big colonial land grants, this rocky hillside of evergreens that persist among massive boulders of granite, on land pillaged and assaulted, there's a sense of fragility, and 'intrusion' becomes the setback to its repair, but not the be all and end all. We push on with hope, with belief, trying to show that land can be restored to health, that respect can be shown to its traditional owners, and that discussions about presence can be had. For us, the key is restoration, to create a buffer against the destruction. But even those huge granites are at risk of being levered out, rolled, smashed. When the people before us ran this place as a horse farm, they made an arena in the top north-west corner, taking out the trees, levelling inclined land by bulldozing and pushing aside the granites, which sit isolated and disconnected around the space. It was then covered with sand so the horses could do their circuits under the eyes of their trainer. When we arrived it was a white square, a squaring of the circle. We didn't plant it out again, but as seeds found purchase we let it refoliate. The ecosystem around the granites has re-established, and rock dragons might be seen on occasion sunning themselves, and there are often signs of echidnas having sheltered beneath rock ledges. We go up to the arena to see how a 'return' can happen without our intervention, even in such a desolate zone. During the last big storms late last year, the largest self-seed York gum in the centre of the arena came down. As some root stock was still embedded, we thought it might survive and take on that odd shaping of so many York gums – new branches sprouting vertically from a horizontal trunk. But, alas, it was a long dry summer and it perished.

Actually, the *shapings* of York gums on the valley wall due to destructive winds, run-off when heavy rains hit, and other micro-geographic and climatic specificities, are quite incredible. The complex bent and twisted limbs lure us in, draw us close. 'Eyes', 'mouthgapes', 'loops of cursive', 'waves', 'humps', 'matrixes', and so many other words might be used to describe the weird configurations of branches. *Other-wordly*, and reminding of a depth of ontology of presence that resists our descriptions, even our immersions. The language I have is inadequate, and I cannot and would not access the language that can talk of it – not only do I not have the right, but I could never decode it. I will never really comprehend its complexities and intensity, but through poetry

I go as close as I can to doing so, I hope. You can't substitute understanding, but you can at least respect it.

One of the most consequential 'intrusions' outside the obvious ongoing colonial injustice (not that there is an outside, because all these intrusions are part of it, as we are, too), one that is so overt and discriminatory against place, life and the biosphere is the annual Targa car rally: high-speed cars racing around a loop where it's barely safe to drive at 60 or 70 k's an hour. When it was first mooted that the rally take in the 'highlands loop stage' in 2012, we strongly resisted. In fact, I wrote a protest submission and lodged it with the shire, and actually managed to stave off the 'event' (this is no Situationist moment – it is entertainment at the expense of the bush with few cheering on the bush) for a year.

This act of resistance had disturbing repercussions. I was vilified in town, and one town official walked up to me in the street as I was sitting in the car, leant in through the passenger window and said, Howz ya therapy goin? Tim was still struggling with the cruel atmosphere at the local school, and every day endured a long bus trip to and from the town. Only days after we managed to stop the rally, the grapevine was in overload, and he was harassed on the school bus with, Your father is a bastard drunk idiot who spoils everyone's fun (I'd been sober for over twenty years!), accompanied pushing and shoving and thinly veiled threats. Linked with children at school telling him that their fathers were going to shoot his parents and cut off their heads, this was cause for concern. In our objection, to which they'd had no time to legally respond, I'd spoken of stress to human life and animal life. Our lives were directly threatened, which says so much about the culture around a sport I had accused of encouraging 'hooning' (which the organisers denied).

The burning of fossil fuels for the sake of burning fossil fuels. Sport? Entertainment?

The next year, the rally organisers and their shire supporters came prepared and our opposition was crushed with a series of manoeuvres well rehearsed in other locales. As we expected, cars raced around the loop at high speeds in the weeks before the event, and for months after. It became very dangerous. And the animals of the valley were clearly stressed. As fuel is burnt to feed the adrenaline and material desires of the drivers, the state of those living here is ignored, though it should be said that beer and parties abounded around the region to celebrate the occasion. It speaks volumes of this colonial expeditioning: an advert for a house and property being sold around this time advertised the house as 'having a dance floor built over an Aboriginal grave site'. You've got to understand some of the subtexts of living here. Most who live here actively defend their 'right' to property and 'white cultural heritage', or live the 'rural life' in quiet denial, wanting not to be bothered by questions about the ethics of presence. Or, at best, paying lip service to the issues while maintaining 'lifestyle'. There are exceptions, of course. Some live in the district to be 'close to nature', to 'restore', to 'protect'. And there are gestures of multicultural respect of diverse participation in 'community', but not in the main. Not yet. We always hope for positive change.

The psychology of a locale, of a district, a region. *Isolation* and *proximity* – the clandestine and the 'outside society' – merge. Australian flags and occasionally the Southern Cross are flown as a statement of solidarity and independence, of 'fuck you, this is *ours*'. As the mining boom Up North (which caught my father in the late sixties) evolved into a fly-in, fly-out workforce, 'cashed-up' workers bought properties around the region 'cheap', to set up their private lifestyles funded by extraction and mutilation of northern Indigenous lands. Theft leads to purchase and claim and a right of dictatorship. But like all such equations, it's also a complex intertwining of class: workers who have never had such access to money and the ability to acquire a slice of 'God's own country' make a statement of presence, exclusion, and their own ideas of community. There's a resistance to the wealthy having it all to themselves.

The new colonialism is one funded directly and indirectly by the mining industry, feeding the world's lust for energy and consumer goods. In articles I published between 2009 and 2012, I wrote of a neo-Luddism – a rejection of all non-vital technologies (vital technologies included many medical and essential service mechanisms); I abandoned the internet and largely avoided electricity. (It was then that I switched off the power to our Red Shed and it has rarely gone back on since.) I received threats, and even letters about coming around to teach me how to tune my VCR. And yet this decision was based in extensive experience rather than ignorance: I was making computers myself in the mid-seventies, and I could program commercial computers from 1978 on. My choice to leave behind fetishised consumer technologies was intended to be ethical. I accept that ethics are relative, but my intentions were to not participate in the consumer technology 'machine'. Not to opt out, but to resist through non-participation.

The *sell* of a 'new' sustainable world of lithium batteries, with the damage shifted from one form of extraction and manufacture to another, I feel might well mean the death of the biosphere. I am not offering a panacea, and I have not found any long-term solutions, dipping in and out of the technological world in a variety of ongoing ways, but I am saying we have to constantly be pulling back – progress is thought, ethics, arts, how we treat each other, and not the manufacture of new consumer goods to create a false fairness. Equality is the right to possess *as much* and *no more* than anyone else, in all things. Property, for me, is only what is held in common. Alongside the right to personal privacy, there is also the right of shared access – the door should always be open to outsiders and newcomers who want to share the responsibilities and the benefits of dwelling. Consensus, not the rule of an oppressive majority. Decentralisation, but with central notions and 'protections' of rights, not through surveillance but dialogue. It's possible, and my family and I have tried to live in conversation with local and broader communities, with the regional and the international. I have called this coexistence 'umbrella anarchism'. At its core are the rights of all living things, mutual aid and mutual respect. We also need to share the hurt – a redistribution of hurt so we all take on the responsibility of bigotry and its consequences. Idealism? Maybe, but it's the fuel of conversations at Jam Tree Gully. It's what Jam Tree Gully is.

Ah, listen! Multiple birds call suddenly from west of the house. Rufous whistler, Horsfield's bronze cuckoo and shining cuckoo. Nesting season will be stressful for some birds, easier for others. Talking with Tim about the sudden appearance of the golden whistlers, which have just as suddenly departed, he notes they were here before the big rain, then moved on. And pardalotes are out there as well. The cuckoos will be watching, watching. Nesting materials gathered and movements noted. Nests will be invaded, 'intruder' eggs laid and raised.

Wild oats are forming their grassland carpet – here they will be mowed and cut in October when they are dry, but on many other properties and on roadside verges they will be poisoned before they seed, and elsewhere they will be burnt (a front to legally illegally burn other vegetation). Each year the same pattern, each year the sickness of the land increases. Its spiritual health resists, but the colonial machine is well fuelled with what's left of a mentality that 'it's there for us to take'. Australia's high standard of living is as selective as middle-class cultural capital – plenty of people live below the poverty line, and there's a huge gap between the rich and the poor which is protected by the state. 'Class warfare' is not an expression used in the mining realm of Australia, but it's what's at its coalface. And coal is pursued with a zest that smothers the planet; it is a commodity of real and conceptual currency in Australia. The nearest coalfields to Jam Tree Gully are a couple of hundred kilometres south-east in Collie, where much of the state's power is generated. Quick bucks. Living standards. Employment. Climate change denial. Carbon capture schemes. Votes. The lies of elections. How we live – what energy we use – is bound up in the reality of an overheating planet.

~

Herbert Clark Hoover is no further away from Jam Tree Gully than my great-great-grandmother was as a young woman in Boston. On the other side of the family, on my mother's side, on her mother's side. My mother's grandfather was the foreman of the South Champion goldmine in Kookynie, out on the edge of the arid zone – he who was saved by a cameleer and a Wangai elder, he who died of dust on his lungs, the miner's disease, in Wooroloo Sanatorium, his children visiting him on the train from the city, so far from their birthplace, the place they only knew as home, unable to fully weigh up the consequences of presence, the power and corruptions of gold. And Hoover was an engineer in and out of the northern goldfields around the same era who invested at Gwalia (maybe the most famous mine in Western

Australia), and who became the premier influence on and driver of the production of lower-grade ore. People still speak of his influence with awe. Awe at his ore. This ranging and targeting colonial(ist) of the New World to the Newer World (ironically one of the most ancient places on earth, with one of the oldest and most persistent and intense civilisations), this displacing of Old World values (he filed his claims in London, capital of the empire) in order to plunder the most ancient of worlds.

Did my great-grandfather know Hoover? Maybe not on a personal level, but he would certainly have encountered him. And if they were both conservatives, and both of dissenting churches, they were different from each other, really. But both were representatives of extraction, and 'tough men'. My great-grandfather's drive was raising his family where he worked. The place also killed him.

And why Hoover comes to mind is because of a slippage, a slippage to different Hoovers who were of Columbus's waterworks, and the flow of the Olentangy River on Ohio which rolled past Tim's birthing in Riverside Hospital, and his rights of presence, born on American soil; a country that would later reject me because of my peace activities, my pacifist 'disorders'. Hoover Dam – named after those Ohio Hoovers, the great dam across Big Walnut Creek. And the Hoover Reservoir we used to visit when Tim was still in his pram.

What is most known of President Hoover now by townsfolk in Kalgoorlie, epicentre of Western Australia's gold world, was the poem Hoover purportedly wrote to a barmaid there – a love poem, a poem of infatuation. Likely written by one of the usual 'goldfields poets' – almost universally racist poets, hating 'Asians' and 'blacks'. Trade routes of hate underpin the colonial experience, the frontier's desiring.

When you're ostracised as a child, you don't align with the social group that expects you to be part of it. I did not belong with the other kids – I didn't belong anywhere. My best friend in Grade 6 of primary school was Japanese – an unheard-of friendship when bigotry left over from the Second World War (and well before) was prevalent. My primary school was predominantly and proudly and consciously 'white'. Though fortunately, not exclusively. Ataro was the only Japanese kid in the school and I am pretty sure his father was connected with mining. He and I were collectors of many things, and in this we found a bond that created its own cultural referents. It's not unusual for outsiders to find outsiders, but Ataro didn't consider himself an outsider – he just thought the other kids were 'jerks' for not getting where he was coming from. Their loss, and he was right. I admired this attitude.

On many occasions I was sexually assaulted by boys, and sometimes girls (usually in groups at the behest of their 'boyfriends', to shame me). This dynamic is not often spoken about, but when you've had your genitals exposed, hit, pulled and crushed, it doesn't matter if it's being done by a boy or a girl. To all intents and purposes, to them, I was neither male nor female. They considered me a non-person whose sexuality was questionable and to be mocked and destroyed. Being dragged out of a toilet cubicle, down the steps from the toilet block, and exposed to the slings and arrows of boys and girls in the quadrangle is not something that's easy to move on from. But as I grew older, I tried to understand what was wrong with the perpetrators, to understand what made bullies bullies, and what made people who weren't usually bullies into bullies when they were together in packs. I didn't want revenge – I wanted to understand, to make sense of it.

When I briefly connected with the circus through a show kid who was at our school for half a year or so, whose mother and sister wore false 'tits' when they performed, and short skirts, and glittered, I felt almost secure. I liked him, and he liked me – though I remember this better than he does, because in later life he made contact after reading something I had written about that period of my life.

I have written about this kid's household before – about Zelda the Snakewoman, and the kid, my short-term mate, riding the Globe of Death on his kid-sized motorbike. Years later, in 1978 and living in Geraldton, I saw him again riding the Globe as the show passed through town. I was with other 'friends' then, who did not really like me and found me weird – one of them was tilting a machine that built piles of coins and scraped them into chutes, and another was drinking green ginger wine behind a tent. I said, I know that guy, as he did wild manic loops inside the metal mesh planet on his now full-sized motorbike, and they just said, Ya bullshitter, no you don't. I didn't try to reconnect with my old friend after the show. I just took the shit and got sadder inside.

You make friends with those who will tolerate your company. What we all had in common, these later friends and I, was that we liked the bush, and camping out. With one of them, I would see a sack of kittens being thrown from a cliff into a dry riverbed under the eye of ancient red-rock caves, and opening the bag find that the poor creatures had had their mouths sewn shut. Another step in unbecoming the hunter I was to becoming an animal rights person. All of these moments in other times and places inform my life here at Jam Tree Gully. Unbecoming what I was, becoming who I might be – but they and I are one and the same person.

How many times across our lives do we tell our own stories, connect the lives of others to our own, make departures, lament lost connections? None of our experiences are stable, and all are in flux – the prevalence of birdlife outside this window today changes how I remember, say, the shooting of an eagle on the outskirts of a farm 'for taking lambs' when I was a small child, and the incredible hole it opened in that place and in my soul. I knew it was wrong. When I first started writing poetry at a very young age, I wrote of that, and I kept writing it into my early twenties, when I finally got a poem to express what I still cannot express in prose. And here I mention it because among all these birds, the great nemesis, the massive bird of the valley is not present. The eagles have been gone for at least a year – dispersed, or illegally killed? So much eagle killing goes on. In the Hoover Reservoir park in Ohio there are bald eagles. They can be seen. In the few remaining patches of fenlands with vegetation in Cambridgeshire, I have seen marsh harriers. These predators we look to for health of what they pursue. The opposite to the outcome of the leisure and self-empowering hunts here, where so much hunting is a white European statement of rights to fuse the technology of the 'West' with the pseudo-primal. It is a mockery of traditional societies by those who get off on blood-letting, who control as many 'environments' as they can. I see it, and I have known it.

~

Alcoholism and rural labouring became a strange kind of synthesis for me. From the age of twenty till thirty, I wandered, working to pay for booze and for a place to crash out. I always worked hard, both because I am obsessional and feel ashamed of a job done poorly, and also to sweat the grog out of my system. I often worked with my brother, the shearer, when he was wandering and not shearing. We hay-baled for Italian-Australian brothers caught between traditional family ways and partying up in the city, with one brother taking over the patriarch's mantle (extending to his grandfather, who ran a large dairy) while the other became the bête noire and a denizen of the city's red-light district. But these brothers loved each other, and brothers working with brothers was an intense sharing. Working with them was exhilarating, as we rounded the paddocks scooping up the cut grass for the hay baler, collecting the square bales and packing the truck like a puzzle cube, undoing and transferring it to the greater puzzle of the shed. It was good to sweat and itch together and fuse cultural knowledges. A strange temporary sense of connection and belonging that I kept looking for in my work.

Even once I had a partner, and a child coming, I shifted about, disrupted and disrupting, going on benders, labouring hard for a few days, making many temporary friends who were as close as people could be with each other for the few days the money and booze and substances lasted. Conversations were had that could never be had in any other way, but they would also evaporate, be left behind, mostly forgotten. Really, what I learnt was that I craved being in one place, but unbelonging made me restless, itinerant. Jam Tree Gully is the centre of the wheel of my life now, but the spokes still radiate out into other places of rest and contemplation, and action. And I know the problems, politically and ethically, of all centres built on false premises of presence.

I often think of my late friend Tom, of Gambier, Ohio, who worked on *The Kenyon Review*. When I first went to Kenyon on a visit to read and talk about my shortlisting for the Thomas Chair in Creative Writing, I spent most of my time with either editor David or with Tom, the managing editor. Tom drove me around, discussed varieties of tree – I developed a deep love of black walnuts and maples – and he introduced me to my first skunk. It was wonderful, though it sprayed the road as we passed by and the stench was in the street for weeks. I would become fascinated with the chemistry of skunk spray.

Tom took me out to where he lived on a small farm (from memory, about 70 acres), and wandering the ecotones, we discussed the edge effect and 'argued' over the work of Barry Lopez, whom he admired and felt *understood* where and how he was living, on the edges, trying to conserve, articulating the slippages. For me, Lopez is a hunter apologist who mediates nature through Western consumer desiring, and for all the beauty of his writing, he usurps the natural world he so 'values'. Anyway, we managed to find common ground in our discussions. And those wild turkeys! And the buzzards! And how houses around the edges can be without curtains and still 'interior', and we chatted over whether or not the lack of fences makes for better neighbours. I like the removal of fences from interactions. This is a motif – these friendships out of nature, inherently knowing where one can go, and where one shouldn't, out of respect. But also listening and learning about codes of presence.

Tom died after an aggressive cancer got hold of him. I wrote an elegy, which I include at the end of this memoir along with other poems of Ohio, because I feel the separation, the protectionist exclusion all the way here in Jam Tree Gully. I think of the trails we walked and about the right to walk them, the way to walk them. Poetry is a never-forgetting and a re-remembering.

Walking has been an important part of my interaction with

the world – trying to tread as lightly as possible, make contact and leave no damage. I want to connect with things, I want to see, I want to record, but I don't want to take. I enjoy walking with others, and that's a bond of friendship for me, but I also like to walk alone. I constantly walk around Jam Tree Gully, as does Tim, but I also walk wherever we're living. An attack of Graves disease–induced thyrotoxicosis makes you agitated and hyper, and Tracy can always tell when I've 'gone over' because my walks become excessively long, then I get home and immediately plan on going out again on another walk. I work as I walk, making lines to the beat of steps as I once made them to drumbeats on my brother's drum kit, and I memorise. What lasts is worth having, I like to think.

When living in Schull down on the Mizen in West Cork, I walk every day, no matter the weather – up into the hills and highlands, between areas of boggy ground. I see the damage of furze fires and the same tricks of burning off as we see back in the district around Jam Tree Gully, and I think of my Irish ancestors escaping English pitch-capping by hiding in the Wicklow Mountains, enacting violent resistance, escaping the famine, and I cannot relate to this response of violence meeting violence, and I founder on their own colonialism in the way they interacted with 'their' new land, their 'settlement' in south-west Australia. But famine pits of the tens of thousands in towns around Schull haunt the nights of all who come close, and ancestry works its way through even the most distancing lives of now.

Tracy's ancestors on her father's side also escaped the Great Famine, to Victoria's Western District. And when we walk together around Schull and Bantry and Skibbereen, we can't help feeling a mixture of joy between the hedgerows with bullfinches and wrens, and the horror of colonialism channelling people towards starvation, the policies that stole food from people's mouths. Walking is never a benign experience. And Tim has just come in from his walk around JTG in the here and now, and tells me the male splendid fairy wrens which nest in August are shifting from eclipse plumage to their brilliant, ecstatic blue plumage. This is the engine of the planet, and it is greater than all the profiteering that ever was.

~

Out here, I do not have much community outside family and occasional contact with people in shops when in town, or the odd conversation (or disagreement) with a neighbour. I do have contact with people when visiting the city, but not many. Much of my social interaction happens by way of correspondence. These days, it's email and occasionally snail mail, though I would abandon email again if I could – I have a three-year plan to leave the internet for a second time, and to leave use of Big Energy in every way possible. I have achieved this for long stretches at various times of my life. It is a continual goal.

When I travelled down from Geraldton to the city of Perth at the beginning of 1981 to start university, I wrote to people (writers, scientists … *people*) to make 'contact' – I instigated discussions. My grandmother (my mother's mother) was always a great letter writer, and as I stayed with my grandparents when I first arrived in the city, she encouraged me to sit down daily and 'do my correspondence'. Letters, and later emails (sometimes long, sometimes very brief) eventually led to extensive collaborative work, often begun in person and then maintained over the distance. I have had the good fortune to make creative works via letter and email with people from all over the world, and even across the region – for example, Yamaji poet Charmaine Papertalk Green and I worked together over a decade on a book confronting the legacies of colonialism, occasionally seeing each other in person and yarning for hours, and often swapping emails and the odd phone call. (I am not really a phone person and do not speak on mobile phones.)

Also, for maybe fifteen years now, I have swapped letter poems with Frieda Hughes – a kind of survival correspondence that has meant a very special and specific kind of friendship in which the private and now public merge, as we are publishing the poems in serial form in a literary journal.

And vital to me, in so many ways, has been the building of book-length works with the brilliant African and Jamaican and American poet Kwame Dawes. In our works we try to deal with dislocation and alienation from mainstream social structures, to find a way of talking out of and across 'black' and 'white', but also to create a poetry of justice. For me, and I think for Kwame too, this has been a lifeline of sanity, of working things out in figurative, autobiographical and documentary ways as part of a process of witness. We claim nothing, but we try to find ways of creating a picture of injustice and oppression, of repair. For me, Jam Tree Gully is the off-centre out of which I write uneasily – a point in my conception of being, almost lost but constantly rewarded (which I probably don't deserve) by healing of the natural world against the odds, the battering ram of 'progress' around us here.

One of the important things to me in all this swapping of fragments of psyche and experience is the use of slower than possible methods. Until a couple of years ago, we were on dial-up internet out here and couldn't swap large files; internet access was slow, often impossible. Now, though somewhat blocked by the hill, the granites and the red shed, there's a signal for wireless, but we have stayed on the lowest-speed broadband through the old copper network. We will wait till the last moment before our enforced *switch* – government seeks to control all our ways of being. We are using capitalist technology, but we update only when we have to. It's a statement – technology can be adequate and doesn't constantly need to 'improve'. I am communicating with you in an old way on an increasingly ageing machine. The manufacture of products for the sake of the market and technological addiction repels this reformed alcoholic, environmentalist and anarchist. My last computer made it through almost a dozen years, though it sat relatively quiet for a couple of those. I tried to file my work – typed on my manual typewriter – via fax machine, to make a point about pace, but review venues I wrote for soon rebelled.

Same with modes of travel. We use the slower ways where we can. We never fly in Australia these days, and haven't for many years – we drive across the Nullarbor as a family, in our small-engined car. Seems strange, but it's the lowest carbon footprint for a family in terms of travel across the country other than the train. On my own, I catch the slow Indian Pacific train to Adelaide or Sydney. In Europe, we catch ferries or ships where we can, and trains, of course. Less impact, fewer contrails, and a point to be made about the pace of life and the use of the planet.

~

In the shaded spots of JTG the moss bed is thickening. You'd think it would entirely powder away after the extreme heat, but for all its drying and dulling, it persists, especially at the points where moisture seeps out of the hillside. And the lichen is crusting and festooning granites and fallen trees with an energy that is exciting. It is faster than people might think. It will be a star-filled sky tonight, the moon falling away. I think of the abrasive moon dust and my great-grandfather's dust-eaten lungs, the chewing of the air sacs and his gasping for breath. He was an explorer of the underworld, down in the humidity below the desert sparseness, the red dust. He knew the names of surface birds and animals, but only second-hand, rumoured. Down below he knew the names of his own ghosts, and those of his multinational workforce drawn by gold fever but labouring in the monopoly mines of increasingly big companies, not a few of the visiting company men frequenting the brothel run by Japanese women so ostracised by the town during daylight hours.

But great-grandfather, you dug bones you did not know, the layers of origins, of making country – graverobbing, without being aware that's what you were part of. What did you learn as your daughter, my grandmother, heard the cries of Wongai children stolen from their mothers and put in government 'care'? And what of your daughter, my great-auntie, who would marry a veteran of Gallipoli, who was reported dead and later turned up with a bullet-grazed head and a bullet hole through his hand (we kids used to insert our fingers into the hole – urggh!), she who would become the last remaining widow of a Gallipoli veteran, and both of them opposing war and violence and working for Save the Children Fund? And she and her husband going up to Sarawak and Borneo to run colonial plantations and sending my mother a Malay language book and Mum's daughter-in-law occasionally casually conversing with her in Malay in regional Western Australia, though Mum studied Indonesian and not Malay, and her daughter-in-law's English is so good they swap few words in Malay now. The tendrils, the threads of family.

And now I am in the back of Mum's friend Auntie Jackie's

station wagon as she and Mum head home from the farm on Sunday night. We kids – my brother and I, and Auntie Jackie's daughter; we are a family of kids – are watching the wandoo canopies flash past in the demi-moonlight, and discussing the evening star. Yes, we've been there before and we are flashing back to the early to mid-seventies – all of us together, on the mattress in the back of the wagon, elbowing each other, hungry for space, for other worlds. And Mother and Auntie Jackie are talking about the week's groceries, our schooling, and where we will holiday in a few weeks. The farm is their security, too, where we can all be a family, an extended family, and work out what tolerance is, and isn't. When the big earthquake hit in '68 the wells dried up, but new tanks were put in and water was carted from the standpipe. We could never have long showers though, and often shared bathwater, because water was always so scarce. It still is out there – out here, too. Remember the hand-me-downs from the farm – country clothes worn in the city? Misfits, but connected to where we wanted to be, the farm. And the kangaroo we had for years, saved from the hunters, living on the back lawn, alone but safe from hunters. Eventually it found a home in a wildlife sanctuary with other kangaroos taken from family. Tendrils of deliverance? Costs.

~

I had that dream again. The one where I am standing in the corner of my grandparents' bedroom in Victoria Park, Perth, looking out through the windows south and west, looking onto Gallipoli Street and Staines Street. A corner block. I am looking across the roses and box hedges that harbour giant praying mantises and over the agapanthus which drunks behead every other year as they stagger past going nowhere in particular, flowers that are starbursts that were ancient suns reaching out through the cosmos. I am looking out across Rutland Avenue over to Kitchener Avenue, and even then I am musing the names of the roads, of their empire-militaristic assertions. This is the house of red brick and portal stained-glass window – kookaburras on a branch – which my mother ran home to, a mile from her school, as a small girl during the Second World War when the air-raid sirens sounded. The planes didn't reach Perth, but they went as far south as Geraldton, where one day she'd be an English teacher. I am staring out the window and nothing is happening other than a train – an older diesel train, not one of the new electric trains – going past towards the city. My grandfather used to catch the steam train into town to Rich Signs where he was a sign writer, and which he later managed, playing cards in the carriage with his mates. I am a child watching, and standing still and breathing quietly so I don't disturb what's going on in the world. I am waiting as others are waiting elsewhere in the house, in the gardens, for my Wheatlands farm relatives to arrive for a family gathering. Years down the track my grandparents will sell this house and move up to the farm, living in a wing especially created for them. And the last time I see my grandmother will be in York Hospital many, many years later, long after my grandfather has died, and she will hold my hand with her arthritis-harried hand and say, John, I want to see Bob again, I miss him, and I am ready. And I will be back in Cambridge, England, a few weeks later and she will leave on her search for her husband of so very many decades.

And I had that dream again. I just watch, and now I fill in the missing sensory details. It is a warm day, but not a hot day. There's a light breeze and the window is open. I am under the gauze curtains, which flutter about my head and shoulders, and veil the world behind me that I don't turn around to see. My grandfather is listening to the cricket in the kitchen, and my grandmother is cooking lunch. I don't know where the others are, passing the time, waiting for the arrivals. I can smell the roses – that deep red and orange smell. There's a New Holland honeyeater trying to stay upright on an agapanthus stem, but it falls away before flying fast to the neighbours' yard – anti-communists who 'escaped' and fear the 'reds', the Soviet secret police, even down here, so 'isolated' from the ideologies and grand narratives of the 'world'. And yet a product of them, retaining and keeping up the values, in this city which had boundary streets where 'natives' couldn't go, and places of curfew, and separations of humans, and theft. And there was a music club I'd vaguely heard of where music challenged the hate and fear and greed and broke down the barriers between 'whites' and 'blacks' in the forties and fifties. I was told, or I had heard somewhere. I listened in that daylit dream, but could only hear a train passing, the New Holland honeyeater, its (re)naming agitating the calm of the scene, and the breeze in the lace.

~

Around those rose beds at the Gallipoli Street house, my grandfather, my cousins and I smashed dozens of large asbestos panels into fragments to cover the sand so gravel could be laid over the top. Dust everywhere, karate kicks and fists of iron – it was a party. Like smashing bottles at the rubbish tips on the farm; like shooting tin cans on the fence down near the great flooded gum, pocked with lead, Dante-esque tree blocking the way down to 'the salt', the vast salt scalds that were gradually being reclaimed through tree-planting, salt scalds caused by clearing in lower areas, waterlogging in the hell-dry climate. But when rain came it filled the basin, drawing out the salt, making cities of crystals which I investigated. Many birds flew in and out of the great flooded gum, the only tree capable of holding back the salt, of saying this is where it stops. It did, and before it was too late and the great tree died under the saline stressing, the newer trees started drawing up the water, helping it out. And there was smashed asbestos on the farm, too – the old outdoor dunny we demolished, the tunnels we dug slowly through the rock-hard soil under the cage of asbestos remaining from our demolition. Everywhere, asbestos. Broken asbestos. And the extension on our house in the city by the river in the days when hundreds of acres of bush were intact just down the road, where the idea of a city was different, pulsing with its desires to increase itself, to occupy, but always verging on nature. As the builder, who was a gun freak, cut the sheets of asbestos, I stood by, showered in it, and we talked of guns. He taught me how to reload ammo and gave me machine-gun cartridges: .50 calibre. He introduced me to muzzle loaders and gave me lead balls that made me think of ill marbles. He was saturated in weaponry and I learnt his trade, absorbing it through the skin, lifting my serum lead levels higher and higher. Powder grains, detonators, rimfire and centrefire, recoil, the press, the moulds. All there, entrenched. And ejected … I was to become an anti-gun activist, and the knowledge of the how and why is still embedded, with the asbestos dust, with the raw asbestos rock – blue asbestos – on my bedhead, from which I peeled the soft blue fibres away from between their hard-rock 'casing', which I tasted and sniffed and felt closer to the earth, the neighbour father working at Wittenoom (a town in the north of Western Australia that is now degazetted from maps because it is such a dangerous toxic zone), who would bring back 'samples' from the mine as gifts.

When we first arrived at JTG I scoured the block for any sign, any fragments or fibres of asbestos, and found none. Though down the loop an old asbestos house had been recently demolished like it was an exercise in keeping fit, an experiment in home demolition. The fibres spread on the wind, the fibres are picked up on tyres and shoes. The fibres go somewhere.

In building our 'eco-friendly' home onto the old kit home here, we had the fibres in the cladding tested, and they came back 'no asbestos' – wood fibre and cement. We need to be vigilant. It broods inside me, and others. Asbestosis was one of the factors that led to the death of my father-in-law, who had demolished a number of asbestos houses over his lifetime. Asbestosis *and* melanoma, another legacy of demolishing in the sun without protection; an abreaction of our ongoing colonisation. Colonisation can also be physically tragic for the colonisers – and it is always psychically damaging; it has no positives, even while the colonisers push for their own advantage. It is never the way – it never 'makes better'. And the legacy of asbestos is hard to consign to the greed of more recent colonial history, of fifties and sixties mining, of James Hardy Industries knowing and denying. For it's still with us, and will be for a long, long time. The town of Wittenoom may have been degazetted, but its wastes are still brooding and dispersing. The fortune built out of such exploitation still manifests in the world today, still influences Australian economic, social and environmental policy.

~

In the small silver shed at JTG is a sign Tim held during the protests against the Roe 8 highway extension. It says: 'Save Our Birds/Save Our Native Bushland/No Roe 8'. It was written by someone in the protest camp, and Tim held it up so motorists would understand. He received warmth and abuse in equal stead. I think about the word 'our' – another colonial conjuring trick, but one meant with genuine shared affection and hope, certainly by young Tim. Stolen land and then protected, but at least not stolen and then demolished. And there were Noongar elders informing the campaign of resistance, and it was certainly *their* bush that was under threat. The right-wing Barnett government of the time used every dirty trick up its sleeve to push the highway development through this magnificent remnant bushland, so rare in the centre of the city of Perth. Banskia-marri bushland, and the home for so many species of birds and animals and plants, including the endangered Carnaby's black cockatoo and the marsupial quenda, or southern brown bandicoot. The attempts to save this urban bushland had been going for many years, but as the bulldozers began their dirty work, it roused many people who'd usually let these things go to come out and participate in the resistance. Animals were removed from the kill zone in extreme temperatures and perished; bulldozers operated behind fences with security guards. We came down from JTG to help resist, and I deployed poetry to thwart the machinery. We had to remove Tim from the protest sit-in because bulldozers throughout the area were unearthing and dispersing dumped building materials that contained asbestos.

A friend and I ventured illegally into the 'wound' (as I termed it) to record the devastation. So many protesters had had enough of seeing the bush butchered before their eyes, and breached the fence in a surge of anger. Young people locked themselves onto machinery, climbed trees and had to be removed by the police. I am no stranger to environmental actions, but what was so amazing about this one was that the middle class emerged from their more distant houses, came down to the working-class suburb, and lent their names and bodies to the Beeliar Wetlands resistance. The spirit of that moment, which stopped the damage, though much wounding had been done, is ongoing. But the asbestos fibres are out there – asbestos from which so much Perth housing was made, which is an ongoing crime of exploitation, especially of less well-off people, of those who have lived in state housing, of those who cannot afford new builds.

~

I repeat details as I build memory. These expanding echoes, thinning yet encompassing more. As genetic engineers invade the barriers against invasion into memories, as they alter to suit their vision of the future, their profit margin, so the construction and reconstructing of memories becomes more vital, becomes an act of resistance. They are here, and their motifs branch into the forgotten to elicit a sense of purpose in the now, but also a tracing of how we arrive at loss and destructiveness. The genetically modified fields of canola are being trampled down in the public's desire for selfies in the disturbingly bright yellow fields – the glow of the new modernity.

~

While living in different countries, different cultural spaces, we have never tried to recreate what we've left behind in our journeying. But we know the longing for absent familiarities. Maybe we recreate them by writing them – I have always agreed that distance clarifies. But in writing the places we've lived outside of the Western Australian wheatbelt, I have increasingly created hybridised poems – poems of many places at once – that rather than appropriate the places we've become a part of, allow the knowledges of 'home' to commune with the acquisition of knowledge about the new places. These conversations I have called 'polysituatedness' – the being in and of many places at once. Place is both fixed and fluid, and I feel a need to trace this. But we never wish to make 'little Australias' in, say, Schull or Mount Vernon or Gambier or La Réunion. We want to listen, learn, respect, but also retain our knowledge of where we've come from, even though it is a disputable and disrupted 'home' and 'belonging' we come out of.

Having said this, anxiety for what's been left behind is a constant. Mum and Guru are our conduits to Jam Tree Gully in our absence, not only by looking over and maintaining JTG, but in the spirit of respecting what we're trying to do and undo in 'being' there. They understand. So, very often, I write poems of the place I am in – observations and experiences fusing with language, always evading 'labelling' – and these poems converse with what I hear is happening at JTG … a mimesis in which the sounds of birds and the swaying of trees in an easterly inform the structure of the poems themselves. We receive 'Guru Reports' about the state of the grass cutting, about the birds and animals he's seen, about what's happening around the district. I should say that 'Guru' is an affectionate and ironic name for John, who is not remotely guru-like, but is vastly knowledgeable about issues of self-sufficiency, communal survival (no fortresses here!), and practical matters of life. He respects our vegan ethics (is a vegetarian himself) and has always been a labourer – he has a strong work ethic, like my shearer brother. But not at the cost of the planet or others.

In our anti-nationalism we never consider ourselves as 'expats' but as participants in community insofar as that community wants us. Our concern is protection of the environment, and that's an international language. Our experiences at JTG can be transferred to other situations of damage and reclamation, but not imposed. But a comparative language of respect for the natural world can grow, rather than a universal language of technology as panacea which brings some equalities, but greatly diminishes others through the exploitation of both people and the environment. (Loss of habitat is a loss for people as well.)

~

Concurrent with the Roe 8 protest was the Cathedral Avenue protest, just outside the town of York. The Department of Main Roads insisted that road widening was the way to reduce road deaths throughout wheatbelt Western Australia. Obvious methods such as reducing speed limits were pushed aside in the obsession to empty the 'long paddock' of trees. Cathedral Avenue is a stretch of road between York and Quairading, so-called because of the massive overarching wandoo trees that had formed a roof over the road. Before the situation could be assessed properly, or challenged, Main Roads started bulldozing these trees, reclaiming 'private' land, and widening the road. As a family, we participated in the resistance to this mindless destruction of trees hundreds of years old. There were other methods that could be used to make the road safer – it was already a high-quality road. Again, writing and reading poems was part of this process.

I have long claimed poems can stop bulldozers, and that comes of reading poems in front of bulldozing in my late teens to try and help stop bush clearing behind what is now Murdoch University's extended campus – which, in fact, connects to the Beeliar Wetlands. I did stop a dozer when a driver jumped down to discuss what I was up to, and we talked unionism and environment. The development continued, and though dozers had their tanks sugared by unnamed parties, the bush was horrifically cleared. But I had made contact, and dialogue happened with a worker, and that showed me it was possible. Again, though many people came together in different ways, from conservative farmers to somewhat radical ecological activists, Cathedral Avenue was largely demolished. Some trees were saved, with slight adjustments to the clearing plan, but by and large the Main Roads got what they wanted. To stop this ongoing damage, a language of resistance needs to coalesce across communities, and across the world. Bulldozers are deadly weapons – and so easily one can fall under their blades. A driver trying to scare a protester can so easily be overwhelmed by the immensity and power of the machine, and can maim or kill even if it's not their intent. I take these machines seriously, and it's part of why I tell other protesters to address the machines but never put themselves at risk – a death helps no one.

This memoir is one possible minuscule conduit in that discussion of how we might live lives outside indifference to damage (what we don't know can hurt!). What was deeply moving in the Cathedral Avenue protest was that a friend, a local newspaper editor and also a 'landowner' along the road, threw himself into the resistance with an inspiring passion. He and I were photographed with our fingers just managing to touch as we wrapped ourselves around one of the massive wandoos – a tree so ancient, a tree that was habitat to so many creatures, a tree that was helping hold together a bareness and blankness induced by overclearing – that is now gone. We tried to advocate for it. We're two big blokes, and our fingers could only just touch, so mighty was the girth of that tree, that living entity, that city of nature, that witness to lives before and after colonisation, that witness to the intrusion, the damage, and also joy as well as loss. The killing off of the witness itself. It's part of the ongoing colonisation, the design of a material matrix to maintain total control.

Around where we live there are many who live anti-government lives, yet they do so with the flag of the nation at their gates – a sign of patriotism that claims something 'deeper' and even more insidious than administration. As with the American prepper separatist, it is so often a looking to the soil, to nationhood via birthplace, as validation of the violent rejection of community, to the dispossessing of First Peoples through a selective and colonial *jus soli* while often rejecting refugees and new migrants. Fused with a patriotism also forged with a racialised version of *jus sanguinis*, a heady mixture of rights and exclusion comes into play whereby the military is seen as a legitimate source of pride as it extends back through the military actions of history (from empire to ally of America), and the government is pressured to be compliant to this vision of 'our country'.

This far-right envisaging of an Australia for some and not others is about the occupation of land and a belief in a right to destroy or 'shape' and 'carve out' that land as an extension of presence. As an anti-nationalist and an anti-militarist, I am even more suspect than the government to these occupiers of chunks of land. For me, to 'occupy' is to dispossess, and even when I was involved in the Occupy events in London and Cambridge, I did so always pointing out that in reclaiming space consumed by capitalism, we also have to be wary of those even less privileged presences we exclude in our 'occupying'. And very often, this includes the non-human.

But I engaged with Occupy in the spirit of anti-capitalism

and anti-oppression and pro-justice and pro-equality in which it 'evolved' and erupted. The control of not only wealth but moral discourse by big companies and big financial entities needs to be undone. Occupy did not achieve this, but it drew attention to the issue in a general way and offered more collective tools to work towards an undoing. Its problem is in its solution – Wall Street and the City of London and other financial focal points are empowered by consumers. The morality they serve up is one co-created with the markets they create and enforce. Seeing occupiers with mobile phones is a contradiction I could not decode. Speaking of ecological resistance to those camping outside St Paul's, and writing poems to the archbishop to not 'move on' the occupiers, and standing and being counted were relevant and essential to me. Non-violent presence to disrupt the flow of business-as-usual is a positive thing. It ended because consumer life calls in subtle ways, on so many levels of the chain of 'supply'. Patience is short. Protest cannot occur merely in short bursts, but has to be a web of activities that retain their connections and do not get sidetracked by dramatic thrill points, points where people can channel anger and other emotions at the expense of the overarching concerns, which are preservation of the biosphere and justice not only for all individuals, but for their collective communities and other life as well.

I constantly ask myself how best to write protest so as to continue protests, to contribute to a shift in language so language is by default more just, but also more 'free'. One factor would seem contingent on another, but as selfish 'self' libertarians will tell you, this equation is not always the case, and rarely resolvable. When I write fiction of protest, I do so with both self-critique and the critique of contradictions in protest movements in mind. I am concerned with *motives*. One needs to unpick these contradictions to move forward. I wrote a story of a forest protest in which men, and one man in particular, exploited 'feral' female protesters because in resisting the 'redneck' and often abusive male forest workers, they assumed a togetherness bringing 'free love' where no permission had been granted. The 'free love' was about the men having their way, not about the women having a right of refusal. And, indeed, I have seen this kind of abuse go on in camps in forests where women have been subjected to patriarchal impositions in many different forms – from having to do the cooking to being expected to provide sexual favours – on the basis that it shows a weird form of unity against the tyrants. Unless we identify tyranny within movements acting for justice, there will be no justice – things rapidly unravel.

But I couldn't write that in a poem – in a poem I act as witness and process the damage done. I don't wish to lecture, but I wish language to process what is seen and to be part of how it's discussed. The poem is a living entity, experiencing distress, searching for joy. It can be an uncomfortable enacting of experience. The poem is an organic entity, often escaping its act/s of making.

~

The dam pump won't work. It's the early eighties and I am caretaking Wheatlands farm for my uncle and auntie. I have topped up the oil, refuelled, worked the choke. It's just not biting. I have a few tools with me, and unscrew the spark plug. Yes, carbon build-up. I have a spare – not a new one, but another I have cleaned up with a wire brush in the vice down in the tool shed. Okay, pull the ripcord a few times … gargle, gargle … a little flooded. Pull back the choke, starve the fuel. Pull the cord a few times to dry the cylinder. Then fuel full on and it kicks. Water is being drawn from the diminished red-ochre pool of the dam up into the storage tank. I pull myself up the rungs of the tank, hands hooked over the sharp top, and peer in, and the bloody water is swirling in, making its Charybdisian whirlpool.

I have been studying the classics and I am enacting the *Odyssey* on the farm as both absorption and irony. I am alone, no one for miles, and I like the state of being. My friend Craig will be driving up from Perth to visit in a few days. I am not a vegan yet – that will come after Craig and I get back from Nepal, flown home on insurance after a horrendous bus crash which changes everything. Witnessing human death puts all death into absolute focus. But I am not a vegan yet and I go down to the dam to pull a koonak trap. I am not even sure if this dam is still stocked with koonaks, a type of freshwater crayfish. The dam on the edge of the salt that ironically still runs fresh *is* stocked – I have been pulling the traps for a few days. I ate koonaks and rabbit, which seems so strange to me now after thirty-three years of veganism that I must slip out of the present tense for a moment into the past. But now I am back in that past present. I am there, I am in that *now* … I think I am close to the land, but I am persecuting the land in ways my epic journey around the farm can't elucidate. I check the water troughs for the sheep, I feed the chooks and the guineafowl. And then I am driving the ute and a ram wanders out onto the road in the twilight and I brake and skid on the gravel beneath the overarching salmon gums, infused with pink light and tamping heat that won't quite let go. Another step on the way to animal rights activism comes in the next moments. The ram has a broken neck but is still alive. I haul it onto the back of the ute, drive it back to the farmyard, go to the house and take the rifle from the elevated kitchen cupboard, load it, and go out into the yard. I lean the weapon against a fence post – NEVER do that with a loaded gun – and haul the dying ram to the ground as gently as I can. It's a huge weight, a massive wool-laden merino – my brother always says shearing rams is hell difficult – and it slowly thuds to the ground. I take the weapon, look into the beyond-description eye of the ram, and I can smell its short breaths, and I shoot it in the head. And that's the end of guns for me. That's a signing-off. The ram's death warrant is also my own death warrant. And the heavy drinking I do afterwards – drinking well into the next afternoon, is a disgrace to the memory of life.

~

My auntie is trying to teach me French verbs. We are on the verandah at Wheatlands farmhouse and the kangaroos are at the garden fence. Twenty-eights are busy in the fruit trees and we both interrupt to say it's a good thing for the twenty-eights that Uncle is out somewhere on the farm. He shoots twenty-eights. I used to shoot parrots too, but I no longer do and haven't for forty years. I want to be able to read Rimbaud in the original. I am at the farm recovering from addictions, from months of wandering the streets and pubs and clubs of Perth. I cannot repair in the city. I have been raging with the punks and resisting the nationalist fascists. I am unable to sustain a relationship, and I feel I can do nothing but walk out onto the salt, and read. And try to learn my French verbs (past tense). Matching the endings of words, working the genders, is fuzzy as I try to realign my focus to a life of hope, of being somewhere outside the certainty of addiction. But my growing clarity is only a hiccup, for I will descend fast and far again and again. And I will lose all I love and care for, only to get it back and lose it again. I walk among the needle trees and let them reach out and scratch me. The finches would prefer I was elsewhere, I am sure. But I love them, too. And I love the wastes of destroying salt because they harbour the needle trees and the finches. All the planted tamarisks are a protective barrier, too. These islands on the scuppered Odyssey I began years ago with no home to return to because I have trashed it. One day I will recover. I will always question what home can be, but I will always love those I should love, even if I treat them appallingly on the way to the place of my *unbelonging* I can care for the damage, I can restore. Deracinated always, but knowing that rhizomes are reaching through. I can barely believe it's twenty-three years sober. My mantra.

~

Rain is predicted for tomorrow, but not a lot. It's clouding over, with patches of sun. On the sunless side of the house, there's (unusually) a sun skink on the verandah. As Tim just said, filming it for one of his nature documentaries, 'A skink in July!' Tim has recorded life on the block for years in the form of lists, reports, photos and videos. He has built up patterns of behaviour and presence (and non-presence) over years, creating a comparative interactive tool that is highly revealing in terms of what is managing to persist, what creatures are coming here for shelter, the various irruptions and fadings.

In the years of Tim's homeschooling at Jam Tree Gully, Tracy built in integrated curriculum that included all the broader education requirements, augmented with the 'here', especially in terms of ethical and political consequences. Further, in her working to create a rich language matrix for Tim, one that calls on his extensive experience living in other countries and cultural spaces, he developed (and develops) a means of talking across places, and respecting the connections between language and belonging.

Tim is fascinated with birdsong not only in itself, but also because of how it communes with 'here'. He often asks us to recount our sightings of birds and the observations we made of them, how we interacted with their lives (and vice versa) when he was a baby and toddler and small child in Ohio. He tries to piece this together as part of who he is, and where he has been, and which birds were there speaking at the time. They are part of him, too. Their song, their words.

Tracy has just brought to my attention Lequeu's *The Great Yawner*, his bizarre designs for 'entries' into 'hunting realms', the follies made of his work. She is translating bits from French articles on 'bad taste' and the 'pre-postmodern postmodernist', and I am considering the 'big yawn' and the clothes of this late-eighteenth and early-nineteenth-century public servant (in essence) and sometimes pornographer, as it exposes something of the terrifying (and murky) depths of 'Westernisation', the machine of cultural certainty and expansion. Such interventions in the flow of the day are commonplace at Jam Tree Gully – our rural 'isolation' is no isolation at all. It is a conduit in a conversation that is neither broad nor narrow but pulsating and necessary. I look out through the library window (study, storeroom of books), and Tim walks past with that look that says he's heard something special – so I listen hard, and hear a twenty-eight conversing with … what … a butcherbird? Tim will report in detail when he comes in. Of that, I am sure.

And in every house in the valley, between the paddocks and sheds and spaces people have tried to empty (they can't) to refill with their utilities, in those houses there are conversations, too.

We read the local news of drug raids and robberies, of domestic and other violence, of accidental fires running away from the *owner's* ability to control them, and it's part of the 'flow', the disruption, the presence. An ant runs up the slat of the vertical blind, suddenly active before the gentle cold front arrives, that warming as introduction to 'weather', it runs up and down, marking its trail for others to follow, foraging. I will lift it gently and take it outside, before the procession begins. I think of Robbe-Grillet and a room and dust and imprints left. *Which* novel was that? – so many years have passed. *Labyrinth*? What did the prints in the dust mean? And did the old steps leave after-traces, motes still trying to settle where there was no longer a disruption of moving bodies of breath to disturb them? That is not Robbe-Grillet's story, not really, but something taken from it mixed with some other memory. *Here!* watching the early afternoon light already trying to be crepuscular, I fixate on a piece of bark maybe 4 metres from the window, flapping in the gradually lifting breeze. Is it a good place for the ant, which is now on the desk, to return to? Has it ever foraged on that piece of bark? Is it familiar with its textures? There is dust on some of the books in this library, but not all, because we use so many so regularly. We do not *own them*, though we purchase them and the law of property says we own them. But no one can own words, not even that which contains those words. They are there and we must read and re-read them, though they likely tell us nothing or little of what's directly outside. But that's not true, because they do. As we know. As you know, too.

Tim is back inside and very excited – he saw a spotted pardalote up close. With the total-recall brain he has, he says, 'The last time one was seen here was by you out near the big tank on July 1st, 2017. And now I have just seen one up close, right next to my face, near the group of young York gum trees on the bank above the red shed. I got some video – not great video, but enough to identify. They have such amazing patterns on their feathers – there is nothing like it, Dad!' And I agree. I see the footage. The bird turns its rump on technology. Incredible pattern you are driven away from, and distracted by. What is it to record, to identify? What technology can be 'good' technology? In the consequences of every part, every aspect of the camera's making – the birds that suffered in its conception, its realisation. We discuss these things. In our memories and words are the best images. We compare notes of all those interactions unrecorded. Consequences. Least-impacting ways.

Suddenly, in my mind's eye I have the statue of Patrick Kavanagh by flowing water in Dublin – yes, on the Grand Canal and he is sitting down, no doubt after a few drinks. Is one encountering him supposed to think, After a few drinks? Would he have wanted it that way? And there's a bird on his shoulder, then on his hat. And that's part of this, too. I could look up an image of the statue online, slowly (how is one slow with the almost instantaneous? Well, pages load slowly out here!), but prefer not to … just memory, my memory, will do. With its haziness and vividness, with its emphasis and loss, what I have in my mind's eye is what I need, and tells me more.

What does it mean talking sotto voce to an ant, and listening to Babes in Toyland's *Painkillers* while thinking about Mahler's Sixth Symphony? It's as if all these threads of here-and-now should separate themselves off, but they won't and can't – nerve bundles of presence. Earlier, listening to the remarkable lone album of the late-eighties, early-nineties southern Arnhem Land Aboriginal band Broken English, I felt I had cross-threaded my sense of how to express any kind of 'being', any kind of receptivity and creativity – just listen to their 'sunset' song and you might know what I mean. No sunsets are the same anywhere, and people never read them in the same way, though they have cultural auras and truths some groups of people can access, but not others. I concern myself with sunrises and sunsets, but I observe within a limited band. I know there's more, much more, than I can see. So much is outside my spectrum, and my years of using hallucinogens did not expand them, though I thought I saw colours that did not exist. There's no knowledge to be gained from flashbacks. I try to write this in a poem to Kwame. We are swapping poems about 'family', about stories and what they make of us.

Some friends have visited us here at Jam Tree Gully. Some have passed on now. One came and was disturbed he could not smoke – I was also once a chain smoker, but this is a no-smoking house. And in dry weather in the tinderbox valley, there's no smoking outside either. He smoked in his car. But he believed in the tree planting, the *semantics* of stopping the erosion of gradients and letting open areas close over – he supported the philosophy of Jam Tree Gully. We worked together in being here together. When he died we were in Schull, West Cork, and we were so distraught we travelled into the Caha Mountains to Barley Lake on the Beara Peninsula, and lamented the cut turf and celebrated the wisps of bog cotton. It was so steep, so risky. And rare choughs were on the mountainside, and rampant rhododendrons so beautiful and invasive and unwanted. The elegy writes into you, a tattoo of absence and dislocation. And the dark reflections of the lake eye to the low sky at the old red rock summit, sheep on ledges, fleece flying tattered from fences in tufts. Spark across the gap? Colonial equivocations, as our brilliant friend, our deconstructivist thinker friend knew. From the Beara to Jam Tree Gully – neither places of him specifically, but informed in us, in our permanent passing, by our respect and love for him. What to do with these residues? How to survive them?

My eyes start to itch, and hurt. They are running. I hear a motor *running*. I heard it earlier as well, and thought someone was just mowing or pumping water. I asked Tim to keep an eye out in case someone was spraying. He couldn't see anyone. An hour has passed since then and the motor is still going and my eyes are really sore. I go out and climb the hill and there on Mount Toxic is His Poisonness, using his ride-on, dragging a motorised spray tank, flooding his entire 11 acres. The taste is in the air. I might add, he's wearing a full mask, so he *knows* what the poison does. Herbicide runs down through the cracks between wild oat lashes, bloodying the eye of the rise. Our water supply, the nurtured unpoisoned soil, is being 'drifted over' again – misted ('merd'). These people are desecraters of the land. They just don't *get it*, and do not care. We are below them and copping their laziness, their unwillingness to look after their 'grass' with the least impact – it can always be cut. If their mower can cart a spray wagon, it can cut the grass. They have chosen school holidays so the kids of the valley can 'enjoy' their labours, their horticultural pursuits. The increase in behavioural problems in schools, the agitation and aggression and inability to concentrate is more than anecdotal throughout the wheatbelt, and the spray culture drifts in like the pollution it is. The chemicals break into chromosomes. Resist the propaganda of chemical companies and scientists funded by their profits, and accept that this is more than a possibility. Any risk is a risk that shouldn't be taken. So, a green Mount Toxic will be sick orange in a week or two's time. We will see the withering, the death. This the husbandry of the hill where they grow trees they hope will poke through and smile against the backdrop, the carpet of death, as an inflection of the agricultural methods that have left so much of Australia's environment so physically and psychically damaged.

The poisoners should look deeply into the research – the research beyond the propaganda – regarding the effects of herbicides on humans, and on birds and animals, and on the natural world in general. It is the mist of colonialism, its ultimate expression of getting between, of intervening, of changing to suit the occupation of space, of floating over once the mass clearing is done. Hanging in the air, the soil. Residues. It is the tool of their satisfaction, and the three of us living here receive their wisdom, breathe it in, wear it on our clothes and skin. A spray day is inevitably a 'fine day', especially as rain approaches – getting the spray in quick. I have written again to our neighbours of the high place (a year since the last letter). Tracy has intervened and softened the letter as she points out that my anger expressed in the letter will not open their minds to the issue one iota. So here's the version I will get to them via the town post office (if I can):

> Dear Residents of the Property Above Us
>
> We … suffer the fallout from your mass herbiciding program.
>
> It poisons our water, the land and the air. We don't understand why you would choose school holidays, and without warning.
> We have a child.
>
> Have you researched the health consequences of the herbicide with which you flood your block?
> We have mentioned this before.
>
> Yours,

There's a jonquil confirming its presence between the septics and the edge of the house-tier bank. It defies the mist. It's a new day and the sprayers have gone. After all, why would they stay in the fallout zone they've created? We are going away tomorrow for ten weeks in order for me to be close to Curtin University, where I have a research fellowship, and for Tracy to do some work, though I will be up once or twice a week from Midland to see how things are, to reconnect. Were we not going away, we'd probably still leave for a few days till the orange revelation showed the truth about what's been done.

We went into town this afternoon to renew Tim's Australian passport – and Tracy's, as it turned out; we missed that it has expired. Tim has an American passport which we renewed when I was applying for a new American visa. It took so many months to get mine through the vetting processes that we'd become entrenched in Ireland, and by the time we got back to Australia the consulate had cancelled it. A constant state of having to prove this pacifist is worthy of entering the 'land of freedom'. As I once wrote in a poem, 'the irony stings the sense'. A life dedicated to pacifist liberty, to the very essence of freedom for all living things and the land itself, and I have to struggle through the 'permanent record', the indelible imprint the authorities so love to wield as authority over one's identity. You are what the law has found you to be, whoever's law that is or has been. It's who's seen and been counted to whom the vigorous refusal is directed.

The post office person said to Tracy, So you're going back home? We guess it's because of having to process Tim's birth certificate, which lists a hospital in Columbus, Ohio, and then his parentage certificate (Australian citizenship), but we always give this sense of us having come from elsewhere, even though we were born here, and our families are here. But living 'overseas' always makes you 'odd' – home is never sure of what you are. Tracy just said politely to the person, who is always friendly, Just a holiday for Tim and me, and John will have work to do.

At home again, the fire set, but it's warm already. This is the warmest winter during the daylight hours that I remember. The nights have been cold, but the days well above average temperature. I have always been obsessed with the weather, and next year I am going to do a Bureau of Meteorology weekend workshop. As a child, I made a weather station which I installed at the top of the silky oak tree … but I have told that story in an earlier memoir and in poetry. It's one of those leitmotivs, like lines of 'constant pressure' – isobars on the weather map. They bind the chaos together for me, because I need both the predictability of chaos and the predictability of order. Both factors 'make' a seeing into the nature of place, and poetry.

I am thinking of my days going wild to the Dead Kennedys – a vent for political frustration that translated, was expressed in my interactions and fusings with Perth and Fremantle, Western Australia. Once, being arrested by an old 'schoolfriend' policeman at the wharf protesting against the Seventh Fleet and nuclear weapons, I sang Dead Kennedys lyrics out loud. And I swore. As my dreadlocks flailed around (my hair naturally dreadlocks; there was no appropriative intent, any more than having bare feet and wearing homemade clothes), I was dragged off in front of the television cameras, silver gulls screaming back louder than the far-right supporters of the Reaganite projection of military power who yelled they'd 'get' me.

Those same far-right anti-protesters conducted the racist campaign in Perth that ended in fire-bombings of Chinese restaurants. Their violence against the 'Trot hippies' was acceptable to more of the public than my singing Crass songs or the Dead Kennedys' 'Chemical Warfare'. (Not that the Green movement sided with 'anarchists' like me – we were too unpredictable in our rejection of all middle-class social values, even though we were vegan and 'peaceniks'.) I was left in the police lock-up cells to rot. I have never forgotten it, not out of anger, but out of a failure to connect, to show them I/we cared as much as the Greens crew did for non-violence and an unpolluted world. But my/our rejection of so much of the capitalist world was too much for middle-class Greens. But then, to be honest, there was also the world of drink and substances and music, and that confused the picture and made us far less useful in working through the system. I/we stood outside the system, and we were 'lost'. If we'd managed to connect with like minds still with one foot in the socially acceptable camp, could we have made a difference? I don't know, but I do know we were there because we wanted to stop all projections of force, wherever they came from. It was never 'anti-American' or anti any other people, it was anti-militarism, anti-violence, and anti-damage to the biosphere, values I still hold firmly.

~

Chemistry, organic chemistry in particular. That was to be my future as it fused with *Finnegans Wake* and the poetry of Rimbaud. And rocketry. Those stories will come in time, subtexts to this narrative of Jam Tree Gully where the chemistry is of understanding invasive poisons and the damage they do to body, air, soil, water. Working in the laboratory during school holidays, I was supported in entering a national science research competition; my subject was chemiluminescence. I was working with compounds of massive molecular weight. I had a theory and could prove it. The head of the lab called it radical and revolutionary. I was reading Kropotkin on mutual aid and was interested in the radical, but I thought the suddenness of revolution was too often a smokescreen for tyranny. How to work that seemingly contradictory equation? The lab had the huge mineral sands plant of Allied and Jennings a few hundred metres to the north; between them and the lab and to the south were large extruded paddocks that were rarely green, and yet sheep nibbled at tufts of thin grass and saltbush. I thought of the fallout, as I also made fallout back at home, the liquid and gaseous and solid residues of my experiments flowing into the yard, into my brother's chook pen, into the DNA of his bantams. As I ran the X-ray equipment at the lab late at night I had access to radioactive standards for calibrating the equipment. A fool boy there on school work experience got hold of enriched yellow cake, removing it from its lead-lined security box and chasing me around, trying to rub it over my genitals. And then one day I took home a jar of thorium nitrate and experimented with that. The exposures were horrendous. Reading Keats and being swaddled in radiation. I know what toxicity is and why we need to resist it. We can exist without the toxicity.

As my home labs grew in sophistication over those high school years, from occupying a corner of a shed, to a laundry, to half a large shed, by blurring the chemical and alchemical nature of 'experiments', I matrixed it all around poetry. I became more interested in the abstract qualities of experiments – in their metaphysics. No gold (though I had a gold nugget to standardise testing), no philosopher's stone, but Paracelsus as a way through to the spiritual via 'material properties'. This odd way of seeing the world was taken with me out into the bush where I often wandered around Geraldton with my brother and a friend. It made me alert to contamination and things being out of place. My friend Peter and I once found a stick of gelignite, which we reported, but not before touching its sweating bizarreness, and on another occasion I came across a stash of hidden or abandoned out-of-date medication. (I also unearthed some when digging in grey sand as a child, trying to turn a garden into a complex of dams and weirs.) And shortcutting through a bush block to avoid a massive beehive in an old river red gum on its edge, my friend and I came across a penis enlargement vacuum device in a decrepit and broken-down box. Some of this stuff can only reside in my fictional stories, existing on the verge of the real and unreal as it does.

Evening is closing in. We get two evenings here – the sun dipping below the hills (which are low, really, at 270 metres above sea level, but with the mainly flat plains just north of here, that's elevated, and there's the winter creek of the valley leading into Toodyay Brook down to the Avon and the greater valley itself), making an orange-purple winter bruise on the lip of hills, casting their haze, and then the real evening of the sun going down over the distant sea. We get two strange effects, like a curtain being drawn in stages. Maybe you have to be here, or be like the jonquil, its petals almost oscillating trying to pick up signals to help it understand what state it is in – neither completely radar nor sonar nor light meter nor seismograph registering the bauxite 'test site' intrusions, or the quarry blasts, or the occasional wheat train passing below the loop … none of these completely, but certainly all of them, as it is with us.

We are going into the absence, the being away – returning to 'keep an eye' and restore our godshaped holes, but away, in absence. But as we are leaving I notice a second, no, a third jonquil. Like Easter lilies, these are markers of colonial presence – planted way back, when cottages began appearing on the land grants. At the bottom of the north end of the loop, there's a shepherd's cottage that dates back to the mid-nineteenth century. The plantings here are much, much later, of course, but they work in mimicry of the colonial garden filled not only with European plants, but plants picked up along the way, especially from the Cape as the ships stopped off at the tip of Africa before catching the trade winds to the 'Great Southern Land'. I had a great-great-great-uncle on my mining grandmother's side who was captain of a ship that went down rounding the Horn of the Tierra del Fuego on the other side of the trajectory, the path back to Europe, laden will bullion. That was the New Zealand immigrant side of my grandmother's family – Scots and Cornish miners and a harbour master of Port Chalmers, Dunedin and then a double emigration to the Victorian goldfields and then the Western Australian goldfields. These displacements and displacings. *Narcissus jonquilla* from Iberia naturalised in colonial beds, bulb by bulb. Easter lilies which flourish also near the septics and on the edge of the fall away to the next tier … origin Taiwan? Cultivated and sold throughout the world at the height of the colonial reach, of the reach of industrial capitalism before the First World War. In the pink flush of their trumpets, constrained and diminished this year because of the long dry. With Easter dusty, I still thought of their journey, their version of the time machine, the use they are put to even when we didn't plant them and don't cultivate their reappearance. We just let them be. As is. As they are. Robust against the drought, if struggling.

And departing, we heard dozens and dozens of gunshots. Far more than usual. Coming from west of the reserve. Maybe somewhere near the NBN tower and its glinting deceptions. No, closer than that. From just over the crest of Mount Toxic. It's a shotgun, or shotguns. I am wondering if someone is clay-target shooting when I hear something small and hard and fast hit the tin roof. I know the sound of 12-gauge shot landing on corrugated iron. It is dangerous to our lives directly and indirectly. The shot will go into our tank when it rains, washed along, sitting in pools in the pipe trap. Lead poisoning. On and *in* the Yorkshire Moors there is so much lead shot from grouse shooting embedded in the peat and sediment layers, birds of prey, never mind humans, are affected by the toxicity. There is the poisoning caused by lead mines, and by their products. Killing that keeps on killing. Some months ago, an attempt to have a property some 15 k's north of here registered as a shooting range was foiled on the grounds of contamination of the creek and the water system. I fear those same shooters are making use of 'property' nearby. This is the most direct kind of incursion. The advocates for this 'club' proudly had their African hunting safari photos of kills – giraffes – and other trophies displayed in a newspaper article on their endeavours. Resisting the heavily armed is always difficult. They claim they are responsible users of guns, and yet one always knows they have the ability to use those weapons at any time. And it's a feeling they work into interactions in many subtle (and less subtle) ways. I recall some years ago when we were living at Mum's place outside York and I heard a lot of shotgun blasts. I immediately headed down to the riverfront in town, and found a gun club 'culling' corellas. 'We have permission!' was yelled at me when I stood in their way. I told them they were exploiters and murderers, covering their thrill kills under the rubric of 'vermin extermination'. One hunter, who had his extremely expensive piece broken across his arm, carefully twisted his arm so that the piece was pointed at me as he reloaded the two barrels. Others were using pump-actions, and I could hear the cartridges sliding into place as they reloaded. With advice to move or I'd get hurt, the imposition of menace was unforgettable – and I am no stranger to such horror. I screamed and yelled and ran to help the injured birds. I was directed to leave the 'scene' *immediately!* by the ranger, or she would call the police and have me arrested. The kill went on, lead shot filling the Avon River pool. In some parts of the world, a weird ecological eschatology paradox has evolved in which non-lead shot is used to kill (and, it has to be said, to clay-target shoot) so as not to poison the ground and the water, but that's not the default here or many other places. Lead is part of the 'tradition', the identification with control over the toxic. To wield.

There have been a lot of corellas in the district. Native birds hated by farmers because they flock and supposedly feed on the grain crops. Lately, it's actually pig melon seeds (an introduced 'weed' that is often poisoned) the corellas are after, dispersed during the recent burnings-off. Tracy says the mass shooting we're hearing might actually be a local corella cull. That may well be the case. I will investigate. Both scenarios are obscene. So many fox and cat shooters in the region go on about how they are keeping 'vermin down', and yet are equally happy shooting native species. The hypocrisy of the sports shooter is astonishing – it was recently revealed that pigs have been bred and released into native forests so they can be shot, because 'controlling the feral pig population' is one of the main excuses recreational hunters use for their activities. And then there's the lie that they 'only hunt for meat' – so much is abandoned, fed to dogs (which often get worms from eating contaminated meat), or 'sampled' and then ditched. I have seen and heard every lie, held them accountable, and yet the power resides with those who ('legally and responsibly') keep and use weapons.

And so we are going to be perched on the edge of the city for ten weeks – in Midland, of the old railway workshops and working-class politics that are in traumatic unrest in terms of development and a total annihilation of green space. In Midland, called the 'gateway to the wheatbelt'; in Midland, where there is so much unhappiness coexisting with the usual ups and downs of suburban life, so much homelessness, so much of a separation between the haves and the have-nots; in Midland, which Tracy calls the city of the sirens – place of constabulary, medical facilities and services, Landgate (apportioning out and surveying and controlling the land grab that is a linchpin in the new Australian colonialism), government services, and shopping … and violence, and an extreme meth problem, and unhappiness … Jam Tree Gully up over the Scarp and inland.

And as I look out of the hotel up at the Hills, I wonder how much more shot has rained down on the roof, will find its way into our water supply with the flush of rains going through.

~

Over the last six or seven years, the right-wing federal government and a far-right government in Queensland, followed by a weak, slightly left-wing Queensland government, have overseen the destruction of bushland and forest amounting to twice the size of the Australian Capital Territory (as attested by *The Guardian*). The fact that this is catchment for the Great Barrier Reef is tragic enough, but the inherent tragedy of the loss in itself is beyond comprehension. As people do their hashtag social media campaigns on devices that damage the biosphere, as they work to improve their material and emotional lots, they literally acquiesce to the destruction of the environment that gives them life. To me this is illogical, self-defeating, and supremely selfish.

My grandmother's Goldfields 'heritage' is always with me, and I am thinking about my youthful obsession with tracing the pipeline from Mundaring Weir to Kalgoorlie – an early state engineering feat by C. Y. O'Connor, who was born in Country Meath and committed suicide in Western Australian in 1902. Water was 'white gold' in the place of yellow gold that was relatively waterless (on the surface, at least). And I am thinking of the fetishisation of gold fever in obscene environmental-destruction television programs like Discovery Channel's *Gold Hunters*, in which prospectors treat the bush like a lucky dip, bulldozing and assaulting the land for gold. Midland, where we are staying, is the gateway to the east from the Perth coastal plain, and the Great Eastern Highway is the conduit for machinery heading to the eastern goldfields. Also emanating from Midland is the Great Northern Highway, a further conduit to northern interior gold, nickel and uranium mining, and the Midland town vicinity is the sales yard and storage depot nexus for huge loads of imported mining equipment which feeds the ravaging of the land, of community, of the soul of country. 'Rapacity' is the word I have used in my poetry, and that same rapacity focuses on the bauxite of the Hills. And Toodyay Road riding up past the sacred owl granites of the national park, and past Red Hill toxic waste dump perched overlooking the city, the repository across the road from a huge blue-metal quarry which feeds the insatiable builds, and will no doubt in time become another landfill site. That's what the government and aligned private industry do – they exploit in every way they can and we struggle against it all. In his fossicking for gold, my great-grandfather almost died out in the desert – hoping to add to his life working for the company, to bring 'extra', or by finding a big nugget that would be their ticket … to the city far south? He went out alone without heavy machinery. Now it's metal detectors and bulldozers.

My father – the other side of the family – is still skilled at working on all heavy machinery. Though he is into his eighties, he keeps his tools in pristine condition and is as organised and meticulous as he was when he was his tech school's top apprentice when he finished his training in the mid-fifties and began working as a bus mechanic.

Even after he and my mother split, and my father had gone north, evidence of my father's trucking life remained at our family home in the steel chests of heavy jacks and massive spanners, the heavy steel vices, and the shed he had built large enough to take two trucks. When my brother and I travelled by bus the thousands of kilometres up to the town where he had been made a foreman to a team of mechanics looking after the heavy equipment for Dampier Salt Mines, we acted as a spark across the residues of his old life and his new. Our fascination with what he did was spliced into a constant need to be in the bush, or, at Karratha, out in the mangroves and on the tidal flats. The contact points and the extreme magnetic repulsions of like poles messed with our sense of what nature was, and how humans might or might not interact with it. Dad was quite literally a child of the bush, and it was where he'd take us on excursions, but he was also servant and manager and sometimes operator of the very equipment that most threatened it. On the huge farm he managed inland not far from the town of Mullewa, where the big machinery and the cleared swathes of flatland spoke their language of degradation and harvest, it first gelled in both of us brothers that this was a complex and confusing relationship – between land and machinery, between ourselves and our father – that would never even approach resolution.

Dad drove around the countryside – and the city, when he was down – with a gun on the back ledge of the car under an Albany Woollen Mills thick-weave tartan wool blanket, 'ammo' in the glove box. This was what blokes like him did. It's not a unique story. Sometimes he'd pull over in the bush and set up a few targets, have a shoot, then drive on. We participated, but we never completely worked it out. And though back home we were being brought up by two women, the odd connection with Dad was always sort of there. But I in particular was an oddity to him – I didn't fit. I didn't play football, and he gave in trying to make me, but he pushed my younger brother hard. But though he played, Stephen had no interest and wanted to be off the oval and out in the bush, or by a river or the sea.

Two and a half years younger than me, Stephen suffered under a range of older-brother tyrannies as I tried to earth the bullying I myself received, but he also stood up for me and comforted me in my frequent public distress. He was a feisty kid who lived by his own set of rules and vision of things. He and I were very close, and remain close. Tim says we are alike, but that his uncle is 'less grumpy' than me. Both Stephen and I struggled through overlapping decades of addiction and wreckage. We looked out for each other, most times. We were incredibly close to our mother, but it was actually on the Mullewa farm managed by our father where one of our intense bonding experiences with fate and circumstance took place. Messing around way out from the house – maybe a mile away – we were climbing into field bins of pickled wheat, and jumping into the seed grain and hauling ourselves out with a rope. We dropped in through the narrow hatchway at the top but forget to retie the rope, which had come loose. Gradually, we began to sink. Together. As we struggled to escape, to move towards the internal ladder, we sank further and further. Believing we would die, we held on to each other. We often fought as kids but we were close, very close. We spoke our own strange language and knew each other inside out. Astonishingly, given the size of the farm and the thickness of the silo walls, our father was passing by on an errand, and heard our muffled shrieks. We were hauled out – or, rather, carefully and painstakingly extracted from the wheat, which was up past our waists. The chances of his being there at that precise moment were almost zero. Our father didn't usually hesitate to give us a hiding – especially me – if we'd done something really wrong, but on that occasion he didn't. (Our mother never smacked us once, not once.) I guess it was the relief and the shock. *Drowning in wheat* marked my life. I have never spoken with my father about it since. It is the ars poetica of my poetry, and my life.

Drowning in wheat

They'd been warned
on every farm
that playing
in the silos
would lead to death.
You sink in wheat.
Slowly. And the more
you struggle the worse it gets.
'You'll see a rat sail past
your face, nimble on its turf,

and then you'll disappear.'
In there, hard work
has no reward.
So it became a kind of test
to see how far they could sink
without needing a rope
to help them out.
But in the midst of play
rituals miss a beat – like both
leaping in to resolve
an argument
as to who'd go first
and forgetting
to attach the rope.
Up to the waist
and afraid to move.
That even a call for help
would see the wheat
trickle down.
The painful consolidation
of time. The grains
in the hourglass
grotesquely swollen.
And that acrid
chemical smell
of treated wheat
coaxing them into
a near-dead sleep.

I used to collect enclosed ball bearings. Thrust bearings and so on that sit in 'cages' around shafts. My father got them through his work. I added them to my various other collections of ceramic telegraph pole insulators (ah, Edwin Denby would come into my reading life at sixteen), rocks, feathers, coins, pressed leaves and flowers, model airplanes and military equipment, bullets and bullet casings (I even had wooden world war ammunition boxes), chemicals and stamps. Stamps defined my life from eleven to fifteen in so many ways.

I didn't just 'collect' stamps – I was a *philatelist*. I collected and obtained them in all ways I could, but there were three main conduits. The first was via my grandfather (my mother's father), who collected stamps in large quantities, including dozens of chocolate boxes of soaked-from-letter single stamps bundled in hundreds and tied up with cotton and wool thread. Of King George Heads, the common Australian stamp of the twenties and thirties, he had maybe ten to twenty thousand samples. These were worth almost nothing in themselves, but hours of painstaking inspection to ascertain perforation size, watermark, and vagaries in printing and colouring would mean a rare or even unique version could be discovered. As with bundles of other common stamps, one would be on the lookout for anomalies, especially spurs (spur-shaped marks off the normal engraved line reproduced in printing, caused by minuscule errors on the plate), double watermarks in the stamp's paper, machine-missed perforations. I found quite a number, and split the profits with my grandfather. Sometimes I just bought batches off him cheap and found them myself; sometimes he gave me bundles and boxes. My second source was stamp auctions, using my pocket money and the money I accumulated from selling stamps at auctions myself. Over the last two years of primary school I went to these auctions with a friend of my mother's. He was a keen philatelist who taught me the whys and wherefores of the auction room, and most particularly, the circuit sheets – sheets of used stamps 'hinged' to pages (or in plastic sleeves if mint), with prices listed, which circulated the auction room. If you wanted a stamp, you would peel it off and add letters or another naming sign on the circuit sheet where the stamp had been and settle up at the end. Dozens of people, mainly men back then, would sit around a long trestle table in a hall, breaking bread in the form of purchasing and hoping to make a profit by reselling the stamps elsewhere. This form of capitalist investment went in deep with me, and I was very successful and celebrated as having a 'shrewd investment head on young shoulders'. As my politics developed, such knowledge gave me a language of resistance against the inequities of wealth generation coming from little labour and a lot of market play. Those who knew me then would find my radical shift to the left incomprehensible. But then, they'd have to remind themselves that I was still a child at the time of my wheelings and dealings.

The third conduit of my stamp life involved working for a philatelist for a year when I was thirteen and fourteen. With my first pay I bought my mother a copy of Banjo Paterson's poetry – she still has it, inscribed by me 'bought with my first pay'. I got this job because when we lived in Perth on the edge the river (and weren't visiting Wheatlands or holidaying in the south-west or we boys visiting our father), I'd catch the bus into the city and visit the stamp shop in London Court, that mock-Tudor parody of a soul of the city. Jackie's daughter often stayed with her grandfather who had been four years in a Japanese prisoner of war camp and was very marked by it, though he did emerge to design the first hydro-electric dam in Malaysia and to invent the wooden cross spars on metal pylons for electric high-tensile power cables to prevent lightning strikes taking them out . He and I were close and he fed my love of physics and science, as well as my obsession for classical music, encouraged by my mother, who taught piano here and there over the years.) The Dutch immigrant who ran the stamp business, and his son who worked there, who was a few years older than me, tuned in to my obsession and offered me a Saturday morning job, and school holidays when I could manage them. It was generous of them, and though we now exist in parallel universes, I've never forgotten it. It's a long story for a short period of my life. I felt, and maybe my new employers felt it too, that I was 'destined' to make professional philately my life's calling.

After only a few months working in the shop, I was introduced to – no, I was summoned by – the Great Man from Stanley Gibbons of London, a buyer for the world's main stamp company who was in Perth searching for interesting collections to purchase (and probably to make sales as well). He wanted to meet the 'young prospect'. I got so excited that I ran through the foyer of Perth's most exclusive hotel hooting about a rare stamp I'd managed to buy a week earlier, and got a polite but intense dressing-down by my boss about how I could undo years of good relations with a few seconds of out-of-control behaviour. Above all else, he advised me, smiling again, his pipe hanging from his mouth as he spoke, Above all else, never show your hand – remain calm, don't let anyone else know you know what you've got. But it didn't last. Mum got her teaching transfer and we moved far away up the coast.

In Geraldton my interest switched almost entirely to chemistry and the bush, and my many years' obsession with stamps faded away. I sold my last stamps in my mid-teens to help pay for hundreds of books and new chemistry glassware. I think of my employers often. Kind people – my Saturday lunches with them in the flat atop London Court were cultural as well as personal occasions.

But what is relevant to this memoir of a rural life is the fact that my favourite stamps, both as investment items and collectables, were the kangaroo series of Australian stamps from the early twentieth century and the Western Australian colonial swan stamps from the nineteenth century. Animals I love. Tracy and I wake to kangaroo does and boomers sniffing outside our bedroom window, or rubbing against the house as they hop past around dawn. The kangaroo is ever present at Jam Tree Gully, suffering the culls and thrill kills of locals, but persisting. And here I am not talking about traditional societies' or Aboriginal Australians' non-romanticised relationships with native fauna (or flora). That is not for me to speak of or about.

And swans – especially the black swan of Western Australia – have helped bind the different aspects of my life together, as a symbol and an actuality of persistence. Strangely, the white swans of the Avon River in the wheatbelt town of Northam, introduced in the early twentieth century by a Russian migrant – a colony enforced rather than a colony desired, managing to coexist with black swans and persist against the odds – are often the target of cruelty and viciousness.

What do these introduced white swans symbolise in the colonial matrix? And should they exist outside this discussion of belonging and unbelonging? They have just managed to hold on, with help from concerned locals, in keeping their basic flock intact, but what would it mean to write positively of them if they had expanded their numbers and become 'pests' through successful exploitation/usage of the place, like the rabbit or the fox? If instead of a local (and tourist) icon, they had become *bêtes noires* with bounties on their heads? It's worth pondering. And as one who respects and values all life, and yet believes all Australian land should be returned to the 'say' of its Indigenous peoples, with negotiations for the presence of non-Indigenous peoples worked out from that point of fact rather than Indigenous peoples bizarrely having to prove ongoing connection to (their own) country, and having their land claims validated by white law and white implementation of law – the same law of the Crown that declared terra nullius and opened the way for total theft of that land – my sense of justice about 'here' is not an easy one. It can't be.

But even postage stamps connect with Jam Tree Gully in tangential ways – signs of deals done to correspond with the rest of the world, to traverse the globe. Communicate. This regionalism mixed with an internationalist sense of responsibility and desire for understanding of difference across the world seems strangely embodied in the symbol if not the actuality of the stamp-collecting of my childhood.

Lightning is omnipresent for me. It strikes in my sleep, it keeps me awake, it constantly threatens, and it is the fuse that drives any 'seeing' I might have. I have written about being struck by lightning (twice) so many times in different ways that the performance of what happened to me, and what I am as a consequence, is a mantra that defines my presence, my aliveness against the odds. In a nutshell, when I was nine years old, I was driving with my cousins after being at the farm rubbish tip smashing bottles emptied from two 22-gallon drums in the back of the ute. We smashed them with rocks, testing our throwing arms. A summer storm was evolving to the north and closing in around the Needlings, always a place of mystery to me, and I realise now looking back likely very important to Noongar people. The Needlings had unusual 'theodolite' granites near the summit, and at its western base a strange 'sinking sand' (*where the sinking sand that ate sheep was*, as I wrote in a poem in *The Silo*). My cousins told me I would be sucked in if I ventured too close to it, and this thought and fear possessed my childhood. In the world of vivid imagination, such places overwhelmed me.

As the storm enveloped the Needlings, we set off too late – getting those final smashings in and risking being caught by the blast. My oldest cousin drove as fast as the ute would go on the gravel, through the crossroads, past the salt scalds, swerving. One of the empty drums fell from the back of the ute and I, being near the passenger's door with three of us crammed into the cab, was shuffled out – my mortal coil tumbling with me – to put it right. The drum had catapulted and rolled into the drainage ditch encrusted with salt crystals, rusted fence wire, eaten jam-tree fence posts that had long since come down, and nodules of salt bush. I grabbed it to roll it along the road to the ute, and looking up I saw a fire had been lit – triggered – in the distance by lightning, which was flashing all around. The pillars of rain and smoke connected on the not-too-distant horizon, and I knew all the adults of the district including my uncle would be called out with their water trucks and wet hessian sacks to fight the bush-and-stubble fire.

I was rolling the drum fast but awkwardly, as it constantly twisted back around me, when the lightning struck. It hit the drum, or near it, and threw me through the air. I could smell the burning. Confused, somehow I got up and ran to the drum and started rolling it again and lighting struck a second time. It threw me and I was frantic and burnt and sick. One of my cousins grabbed me and dragged me into the cab, and we hurtled back to the farm. My auntie said my eyes were 'out on stalks'. A doctor tended me – one of three times across my life on the farm. A long call-out, some 20 k's from York town. But what sticks with me more than anything is that my cousins have little recollection of this event, and my aunt a hazy one. It was the pivotal physical and mental event of my life.

One night many years later, when I was running the X-ray equipment in the lab outside Geraldton one Saturday night, a dry lightning storm struck and sent the equipment crazy. I thought I was going to be annihilated as the cathode gun went out of its arc, strayed from its set movement and started shooting beams outside the protected area within the casing of the Siemens device as I was trying to adjust it. The telex machine tripped and started sending messages from nowhere. Lightning!

And once in the mid-nineties I was flying from Buffalo to New York City after a reading. This was when I went to the US after winning a 'Keating' (an award given to writers by the then prime minister), having being refused entry so many times, rejected by the CIA interviewers as unsuitable. It was a smallish plane that was otherwise filled with a local football team. The plane was struck by lightning and lost thousands of feet in in what felt like seconds, and the footballers were crying and shrieking and I was thinking, It's lightning again. Maybe not chasing me, but knowing me as I know it.

Lightning led to a disturbed interaction with a casual friend when I was on the Cocos Islands, watching sheet lightning turn to fork – an interaction throttled up many notches not because of anything said, or any real change between us, but because the atmosphere was so charged. Cause and effect? Lightning was a story my brother would tell me of driving with three other blokes from a shearing shed near Williams town when ball lightning passed through the car. Many years later, lightning struck overhead, blasting and singeing the roof just above where I was working, looking out at Walwalinj from my mother's house – that electric burn smell you can never escape. Lightning was the shock when I was repairing a power point at my grandparents' house when I was eighteen and down in the city for university and someone accidentally turned the mains power on, sparking and throwing me across the room. Lightning was being with Tracy at Jam Tree Gully when a storm came in suddenly and a bolt struck upwards from a star picket towards the clouds, reversing knowledge of place, ground up, earthing, the leader a prophecy of the path we couldn't take, a few metres away from us, a massive joining of the elements, burning metal and leaving its odour. And it was the bolt that blasted the great concrete water tank, blowing a 10-centimetre chunk of concrete out above the pump. To not retell the story that opened the account is to not tell the story of now. I am no storm chaser, but they chase me. Make of it what you will.

~

One night some twenty-eight years ago, I was driving down from Perth to Happy Valley Farm where my brother lived on the edge of the great Dryandra Forest. (He lived there for eight years and I went back and forth for four years, living half the week with my then partner and our son, and the other half at Stephen's place.) A lightning storm distracted me on the gravel, and seeing the long line of a carpet snake stretched across the road, I was unable to stop in time and slid across it. I pulled over, ran back in the half-light, guided by lightning, and picked up the massive python, and put it on the back seat of the car. It was dying. Arriving at Stephen's, I took the snake into my room and put it in my sleeping bag. I drank myself stupid and talked with my brother, then went to my room and climbed into the sleeping bag with the injured snake. In the morning, I woke to see the snake slowly circling the room as the mid-morning sun chewed around the holland blind. It was alive, it was moving, it wanted out. We caught it and released it up at the old abandoned homestead, not far from where I'd run over it. It lived there for years. Lightning snake, snake brought back to life by my warm if wasted body.

Sleeping with a southern carpet python

Driving south to stay with my brother in the house
on the edge of great Dryandra Forest, refuge
of the stripy termite-eating numbat, I grind the gravel
across the one-lane bridge with its brief bitumen
respite, working strobe-lit shadows and corrugations,
keeping the vehicle centred. I am a young, embittered
father moving away from family ensconced in a low
and swampy suburb, a reclaimed rubbish tip at the base
of the Scarp. Now, eucalypts and parrots cluster
at the roadside, sheep working gnomic lines to dams,
the tinge of green of the new growing year, rancour
of salt scalds – I convince myself all call me *home*.
I grow steadily distracted with the brute subtleties
of dragging the back end of the car into shape,
a soft spot in the gravel pulling away from direction,
gyroscopic interlude. And then, before me *within*

braking distance, within the realm of breaking thought
to control the slide without three-sixtying into oblivion,
is an eight-foot southern carpet python at full stretch,
slowly negotiating the road, its cryptic rippling
a camouflage separated from its realm but working
black and gentle yellow-olive into the orange of gravel,
willing the gap to close, openness a trauma to be filed
under 'instinctual', an inverse constriction of mind
over matter. I skid right over it, crushing its tubular
body. I handle snakes. I have handled snakes since
the time I was warned not to go near, not to *touch*.
Deadly dugites and mulga snakes by the tail
or behind the head. To carry to safety, lift from roads
where they are … crushed. The most intensely alive
moments of my life I replay. Incidents that timeline
character and make speech. And this great snake,
distressed and writhing, python in need of a meal,
winter shutdown fast approaching, I lift and place
in folds of a tartan blanket on the back seat. Compacted,
splayed, its body hasn't burst: its hunger a blessing.
I drive to my brother's, where I place it deep down
within my sleeping bag. Warmth. (I still drank back then.
Heavily. And I drank to oblivion.) When sleep drags me
to my sleeping bag, I don't think twice about crawling
in with the crippled, dying python. My life is lived
with sleep in glimpses, moments of nodding off,
so any sleep that comes is sleep I embrace – a sleep
with snakes is not a temptation, nor a loss. Insomniac,
I sleep deeply and in a dreamless stupor, though it has
since fed my nights with images and dark rumours.
Living dead, I still make body warmth and the cold

blood of the snake exchanges its knowledge,
its stock of stories and experiences. When I wake
with the morning streaming cold light into the room,
I shudder with poikilothermic thirst, clutching
the walls of my cocoon close, synapses tuning
to the expectation of snake at my feet, retracting
my toes and huddling to a ball. Emptiness.
I reach for my glasses and focus. The southern
carpet python, carpet snake of my childhood
I saw often on the farm coiled around log rafters
in the hay barn, rat hunter and friend of the farmer,
warder-off of ill charms of presence, is sliding
alongside the walls, rounding the square room,
full of my body warmth and raring to go.

~

When my oldest son was six years old, my then partner and I split for good. It was a distressed relationship and though for a year I had access visits, it was so traumatic for him moving between the two of us that I let it go. I regret this now, but thought it for his own good, for the best. I wrote one poem about it, and storms were part of that poem because lightning is always there, for good or bad. It's a life loss for me, though he does well now and engineers dams for a living. When he was a small child, we took him to the farm, but also to the dams throughout the Hills. He loved those excursions. I wrote dam poems about them. I wonder how much of a role they played in his choice of career? We don't see each other, and dams are so often connected with mining – tailings dams and the like. I am not sure how we would get on, the different politics of being, the sudden stop to our mutual history. Machines taking over nature for him. But nature still holding out against the machine for me. He lives in Queensland now, where lightning storms are not uncommon. In fact, the well-known song 'This is Australia' by Gang Gajang talks of the cane fields and lightning. A complex history of presence in all directions. One not obfuscating another.

~

Being down on the coastal plain, in Midland at the base of the Scarp, is defamiliarising. In the early seventies the Hills were relatively secluded, and the home of 'cults and nudists'. (There's still a nudist colony up among the jarrah and logged spaces, and I don't doubt a few cultists, but not quite in the same self-advertising 'alternative' way.) It was the place to be: the doomsday predictions that emanated from the folds of the Darling Range frequently referred to the 'great earthquake' and 'great waves' that would follow, deleting the Swan coastal plain and all on it. (The term 'doomsday' is relevant to the destruction of the biosphere through human rapacity and violence, but I use it here in the context of the millennial apocalyptic urge to some kind of external judgement of 'sin' – largely religious in nature.) Pyramids, crystals, dope and magic mushrooms, religious fervour, sexual liberation and sexual denial, all worked in a heady mixture as a way out of the 'rat race', with Perth's isolation from other capitals and major centres of population emphasising this alienation.

To live rural, alternative, small-scale, being a hippie, or religious, or an artist was not unusual. Considered weird down in the city by many people, but not unusual. A close friend who I travelled through parts of Asia with, and who later drowned in the Swan River, actually bought into a commune down south, and shared the trials and tribulations of the community largely from a distance. I never wanted to be in the city – always *away*. In the mid 1980s, the massive multinational mining companies, locally Alcoa, still had their eye firmly on the mineral 'resources' of the Hills and the south-west, and jobs were pitted against environment. Prototypical environmental scientists, funded by mining companies, were brought (and bought) onside through 'rehabilitation of mine site' programs, rehabilitations that were in denial of the fact that destroyed ecosystems cannot be replaced through conventional tree-planting programs (or any programs). It was an era of increasing tension over the wholesale destruction of the great karri and jarrah forests, and the drive towards woodchipping ancient trees (for paper pulp). In fact, in Manjimup, one mill was actually bombed and the perpetrator became known as the 'woodchip bomber'.

Positioning myself against the use of violence as a solution, especially because as a drunkard, violent reactions to things were not uncommon to me, I strived to beat addiction by attending rehab programs and the like. My aim was to reduce anger and frustration and not redirect it. I decided that blocking, standing and yelling poetry at the destroyers were the most effective methods of nonviolent action, with the least hypocrisy.

But violence came from the loggers. Once upon a time in the south-west, when my brother and I, ontologically lost and searching, were hitchhiking through forest areas, we made obvious our protest, our objections, to logging trucks, and were chased and shot at. We were hunted. We hid in the forest near Walpole. Later, we were given a lift by a 'dude in a ute' who was suffering some kind of psychotic episode, and was convinced we were searching for his dope plantation hidden 'down near the coast'. (We weren't.) He let us off at the corner of the main road

– few vehicles other than logging trucks and dairy trucks at that time of year – and a dirt road to the coast, and as he drove off we immediately ran into the forest and hid. We knew he was going back home to get a gun. And indeed, half an hour later he was back, roaming the forest, shining a spotlight onto and between tree trunks. We hid and shook as the great yellow tinglewood trees, so rare, shimmered their canopies a hundred feet up. He yelled out, I know you're in there somewhere, and you'll never get my grass! Eventually he withdrew. At dawn, even more bedraggled than we usually were, we ventured out of the forest and started hitching, our eye steady on the dirt road. We were picked up by a pair of hippie women who let us jump onto the back of their tray top. They drove us to Denmark. Alternative lifestyles?

So looking up at the Scarp, I don't see the 'alternative', but rather the *crossing over* to an existence in which there was a tension between nature and modernity, between belonging and unbelonging, between the reality of colonial theft and a deep desire to protect the land from damage. Last night, walking as I always do after dinner, I looked at the crescent moon (viewed from a street called The Crescent) with the evening star at seven o'clock about a thumb's distance away, and then up at the Scarp, the haze of showers cleared away, and I thought, This is a most sacred place to the Noongar Whadjuk people, here in Midland at the confluence of rivers, the Helena and thc Swan (which is known as the Avon River up in the wheatbelt), which have their own names – Noongar names – and which are the matrix around the endless complexities of language and the certainties of an ancient cultural law. Long strings of thought. And the compilation of buildings and many people surrounding me as I walk doesn't erase sacred cultural presence in any way at all. It is part of the reclaiming. I have always known this, but now I want to speak to the elders of here and talk about restitution, in this place where Tracy was born, then later taking her first steps up in the Hills in the townlet of Kalamunda. And this place where I am walking under the sliver of moon is where I was saved from thyrotoxicosis in a nearby hospital, the same hospital Tracy was born in, a hospital now closed down so a new hospital across the railway tracks might rise up and serve the district. And walking under the fingernail moon, where so many wheatbelt people of all heritages come down from the plains through the hills to this town on the edge of the city, and do what they have to do – shop, seek medical treatment, interact with government services – and go no further before turning around and heading back to whence they came.

~

One of the things about colonial self-isolating or just 'life's fortunes' isolating you and those close to you is that it creates a kind of paranoia and anxiety of presence in itself. Ghosts will be encountered, UFOs seen, and ways of describing experience will fall away from the normative. Or at least this was true prior to wireless communications technology's enveloping of space, and the social media reworking of experience and witness.

Growing up, I not only heard many stories of 'strange encounters' in paddocks and on back roads with 'unidentified' and 'mysterious' and 'unexplainable' lights, but in 1975 I was involved in an officially recorded UFO sighting. But that was in a suburb of Perth, on the edges of the city near the Canning River, with a lot of bushland still around. A light *followed me* from a local park – the same park where I had been beaten up and bullied on a number of occasions – all the way home, like the cars that had followed me, their drivers trying to get me into the cars. When I got home, I called my mother and Auntie Jackie, and they watched it hover over the house and neighbourhood. Mum rang the air force base just outside the city and reported it. I was frightened, but considered myself a scientist at the age of twelve, and said it was a min min light, or a lightning phenomenon or maybe a weather balloon (which was illogical). A day later there was a small newspaper article about 'sightings of lights across the city'. A few days later we received a phone call from an air force officer who wanted to interview us about the sighting. And we were asked to keep it to ourselves. What was said still remains close to my chest. But I am not trying to appeal to the conspiracy theorists out there, or the true believers, but to make a point about the grotesquery of colonial presence, and a failure to understand both land and cosmos when tens of thousands of years of understanding of presence are denied, erased (attempted) or ignored. Even in a city, the codes of belonging are ignored. It's not impossible to belong, but it's impossible to understand without empathy, respect and a desire to learn. Electrical activity in the atmosphere is as spiritual as we do or don't want it to be, but to appreciate its complexity is part of understanding where and how you live. Isolation is relative.

A bright cigar-shaped object hovers over Mount Pleasant

It starts in the park near Brentwood Primary School
and moves rapidly towards Mount Pleasant
a bright cigar-shaped object that darts
and jolts across the demarcation lines
of class that aren't supposed to exist in Australia
but do because even Labor voters prefer

to be on the Mount Pleasant side of the divide
if for no other reason than it pushes property
prices up. It follows the line of my escape
route from school, the same route a man
without a face in a dark car crawls along,
calling to me as I break into a run,
the car door opening and a clawed hand
reaching out to drag me in, the cigar-
shaped object stopped stock-still
and hovering like the sun, hovering
as if it's always been in that spot, always
been overhead, as hot as hell despite
the cold setting in, the sweat emanating
from my forehead, the light bright in my eyes.

I've long been disturbed by Goya's *The Sleep [or Dream] of Reason Produces Monsters* – he of that most colonial of powers, Spain – as it reminds me of settler dreams of occupation of land, of owning another's spiritual country to the exclusion of their inherent rights, then the sleep of dispossession produces monsters, too. I wrote a book of poetry, *Visitants*, about these issues and 'paranormal' experiences that can be explained through confronting the harsh realities of belonging and unbelonging. Art and science and superstition are all tools of controlling stolen and reconfigured environments. The erasure of whole forests that now only exist as perverse suburb, estate or street names is in part excused by the vestigial sense of it once having been. 'Burning' fake logs in an electric open fireplace fed by coal ripped out from where other forests once stood is a disturbance that is self-fulfilling.

I was once asked: So, John, what has your life meant? I mean, all you seem to do is protest! My reply was, I don't see it as protest – I see it as an affirmation of a better and more respectful way, in terms of how people treat the world outside their own spheres of reward and comfort. And I stick by this. In my drinking days, I often protested ineffectively because police and others saw my alcoholism as the reason for my actions. This was rarely the case, though it was frequently true that alcohol and substance degradation rendered my protests less effective, less efficient than they might have been. But I didn't get 'out of it' to find the resolve to stand up against what I considered to be injustices; rather, my addictions were unfortunately part of my quotidian. They enabled nothing, they disabled much.

One incident stands out in particular – a spontaneous intervention against the imminent vivisection of baboons ('for research') at the University of Western Australia. I found out where they were being held, forced my way into the building, and saw the many horrors enacted on the premises in the name of science and with the sanction of the so-called university 'ethics' committee. I saw things in that building that torment me to this day.

What goes on in institutions around the world in the name of human advancement is a disgrace. Tucked away in 'schools' in Australia, we are often unaware of or don't want to face up to the fact that Big Mining and even the military (private and state) are never far away. Sometimes they are embedded as colleagues, under the rubric of 'defence'. Meanwhile, cultural-ethnic battles are being fought over what defines Western knowledge and cultures, and governments enact their policies via control, over funding. Private industry is never far away, with collaborations and 'outcomes' constantly being pushed. Poetry and Big Energy? I don't think so! Surely, not everything can be bought. And vivisection finds its symbiosis with the arts, as ethics committees approve the abuse and exploitation of animals for creative purposes. Interdisciplinary? And once we step outside the humanities, into the hard sciences, well, all is possible.

Recently in Germany, I wrote poems against research on monkeys in universities, and once I did a reading tour of Britain and had the proceeds paid directly to the Dr Hadwen Trust for non-animal medical research. Of course I care about medicine for the benefits of all humans, but not at the expense of other living things.

In that 'animal house' at a local Western Australian university back in the early nineties, I was unable to locate the baboons and somehow set off an alarm or was picked up on the security cameras. Guards descended on the place, worked their way through pens of suffering farm animals (for example: windows are inserted in the sides of cows to observe how they digest different food materials), and pursued me up a ladder and out onto a loading gantry, where I crawled out and positioned myself on the end of a steel beam, warning them I would jump to the bitumen below if they came any closer.

Unfortunately, I was carrying a bag with a bottle of sherry in it (along with books and drafts of poems), and when eventually they coaxed me off the gantry, this was used as evidence against me, invalidating the political and ethical nature of the protest. Locked up, I had to call a friend to bail me out. Though I was charged, these charges were dropped; I guess authorities wanted to keep the whole thing out of the media. Afterwards, I ended up in rehab and the baboons were vivisected. Had I been sober I could have seen it through – commitment, reliability, and a certain amount of social immunity (or 'respect') is necessary to be effective (sadly). I wrote a poem about it, and I have campaigned against vivisection over a lifetime, but the baboons were still tortured and abused and killed ('put to sleep').

~

Cryptozoology is rife around the valley. More sightings of the Toodyay 'panther' around Katrine, where the family of the colonial poet Elizabeth Deborah Brockman is buried, and where we often visit. There's a small church there near a river crossing, and small patches of bush surrounded by quite imposing and steep hills. Cormorants, white-faced herons, egrets and sometimes pelicans can been seen roosting and perching on deadwood at the crook of the River Avon (it becomes the Swan River when it passes down onto the coastal plain through the Hills). When the river is flowing, it can flow fast through there. The Toodyay panther is clearly a large feral cat. I have seen many massive cats in the bush and paddocks over my life, including 'the Tiger' I wrote about in my traumatic poem 'The Hunt'. In trapping and poisoning the animals, farmers deploy similar techniques to fox-baiting – dragging bloody rabbit carcasses in hessian sacks behind vehicles to lay a scent trail, setting strychnine baits and multiple rabbit traps in clusters. If you've ever seen a large cat chew its own paw off to escape a trap – and as a child I saw the leftovers of such desperation – it imprints upon you forever. These feral cats can get as large as an American bobcat or lynx, and can bring down even an older lamb easily. Locals and especially visitors want to believe in the magical animal, even the circus escapee that has 'made it', because they need to answer their own anxiety about their presence. The fear and desire around the Australian bunyip by colonials is part of a fear and desiring of the inherent qualities of country they can't read. Aboriginal knowledge about threat and taboo is inherent to culture, and such taboos are often built in science, but in colonial terms they become abstractions of displacements.

Living in Cambridge, England, I would hear stories from old fens people of the so-called 'Fen Tiger' – another large cat, but Fen Tigers were also labourers in those reclaimed lands in which indigenous culture was assailed by technology and its language and ways were deleted as the fens were drained. Where land has been damaged, or where a 'frontier' is perceived as still holding on or existing, or where it might be wished to exist as a challenge or evocation of some internal longing for undoing the colonisation, of being 'one' with what the colonists can never be one with, you find cryptozoology at full strength. Invaded forests and mountains, even lochs – the Loch Ness monster might be read in terms of English colonialism's ab-effect and desiring for (touristic, almost) difference. Strangely, in the wheatbelt Western Australian town of Corrigin, along with a dog cemetery, there is a local Loch Ness monster shaped out of arches and uprights (with a face) to make the humps and neck of the imagined body. Another colonial trope, the focal point of a town's visitors' walk. The same town has an annual ute muster, in which utility vehicles gather in packs and speak 'bush values': dogs, guns, country music, the pairing of men and women, and a far more subtle array of 'values'. I would never suggest these things are simple constructs – they're not. They're as complex as any other social interaction anywhere. Advertised as stereotypical, it doesn't mean they actually are. They are, in essence, unpredictable events in their social and cultural implications.

In a couple of weeks it will be the big annual event of the region, the Avon Descent. Canoeists, surf skiers and powerboaters come from all over the country (and some contestants from overseas) to do the whitewater run from Northam town weir down to Perth city, down through Katrine and Toodyay and Cobblers Pool – from the Avon River into the Swan.

For us, and for the riparian environment, it's the Descent into Hell. The damage wrought, especially by the powerboats, is denied by most and obvious to those who care. It can be guaranteed that though the Toodyay panther would be driven far away by the noise and 'excitement', there will be a rash of unconfirmed sightings along with the usual hazy photos and videos taken on phones. As Tim always complains, Why, with such anyone-can-take-a-decent-picture technology, are the photos always so rubbish? Indeed.

I am thinking about the church at Katrine – one of the sighting zones of the panther, it would seem – and I also think of the pine growing there said to be from a seed from a pine cone from the actual 'lonely pine' or lone pine that stood before the Battle of Lone Pine destroyed it during the Dardanelles Gallipoli 'campaign' of the First Word War. A bloody diversionary conflict that grew in reality and in the mythos of 'Australia', especially for its 'patriots', over the last century. I placed the pine of Katrine in my remake of the *Divine Comedy*.

~

It's scanning the memories of ordinary days that makes memoir, not the big events. So many of my alcoholic stupidities make for drama, and yet it was such empty drama. Being out at Happy Valley 20 k's from town and trying to open an olive oil drum with a knife and slicing through my hand and my brother's then partner having to drive me at high speed along gravel roads to

Narrogin hospital where I needed dozens of stitches having lost enough blood to make me pass out was more the norm than the exception. Sober for these decades, I still make physical errors, of course, but far fewer. I concentrate my abilities on lessening drama, not advertently or inadvertently causing it. But this doesn't mean my commitment to what I believed in then (as now) was any less, or any less reliable. I make this point because a politics is so often seen as being contingent on one's period of life and circumstances. In some ways, my pacifism formed out of a growing aversion to drama. As an anarchist I do not subscribe to chaos, and certainly not disorder. The 'version' of anarchism I follow is about equality for all living beings, about consensus, collaboration, and communities of individuals that are mutually supporting. It has the social angle, it has the respect for individual difference. I do not attempt to tell people what to believe, but I do attempt to draw their attention to the damage being done.

Rural communities centre and decentre (not centralise and decentralise) in so many very different ways. For the drinking communities in Western Australia, the pub or the sports club bar are major meeting places, and this might or might not overlap with the various denominations of church. There are towns with non-Christian religious buildings, such as Katanning with its significant Muslim population, but in the main, it's a case of various denominations of Christians. On the goldfields it was different, with Muslim Afghan cameleers, Hindu Indians, and other smaller groups of different religious belief, bearing in mind always that the spiritual beliefs of Aboriginal peoples are the core beliefs of country there (and here) – however, this was ignored or denied or taken for granted by colonisers and later migrants.

My grandmother, of Kookynie, was Presbyterian with an inclination to Methodism, and she fought a lifelong imaginary battle with Catholic Irish not because of dislike but because she felt that when she was willing to go into their place of worship, they should be willing to go into hers. The irony of all this, as I intimated earlier, is that one of her daughters married a man of distinctly Irish heritage, whose great-grandfather had been one of the first Catholic schoolteachers in the south-west. Mind you, there are those 'mitigating' circumstances, in the sense that my paternal great-grandmother, in distress that her husband had put his age down to go to fight in Europe during the First World War, taking his son, who had put his age up by two years so as to join his father in this 'expedition', took the rest of the children (including my grandfather Claude) to the city, Perth, until the end of the war and 'converted' them all to Anglicanism. This caused a split in the family that lasted until my childhood.

My mother, interested in all religions of the world equally, and a great traveller, went from being christened a Presbyterian to teaching Sunday school and playing the piano for a Methodist Church as well as going to a Church of England college, to being confirmed an Anglican at seventeen or eighteen, to developing an interest in the Gnostics, to having no religion at all (but not no belief or faith) along with total cultural respect for others' right to follow their religions. Like her elder son: all religions and no religion. And like her father (and like me), resisting all cant – decision-making is in the hands of the individual, not the organisation. Mum says now: 'I understood what Wordsworth was on about while studying him at university, and I think I like his idea of "Wisdom and Spirit of the Universe" more than going to organised religions.' In this, she and I are both pantheists in our own way.

I left the church when I was sixteen. Having said this, when I was nineteen I thought I had a vocation and spoke to the

Anglican Archbishop of Perth about going to Wollaston then maybe to Cambridge to study theology. As addiction got hold of me, this vocation dwindled, though my rejection of organised religion had come long before. I left the church on Christmas Day at St George's of Bluff Point, Geraldton – a nineteenth-century colonial building overlooking the sea – because the sermon compared Christmas with a cash register in terms of what was put in and what was taken out.

My Auntie Jackie and my mother had parted after eight years sharing their lives, our last year together being spent in the colonial mansion that had been the old nurses' quarters of the Geraldton (colonial) hospital. At the end of that last year of our non-nuclear family, a major cyclone messed up the coast and inland in unforgettable ways, and Auntie Jackie went off one way, and eventually my mother started seeing a young man who'd just completed rehab for alcoholism in the rehab centre next door (the centre is still there). Jim and I got on very well, and remained friends for many years, and in his sobriety he helped me out of many sticky situations that my already entrenched though then well-hidden alcoholism had got me into. He'd come along to that Christmas Day service when I was almost seventeen, though his own mother was tending towards Mormonism and in fact eventually became a Mormon. When the cash register came into play we just looked at each other and walked out, shaking out heads – both standing in the heat on dead grass looking away from the sea (hidden by dunes and buildings) towards the flat tops of the Moresby Ranges and talking about the Chapman Valley.

Aftermath. I walk Midland on a Saturday night to make my stomach work. I am becoming family with the homeless guys who set up their shopping trolley walls and settle in for the cold night under the post-eclipse moon. The moon in the aftermath of the next stage of its defining moments is illuminating the fractures of cloud with an orange-blue metallic glow. A bunch of guys who are drunk are pissing on a fence and yelling at cars driving past. I cross the road, turned away from the aftermath of the blood moon. I walk towards the Midland clock tower, its face glowing as a statement of heritage presence, of officialdom and a welcome it feels it should have but is uncertain of. This is still a pragmatic place, despite the ravages of meth. Karaoke is playing in a restaurant that is barely filled during the week, and I turn towards the Tower, studying the silhouette of the hills. Mum was up early this morning under Walwalinj to photograph the eclipse – the skies were less cloudy up there. All the damage done under its remit, the moon came out of the eclipse to continue a little longer, at least.

~

Tracy and I never go to pubs in Toodyay, our nearest town, and are connected with neither drink nor church culture, or really anything townwise outside general interactions that come through using the town facilities. At Jam Tree Gully, we keep to ourselves, unless someone needs a hand with something (which is rare as our lives don't greatly overlap). This separation has intensified since the bullying that meant Tim had to leave the district school. Once the school bond was broken, we found we had fewer social and community interactions with people.

The relationship between Jam Tree Gully and the broader

district is a little like Thoreau's presence at Walden Pond and its relationship to the Concord community in so many surface ways, but it is also extremely different – because of the threat level from external forces, and because we acknowledge that as it is colonised land concrete restitution to the traditional owners is required. Although Thoreau – an inveterate collector in his childhood and youth of 'Indian arrowheads' – acknowledged the destructive consequences of the colonial, he appropriated and grafted his identity to Native American knowledges in unacceptable ways. But *particular* correlations arise, even if they are so different in their realities and implications. The railway ran close to the pond that Thoreau so closely observed, and though we can't see it from Jam Tree Gully, we hear the grain trains going through down in the valley late at night. And Walden, after all, is America, and a very specific time and place in America. Not Australia. Not wheatbelt Western Australia. When I used Thoreau's *Walden* as a template for my book *Jam Tree Gully*, I did so with the ironies of difference constantly echoing (and, sadly, ricocheting).

~

I switch the hotel television on and there's a trucking program. A big rig delivering machinery into the 'heart of the Victorian forest'. The driver and his big rig are romanticised as tough expressions of frontierism, and their arrival 'without a scratch' is a success story. Around them is the devastated 'heart' of the forest, with a few bare trunks sticking up out of the wasteland the loggers have created. Machinery.

Jim, my mother's former partner, was a reformed alcoholic whose formal schooling stopped when he turned fourteen. A very smart guy, he worked feverishly hard and 'improved' himself by taking certificates in things like rigging and even pest control. Prior to this, he'd worked on mines in the north of Queensland, and in an abattoir. Over time, he was to develop a fiercely unionised left-wing politics, and after seeing a lamb born on Wheatlands farm became a vegetarian. My veganism gave him the evidence that it could all work. This is the thing about 'radical' ethical and political choices – they so often come out of opposite experiences. When I became vegan I was quite proselytising, but for the main part of thirty-three years I've lived a strictly vegan life as an example that it can be done. Tracy and I have raised children vegan, always conscious of their wellbeing, ensuring their dietary needs are met (Tracy has a very sophisticated understanding of diet), and leaving the ultimate choice in their hands. Tim was conceived as a vegan and has a highly articulate and self-directing sense of why he chooses to continue to be vegan. It's no case of imitating his parents. He has agency, and he believes animals have agency, too.

Recently I was asked to write an encomium for a book of poetry – a remarkable book of poetry – in which the poet discussed their upbringing in a family that made its living working in a small-town abattoir. This was a book about Aboriginal Australia, about identity, resisting colonialism, and about a hunting culture occluded by the meat industry. It was not particularly sympathetic to animal rights activists like me, but I felt it was an important and tough articulation of a mode of life, a viewpoint, and a reclaiming of country and space for cultural expression. And as such, I supported it. This would likely seem a contradiction to other animal rights activists, but I see no compromise and no contradiction. If a dialogue of difference doesn't exist, and we deny the origins and reasons for the meat industry, we cannot hope to bring change. And change is not a blanketing right. I have no right to bring change to Indigenous culturality, and I have no claim over the choices of others and no say over country. There's a mutuality in our co-determinate resistances, and our concerns for connection and respect, but I do not appropriate a totemic relationship – though I was delighted when a respected Noongar elder bestowed on our son Tim the totem of tawny frogmouth. Tim, worshipper and writer of birds, felt he'd been understood. Bridges need to be made and intactness respected.

My writing an encomium was an acknowledgement. And having neither eaten nor used animals in any conscious or willing way for thirty-three years or so (and I am thorough in how I check things; the only time I have been caught out was with an anaesthetic called 'milk of amnesia' which horrifies me still, and the memory loss it's supposed to induce is, in my case, full of trauma and remembering), I feel I am in a position of consistency and mutuality. Through living alongside wild animals, sharing a communal family existence with other vegans and in extended family who are vegetarians, I feel I can speak confidently about these issues. But what I do know is that I am in no position to judge anyone – we all make our own ways through life and decide for ourselves. As a believer in natural justice I don't set the rules. I do what I feel is right, and I respect difference. And there's plenty of mea culpa in my life, as there is in any life.

Jim once said to me that every bolt he fired through a sheep's skull into its brain was like a needle in his soul. That doesn't mean it's the same for all who look back over a life of killing animals on a factory production line, but it was the case for him. Disconnected from the world, with drinking his only form of communion with others, and alone in his hunger for knowledge, he was unable to tap into this until he met my mother (a school teacher); he went from one job to another from the age of fourteen. He was a pest controller, not in some Burroughs-esque confrontation with the malign and an embracing of evil, or a toxic rendition of the grotesque, but because he had no other way out. He was exposed to deadly organophosphates, and this exposure probably eventually killed him. But as he trained more and grew more and more articulate, he left that behind, too, and condemned the exploitations of the industry. And, what's more, he'd been a pest controller who didn't want to kill anything. I have a strange role in this, in that I helped him swot for his exams to get his certificate when I was in my late teens. I despised what he was doing, but understood the desperation. I provided him with a politics of opposition to the destruction, and also the chemistry knowledge he needed to pass. But out of this intense interaction began Jim's move to left-wing politics which would embrace both of us in fierce anti-apartheid activities in Australia, and verbal and written opposition to the Contras in Nicaragua. He paid me to write his letters of protest, and I did so willingly. And together, we became very active for animal rights and also in protesting the use of organophosphates and other destroyers of body and land. So, relationships are complex, and as Derrida intimated at various times, things ought to be complex because they are.

≈

I find it disturbing living in this self-catering hotel surrounded by the homeless. The people working here are fine and interesting, and supportive of the community they are part of, but so much of the business side of the town seems indifferent to the homeless. Having said this, there are many religious support services, and private drug and alcohol recovery agencies, and some government infrastructure, too. But after dark, when I walk after eating, the homeless walk with their shopping trolleys and vulnerabilities, and a different Midland becomes evident. I know the world of the homeless, for it is a world with its own rules, and its many threats. For years as an addict I wandered, and though I mostly had family to return to, it was not always possible and I lived at times on the streets and in the bush – to make the leap 'back' was often humiliating and confronting, and impossible as long as the addiction ravaged lives around me.

I will say that though I induced despair, and all advice was to cut me off, those who were closest to me never did completely, and never stopped loving me. It's what kept me alive in the end. But I lived on the street, in a cave, in the Supreme Court Gardens, in run-down hotel rooms in the city and in country towns, on the beach, in abandoned houses, and wherever I could crash for a day or two. These periods came and went as I 'got my shit together', and for long stretches I managed to be with a partner and child, though my addictions brought great costs. One of the most characteristic aspects was the bender, where I would disappear for weeks and entirely lose myself, and my sense of what life was.

When I was a child, my brother and I (but often just me) would go 'out' for the day, by which I meant an 'expedition' out onto the farm, or out away from home or wherever we were living or staying. I would take a packed lunch, tell people where I'd be, and 'explore'. It was a narrativising for me: the creation of a fantasy of encounter that was underwritten by a real journey. There was nothing unsafe or subversive about it, in any familial sense of responsibility – I went where I said I'd go and got back on time – but there was a transgression of conventional behaviours insofar as I wanted to leave society, wanted to live as part of the land but also separate. The politics weren't there as such, but I was unconsciously formulating a sense of isolation fused with ways of communicating with non-human space.

I yearn for Jam Tree Gully, not to hide from the homeless, a confrontation with the reality of so many, but because I can wander and have those contacts with a non-human spatiality which determines me in the belief that by helping protect the natural environment I can best serve humanity as well as nature, as part of nature. But that doesn't mean I should close myself off in a bubble – which is not possible anyway, with the various (often violent) incursions because of the rapacity of some humans – but rather, I should use what I have learnt to feed back into helping all those I can help. To write of the homeless is not to fetishise the homeless, but to reconnect, to empathise, to open a door to sharing and conversation. We can never isolate ourselves from mutual responsibility – to do so is its own indulgence, and its own spiritual rapacity.

I will make contacts in this community while I am here, sharing space. I will contribute what I can. I will not deny, I will not pry into what shouldn't be seen as I walk, as I wander. I will swap poems with Kwame – doing so helps clarify what memoir is, what conversation is, what sparks across space might be, what family is, what community might be. As with my dialogues with Charmaine and Frieda, these are the keys to escaping beyond the self into shared responsibility, into finding a language of mutuality while respecting difference. Now, I will walk. It is a blue cool day with a massive front due tomorrow, and another on Sunday. The land is constantly being rewritten. We don't have to be stuck with the damage – it can be undone.

~

My mother delivered a vegan meal and a vegan cake to us the other day. She and Guru drove down from York as they had an appointment in Midland (as so many wheatbelt people regularly do). They understand how much we're feeling the 'being away' from Jam Tree Gully. Tracy is something of a legendary vegan cook – having developed vegan recipes back in the nineties that gained some traction. Mum took to vegan cooking as well, and is also highly inventive. Anyway, Tracy and I were talking about the shifts between old-style 'farm cooking' and veganism – the shifts aren't as dramatic as one might think. My auntie of Wheatlands is a renowned cake maker, and like so many women of wheatbelt farms (and I am talking from the fifties on here) is considered a 'fine cook', and yet she can *also* turn a dab hand at making a vegan cake for family. But if change is going to come slowly anywhere, it's the wheatbelt. Nonetheless, Tracy's vegan cake entry was able to win an award in the 'health cake' section of an agricultural show, twelve or thirteen years ago. Our daughter also won with vegan biscuits she submitted in the kids' section.

The annual agricultural shows are a highlight of the rural calendar, and though there are many things I obviously don't like about them (exploitation of animals, promotion of agricultural monocultures, poisons and so on), there is much I like about them as well. Community is pivotal, and I understand this, even if we spend little time in it and live apart in so many ways. But many trees I have planted I have bought from seedling stalls at such shows that specialise in local native vegetation, and my lifelong fascination with grain growing always gets a boost when I look at the sheaves of wheat, oats and barley that have won 'best crop' samples for the year. And then there's extended family playing in sports competitions – it's good to watch the cousins giving their all in the hockey; the same cousins win almost every competition in almost every category they enter in the show. It's a chance to catch up with family and locals we see once or twice a year.

But there's slippage here. I am primarily talking about the York show – the town we lived just outside of for many years, where my mother and Guru live, where many family members live in or near or in the region of – and sometimes the show in the larger regional centre of Northam. I am not talking about the Toodyay show, which is the closest one to Jam Tree Gully. There's nothing wrong with the show per se; it's much like any of the other small-town shows that occur across a two-month period from the end of 'winter' into the 'spring' (September and October) – essentially celebrations of the season. But Tim would run into the violent bullies who drove him out of school, and we would inevitably have to deal with people whose right-wing beliefs regarding land, Aboriginal rights and immigrant rights we have opposed, and who respond to our 'greenie', 'leftie' views with aggression.

Agricultural shows concentrate people. Then again, we have attended the Moondyne Festival on the main street of Toodyay town on multiple occasions with few problems, though in its celebration of the colonial we do so more out of scrutiny than celebration, and don't participate in the 'activities'. At the regular shows, Tim and I (and once with my daughter) inevitably ride a few of the sideshow rides – I still haven't completely relinquished my adrenaline–vertigo addiction – and talk with people on various stalls. A different dynamic, though the colonial still lurks below the surface, raising its head in disturbing ways. There are always conservative political party booths (the 'left' never show), army recruitment booths, and the usual farming promotions – after all, that's what the shows are about. But over the years a slightly different subtext has started creeping in – land conservation, tree planting and other slightly 'green' notions.

~

I often find myself thinking about the nature of houses, especially as the homeless here (everywhere) are in such need of support. I think of the four houses we lived in in Ohio, and how each of them could have housed three families. We loved those houses, and their histories fascinated us. We talk of them often, especially the Sears house. Especially the woods nearby. Strangely, when I think of the house we took a newborn Tim home to, I think of the toys he first handled, first saw, first rolled over to reach, first crawled to. He was a baby who was fascinated by things. I wrote a sequence of poems entitled 'Timothy's toys' which, for me, captures something of what it was like living away from the wheatbelt (or the fens) and having a new child. Timothy was conceived in America, born in America, and learnt to walk in America, which by Noongar reckoning (and I do not wish to appropriate this, but simply recount what I have been told freely) makes Tim essentially of the central Ohio region. Mum and John being there helped so much, and the support of the Kenyon community was absolute, but it was still an intense and differentiated experience (we were still considered 'foreigners' by some). What meant so much, and this is embedded in the toy poems, was that the toys were mostly gifts given by students, and the families of students – especially one family of a rural background who 'got' us. Material possessions are always a problem for us, but we know how to accept a gift. And the notion of the gift for us came not only via Lewis Hyde and our association with Jacques Derrida and his work, and our sense of what prayer can be outside religious institutions, but because we believe that a gift is an act of non-ownership – it is a temporary possessing to help another physically, spiritually, emotionally. And as such, those gifts of toys for Timothy helped us feel belonging.

Timothy's toys

Caterpillar

Crinkle expression
scrunchy-eyed one with pink antennae
that glow sucked toothless
as limpet, parrot-tongued
the alphabetical beak squeaks
security, this Walmart
labour-drain, sewn
to distract gripe or over-
tiredness, piercing
blue eyes changeable
as days slurp and orally
fixate, to sample
like whiskers seeing, or the platypus's
bill beneath the surface, drool and dribble,
a liquid self, caterpillar scrunches, crinkles,
articulates.

Duckie

Scoff the web-foot of rotation, the bright
emoticon facing the world of the rug,
to almost roll towards a clockwork
rubber duck song, timpanic and bridgeless
to reach across, as toes to mouth,
and duckie there, assuredly giggly,
tipping over and singing on,
oh duckie, duckie, almost

close enough to reach,
yellow-feathered, soft.

The tower of cups

Star pulsar, twist of colour
as down comes the tower,
a tiny foot that rocks foundations,
splashing colour, muffled clamour
of rubble tucks inside each other,
one another prayer-intoners,
om om speech speech up high in the bell chamber,
red-capped eye-strainer
of a plastic clatter, of a climb up and out
of growth suits and onesies,
collapsing odes to technicolour,
industrial music.

Links

Chain of nubbles with link-slippage,
as grunt and shout, and squealing overture,
these raspberries, sibilance about the spout,
to splutter and bubble, to grip and hold,
lock across the body and gloat
as tongue lolls about syllables;
on consonants, on gutturals,
as mauve chain links yellow links
red and green and we can change them back again,
gummy as a sneak of a tooth shows through,
sneak of a tooth,

the eye-switcher switches colour
as bright lights overhead distract
and a roaring laugh glows
as bright as birth lights
chew the langue-ee links
that were never
in the moebius plan.

Wrist rattles, ankle rattles

Snubby chubbles about the wrists and ankles,
to starburst and reflex action the newly gripping
hands and encircling feet: these velcro rings
of opposable thumbs, to pincer-grip
the snug foot-fittings, socks of lion
and elephant with the tied-up stretch of snoz,
the bright shapes, as close they come
and cross-eyes quartet the scrum
of digits and crinkly coats,
rattles for brains, playground and stage
the striped tube that hides the wrigglers
we later call toes, and those waving
fingers – trimmed nails
still etching skin in sweeps and hooks;
as the massive calm comes from without,
the room of the loomers, the large,
a vestige of market research
and the bright packaging
that calls a talk all of its own.

I have wittingly and unwittingly alienated people I have loved and cared for throughout my life. Some of them probably never really knew that I loved and cared for them, or that I respected them. I regret all of this. As we move on, we inevitably wish to repair these separations, dislocations and distancings. But many such interactions are best left as they were when they 'finished'. People don't necessarily want to revisit, to grant closure to themselves or others, and this is fine. These things have to be put into perspective and sometimes we have to let go, forever. In this, I think of Henry Crabb Robinson's somewhat uncomfortable reminiscences of William Blake, in particular over the question of eternity and God. As God for me is an idea as powerful as any, and because an idea is always fallible for me though the essence of right and wrong is essentially clear, there are contradictions that drive the why and wherefores of how I react and respond to experience. As the years of my sobriety build, I increasingly feel that God is an act of responsibility in all its manifestations, and realising that I am essentially pantheistic, and that all is in everything and that every leaf of grass is vital to me, I understand that I cannot separate myself off from a notion of God. I am the unbeliever who believes, in the same way that I once (uncritically – now I have issues with her thinking) subscribed to Simone Weil's 'Every separation is a link'. As Crabb observed as he talked with Blake:

> As I had for many years been familiar with the idea that an eternity *a parte post* was inconceivable without an eternity a parte ante, I was naturally led to express that thought on

this occasion. His eye brightened on my saying this. He eagerly assented: 'To be sure. We are all coexistent with God; members of the Divine body, and partakers of the Divine nature.' Blake's having adopted this Platonic idea led me on our *tête-à-tête* walk home at night to put the popular question to him, concerning the imputed Divinity of Jesus Christ. He answered: 'He is the only God' – but then he added – 'And so am I and so are you.'

I am not a 'Christian', but I respect the goodness inherent in Christ the activist. I also respect much about the prophets of many religions. But there's much interpolation of control and oppression of personal and communal liberty through texts that I don't connect with. But even there, this does not mean I close my eyes or mind to the way others value and interpret these texts in the sense of their own lives and heritages. For me, everything is 'per se' – which, in fact, is the title of a collaborative work I am engaged in at present with scholar Russell West-Pavlov. Collaboration teases out ideas, helps remove some of our own prejudices. I write this as a cold front crosses Midland. It is disturbing to hear a plane try to come in as winds pummel the hotel and rain drives horizontally into the Scarp. Safe arrival, safe return.

~

The Tampa incident took place in August 2001 – the Australian government refusing to allow Norwegian freighter the MV *Tampa* to enter Australian territorial waters because it was carrying hundreds of Afghan refugees rescued from boats, and instead ordering special forces to board the ship. I tried to contribute to the effort to support the refugees and the captain of the ship, who wanted to take the refugees to Christmas Island, by writing and widely distributing poems as well as general messages of support. I received death threats for doing this, and those threats were extended to my family. Out of the horror that was the Tampa affair, the government of John Howard put forward the Border Protection Bill, which has been the underpinning of a vile, racist and bigoted (anti)refugee policy that has as its basis a 'turn back the boats' domestic psychology targeting the trade of people smuggling, to distract from the quarantine-like warding-off psychology and brute reality of the act. The barbarity of the subsequent so-called 'Pacific Solution' of off-loading unvetted refugees (that is, refugees who have not been processed through official channels before departing for Australia) onto Nauru island and other 'offshore detention' locations, supported by multiple Australian governments of both 'denominations' since, finds its roots in the Tampa moment.

I have a firm belief, as does Tracy, that people under duress *must* be welcomed into any country, and this should be done as part of an ongoing process of consultation and with respect to indigenous peoples – as should it be the case with all people who arrived via colonisation, and with new migrants arriving through formal channels (who, to our minds, should be welcomed and placed in immediate conversation with the traditional owners and custodians of the land – the only 'ownership' I recognise and acknowledge, as it takes precedence over capitalist notions of property). In recent years, male refugees have been imprisoned on Manus Island as part of offshore detention, and have suffered unspeakable brutality at the hands of the Australian officials and understandable rejection by locals who have had the Australian government's responsibility forced on them. With my friend the Western Australian poet and walker James Quinton, I have written and co-written poems of support for these refugees and against Australia's brutal policies. Under an arrangement brokered by the Turnbull government and the Obama administration, and maintained (under pressure and not 'happily') by the Trump administration, some of these refugees have been relocated (against their will) to the United States, so as to maintain Australia's border protection policy. It amounts to legal semantics; people are played as pawns. These are people who have been kept incarcerated for years, losing their identities, altered forever in their humanity. What should a poet do but resist such acts of official cruelty in all its manifestations around the world?

Do poems help in such situations? Yes, if they bring hope to those suffering; yes, if they make conversations where people were quiet; yes, if they result in positive activity where there was none. But they can't work alone – and I was saying as much in a textual conversation with the brilliant 'anti-colonial' (as described by certain critics) artist Helen Johnson. To be creative and respond to wrong through creativity is not enough, it must work together with non-violent direct action.

Jam Tree Gully is a small place on the world map, but what comes out of it has a responsibility to all humanity and all life. 'Isolation' is a term of convenience imposed by imperialists on what they want to possess, or used by those who wish to step away from the imperialist machine but possess something unique or 'separate'. Both versions of 'choice' and 'agency' bring their own possessings and dispossessings, and though Walden moments can help one's own spirit, and can even protect ecologies, and the story can be 'got out' and shared to bring a greater understanding of how those of us produced by the colonial-capitalist machine might critique our own positions of mass consumption, in the end we are serving our own fetishising of relative privilege. We can never close our doors. And the firebreaks that surround us are about stopping fire ravaging more and more (fire often caused by colonial invasiveness), not keeping people out. A healthy planet is a shared planet, not one separated off into healthy and unhealthy bits, surely.

'Jam Tree Gully' is just a name we've given to where we live, not because that's its real name – it has many names that we know of, but its most relevant name/s is/are hidden to us – but because it's how we identify our relationship with that bit of land. But it's a name that, to us, means an invitation for others to scrutinise how we discuss our belonging and unbelonging to a place where we sleep, eat, and speak to each other, and how we speak out to the rest of the world where we can, however we can, if we can.

~

A journey up to JTG and back – to check mail in town, and do a few small things around home. There had been a lot of rain over the last week – looked to be about 30 millimetres all up. Journeying, I considered the necessity of repetition to being, and when an interruption or loss happens and the repetition is broken, it hurts. In a single week, more roadside vegetation has been peeled back, more trees removed from paddocks. Some familiars, or occasionals, maintained. The increasingly rare and endangered Carnaby's black cockatoos – which I tend to call white-tailed black cockatoos to get away from Euro-naming (but not to thieve or borrow the Noongar naming without permission), but my doing so is imprecise insofar as there are two species of white-tailed black cockatoo, the other being the even rarer long-beaked Baudin's black cockatoo, which we sometimes see in the region – were on their cold-weather move over the Toodyay Road, and characteristically perched in the limbs of a dead tree opposite the Morangup Nature Reserve, and in living trees in the paddocks, both affirmation and haunting. One of Tim's bus friends told him of a neighbour of theirs who pays a young guy to shoot them. These are the crimes against the essence of life. These acts of violence are expressions of ownership and possession of all that's listed on the title deed, and all that exists within the notion of 'nation' – as if the shooter, the clearer, owns the very rights to all life within their purview, in range of their property deed. 'God's own country' – as it is called by some – is 'their' realm because they believe in such gods. No understanding or respect for *country* (for Noongar boodja), just for their own frontierism which exists as an extension of the new colonialism, the new settling of Australia that makes little effort to correct the crimes of earlier 'settling'.

I passed a ewe earlier that had died giving birth in the last day or so. There's been a sheep weather alert, but the paddock it died in has no shelter – every summer two horses bake in that same paddock without shade when it's over 40 degrees. This sheep was already waterlogged, a half-birthed lamb hanging out of its distended uterus. A dozen crows were picking the two to pieces, which, as I wrote in a poem draft just now (a poem called 'redaction', which is also a response to the influencing and corruption around the recent American presidential election), don't act as exploiters of death, but rectifiers of human abuse of nature. Crows transition flesh and tissue between life and death, death and what follows.

During the extreme weather of the last twenty-four hours (down south, Cape Leeuwin recorded a 124-kilometre-per-hour gust of wind, while along the coast of Perth a gust of around 100 kilometres per hour was recorded) we were 'holed up' in this bizarre tower of self-catering apartments in Midland listening to the furious wuthering. The wind was wrenching at the windows and threatening to draw us out. We eventually fell to sleep weary with a sound that I am very familiar with from living up on the coast in Geraldton, and also inland in Cambridge, where the winds peel the fens, and even more so in Schull, where the great Atlantic storms batter the town even with its protection of Cape Clear Island out in Roaring Water Bay. We were in Schull when the once-in-a-hundred-years storm hit Ireland and destroyed six million trees – and Ireland has few trees left to 'spare'. We saw whole forests demolished on mountainsides. Journeying back to JTG today, there were trees down, but only a few and nothing comparable to the trees knocked down by private land owners, government and private industry over the last week alone. Jam Tree Gully had withstood the front, though the winds were far less virulent (can one say such a thing, really?) that far inland, cocooned among hills on the edge of the great plain of wheat starting to shine in its *florescence* – long a favourite word of mine. It captures something, despite the mono-agricultural damage it embodies. It's a hope for bread, for food, for life.

But florescence might also be considered the shadowy glow of property, and in that it is a negative symbolism. The 'road closure' signs have gone up on the loop – the Targa car rally is about to take over and traumatise the natural world (and a few humans as well – also part of nature!). Usually, the rally route changes every few years, but since I won that protest on legal (public consultation) grounds that first year, there's been a clear commitment to keeping the greenie opposition suppressed, and showing that cars, fuel, competition, and roads built with taxes will triumph over 'alternative' lifestyles. Competition, partying, thrills – to give purpose to lives, to make existence endurable for them?

But a few acacias are in their winter (or storm season, really) bloom, or coming into bloom. It's early for them. But everything is earlier, and 'later' has turned on its own tail. No seasons are alike now, and no seasons are what I remember them to be. For all the desiring of farmers for 'old-fashioned' seasons, or 'reminds me of', the reality is that there's chaos. Chaos has its own patterns, of course, we know that, but it's not the surety that a conservative's desire of/for a compliant land, one forced into the shape they wish for by their own hands, will serve up. Profit that comes from exploitation will always cost. Remove all the vegetation and the rain pattern will change, especially the further inland you go. And the higher temperatures change cropping faster than industry agronomists can outfox. A real fox will always understand more, know better.

~

When the ice storm hit during our final winter together in Ohio, the wind chill factor was near -30. The power was out for a week, and as we had few resources to fall back on, it was a time we will never forget. In Mount Vernon, with the pipes frozen and dagger icicles on everything – even beyond the usual winter freeze – the expression 'ice storm' took on a different meaning. For Tracy, it was the realm of Jadis, the white witch of Narnia, and, of course, the Snow Queen. Both of these manifestations of power and suppression are colonial in their application, and as we felt isolated and outside and not wishing to appropriate other stories, it's where our image default turned to. When I wrote the libretto for a new opera version of *The Snow Queen* (composed by Gordon Kerry), it was from that experience, that exposure to an extreme elemental scenario, that I drew on.

I have been in many cold places, and I once walked off a plane in Edmonton in midwinter in my shirtsleeves, which I wouldn't usually even register (I do not feel the cold at all, even when my health is at risk; later, I would discover this is a result of Graves' disease and my extremely overactive thyroid), but as it became a talking point among the university poetry community there, I am still occasionally reminded of it. Extreme heat is my default setting (though this is what a Graves person is most vulnerable to).

From having to warm two-year-old Tim between us under piled blankets in the aftermath of the storm, to our daughter trying to warm herself under half a dozen blankets and four quilt covers, we realised we had to get out of the frozen house. The Kenyon Inn, though under pressure in terms of space, took us in and we were supported by the Kenyon community, though it was suffering as well. It had been suggested by someone in one of the shopping centres, which somehow managed to stay open, that we use a propane stove to cook on and warm ourselves by. So many deaths by propane – and we weren't willing to risk the children that way. It's strange looking back at the few photos we have of that year – I am swinging on the porch seat with young Tim with his sister standing by, looking out onto a leafy street, in a brilliant spring. Months before the ice storm. That street was an underground railroad street; that street would become a street of over-the-top Christmas lights (as it does every year); that street was so shut down during the ice storms that only the Mennonite family at the northern end kept going as usual – they were off-grid.

Off-grid is always the way to be, if possible. I think of this in the Tower as the fronts of the last few days accumulate, feeling compelled to move along with them over the Scarp, inland. When the heat comes it too can disconnect people from the grid. And there is nothing stranger than trying to make a home where one unbelongs, where one can't ultimately 'fit'. We don't believe in possessing, in property per se, but we do believe in the right of all people to be 'homed', and to be allowed to feel 'home'. Home is not about theft or dispossessing, it's about a right to respectfully coexist, and to define small-scale interactions against the backdrop of the larger world. Interestingly, the Mennonite women who ran the health store in Mount Vernon, though not vegans themselves, understood where we were coming from, and in supporting our needs they expanded that possibility of 'home'. Difference, for them, wasn't alien, but part of presence.

We keep no pets because we feel a human should not control the destiny of an animal. Having said this, we also acknowledge the respect many people have in their interactions with 'domesticated' animals. I grew up around many animals, and even up to when we left York for Jam Tree Gully, there was a 'family dog' not kept by me, but by Mum and Guru, though it was actually Stephen's dog. Not that my brother thinks anyone can own an animal! Shep – that old name so beloved and committed to working dogs – was saved by my brother from being shot by a farmer because he was lame. Yet Shep was the most enthusiastic dog to ever grace a shearing shed, and never lagged behind the other working dogs. After he took very early retirement, his main social interactions came through humans, whom he followed, 'protected' and 'played' with. We all loved Shep and considered him as part of the human family. However, I would not be responsible for feeding him anything animal in origin (there are now many vegan dog foods, believe it or not, which do a more than adequate job), and left his bodily wellbeing to my mother. This does not mean that I didn't care, and I loved his company, but my days of 'keeping' animals were long past. I will always help an animal in need, and will always save an animal suffering duress no matter what, but I will house it ultimately with someone else. I want to provide a safe space for animals to be what they are without human interference, or with as little human interference as possible, and not to gain pleasure from their reliance on or servitude to people. JTG is a refuge for free and wild animals.

I love animals, more than I can say, but many pet owners (and I use the word 'owner' markedly) consider me far less of an animal lover than they are. When I point out that in deriving comfort and solace from a creature that ultimately has no real agency, no freedom, no choice outside the relationship its 'owner' has constructed for it, which suits the owner in all meaningful ways, the 'pet lover' is talking more about themselves than the animal, they often find my saying this offensive. There's no need for them to feel this, and I say so. I respect anyone who does their best, is not cruel or overtly exploitative. I understand the closeness of human–animal interactions. But as a vegan animal rights activist, I feel I must act in a way that is consistent, and that ultimately attempts to place the animal on an equal footing with myself. Save animals in all ways we can – but make fewer pets of them and let them be the creatures they are and wish to be, as much as possible.

The saving of animals, especially when one is a child, is fundamental to developing a nurturing self and finding a way of extending this to people. Throughout the bulk of my alcoholic-addicted years I was a vegan. I checked what I drank and took, no matter what state I was in, so as to reduce the exploitation of animals: not drinking vats of wine that had been clarified with isinglass, which is made from fish bladders (Guinness, too, used to be refined with this). Strangely, in my states of utter degradation I maintained these values, and I think this helped me survive. As children, my brother and I were often saving birds fallen from nests (dusky miners in particular), or raising orphaned kangaroos. Though I was a hunter and a fisher and a destroyer of bushland through carelessness (building cubbies, clearing patches to make camp, and so on) as a child and early teenager, I still believed in this nurturing. One of those driving paradoxes of my life, maybe of many lives. Feeding the blind chick through a dropper, the rubber teat on the Coke bottle for the lamb at the farm, the aviary for the parrot that had lost its tail feathers went hand in hand with shooting parrots, trapping rabbits, and fishing.

About eleven years ago I was driving from Northam back to York after my daughter's ballet lesson. Ballet was one of those pastimes she'd held onto in the various countries we'd lived in, and we'd actually had bespoke non-leather ballet shoes made for her in Cambridge in the late nineties, well before such things became commercially available. She and I were often on the road, as distance defined social interactions, and we often encountered 'roadkill', and sometimes accidentally hit animals with the car. Hitting a tawny frogmouth at night remains a traumatic moment for me. I turned the car around and went back, got out, went to it, wide-mouthed and stunned on the road, headlights blazing, touched it gently, and it flew off. Another time we came across a snake that had been run over (likely intentionally) – an eight-foot dugite – and I could see the end of its tail was crushed. I got out and picked it up behind the head (as one is supposed to if trained in such things, which I am not, though I have handled reptiles all my life), and removed it to the side of the road. It was a silly thing to do (it is one of the world's most deadly snakes) and Tracy told me so, but I am pretty sure it wouldn't have survived otherwise. If it had stayed on the road it would have been targeted by another motorist, and finished off.

Anyway, I digress … So, my daughter and I were driving home in the late afternoon and we saw an injured twenty-eight parrot on the side of the road … or did we accidentally hit it as it swooped in front of the car on its loping way between trees? We turned round, went back, picked it up. It bit me, tearing the skin with its machine-like beak, as they always do, pushing its kernel tongue against my bloody finger skin, a feeling I remembered so well from childhood – this grain-eating bird, so persecuted by farmers, still had life in it. I wrapped it in my daughter's jumper, and she nestled it in her lap as we drove home. I managed to place the bird with a wildlife carer that night and we heard later that it had survived and was returned to 'the wild'. This is not a rare story, but it's a necessary one. In Geraldton, my brother has made a name for himself as a wildlife saver – he sees many injured animals on his long journeys to and from work, and rescues them and takes them to carers. It is part of how we were brought up. Part of the paradox of any upbringing.

~

A radio program I did with Yamaji poet Charmaine Papertalk Green was just played on ABC Radio National. I didn't hear it, but my mum emailed me about it and so did my Auntie Lorraine from Wheatlands. This is the exchange:

> Hi John,
>
> Gerry and I have just listened to you and Charmaine on the radio and thoroughly enjoyed it. Found it very moving indeed and loved the obvious connection between the two of you. Sorry when it was over!
>
> -------------

how lovely to hear this, auntie lorraine! thanks.
do you know, it was uncle gerry taking me to meet the Aboriginal stookers on the farm next door when i was a very small child that made me so amazed and respectful of Indigenous australia? i stood there kicking the ground while this noongar kid did the same …
i knew at the time it was important, and it was.
uncle gerry was taking the stookers tucker or water or something – i have no idea why. it must be near fifty years ago!
love to you both!
john

And then Auntie Lorraine came back with a reference to my grandmother, her mother, on the goldfields at Kookynie being haunted her entire life by the government agents coming to remove Aboriginal children from their mothers: the Stolen generations.

All her life, Mum carried with her the memory of the times the men came to take the little Aboriginal children away.
And so, of course I carry those memories as well.
I can see, so clearly, the terrified little girl, grabbing her little brother and racing to hide – never quite sure that the men wouldn't take them too.
And the wailing of those poor mothers that went on for a long time.

And she also wrote:

Stooking hay was an awful job. (I tried it once!) It could only be photographers that regretted the passing of those

> fields of golden stooks! Bales of hay don't quite have the same appeal – except to ex-stookers!

I include this because though Wheatlands was the product of colonialism in its most overt form – the occupation of large sections of land for farming – it was also where and how I came to understand the need for land return and for cultural respect. It's not a straightforward binary of good and bad, even if what needs to be done is straightforward, and the 'good' and 'bad' of it all is clear. One of Mum's friends once told her that 'Noongar families know who the good and bad white families were … and they don't forget'. Mum drove to school most days with this remarkable woman, who shared some of her knowledge with Mum. The conversations are there to be had, if the colonials and later migrants are willing to listen.

~

There's an incident taking place in the car park below. *An incident.* Bikies, police and ambulance. Incidents. It is strange to be above a car park, seeing but trying to be discreet. I spend so much time sitting in the car parks in Northam, waiting. I have seen many *incidents* – most of them racist. Most of them with Noongar people being hassled by officials, or by bigoted whites who use verbal put-downs or aggressive body language, or walk away to make a point. I have mapped such incidents over the years as an act of witnessing. Sometimes, when it's needed, I will intervene. I have written of this in exchanges with Charmaine, as she has, always confronting and reclaiming, as she must. She talks about white people being so readily 'uncomfortable' when confronted with the realities of land theft, racism and inequality.

She talks of subtle and not so subtle racisms – the fact that racism is embedded in the official state. And in rural car parks around shopping centres, these bigotries come into social play. A few weeks ago we were delighted to see and hear a Noongar guy singing both African American protest songs and Aboriginal protest songs. Interveners into culture try to separate resistant cultures, saying they have nothing in common, but that's untrue. I recently read a fascinating piece on the ABC website about the Fisk Jubilee Singers, an African American choir, who visited an Aboriginal mission in New South Wales as part of their world tour, and spent six years based in Australia

~

At the moment, I am in one of my living, almost embodied flashbacks, triggered by the facade of a building in Midland reminding me of a building I saw in Chicago – a street corner shop. I am walking through an outer suburb of Chicago … thinking of Tracy's mum's sister, whom I never met … and of Tracy's aunt's husband, an Italian American marine she met when he was stationed in Perth during the Second World War. He had to leave Chicago because his family rejected him when he married her, a non-Catholic. They both eventually became Baptists as a response to their son being drafted into the Vietnam War … I am thinking about religion and peace and variations on the usual. Each desire for *needs* to be met through a belief is so different. The problem is expecting a generic condition. That's how things get misread, surely? I was, as always, tracing birds flying up onto a rooftop, into trees. The shop was incidental but I can see it now.

~

Two of my great interests as a child were the space race and magic. I have written about these 'worlds' (as they were to me), which were part of the alternative reality I longed for, but what is relevant here is how they did or didn't transfer into rural settings. The fact was, they largely didn't. Making rockets in a literal sense, later, did, as we fired them from the lab into paddocks, but when I was on a farm or in the bush, or 'down south', I most often left these obsessions behind. I find this strange now, as with access to so much big machinery, to rocket-shaped silos, to 'isolated' spaces, it would have seemed logically fantastical to transfer my space program from urban and town spaces. Strangely, though, what did transfer, as I mentioned earlier, was space coming to earth in the form of weird happenings, UFOs, star-gazing and astronomy.

And magic. I did one magic show down in a seaside country town, using an old chest, but mostly this was the preserve of my grandfather's urban spaces and secret meetings of the Magic Circle, a group of professional and amateur magicians who met regularly in Perth and had sworn to keep the secrets of their craft. Magic, though, was there, taking on another form – one not controlled by sleight of hand, but by the inexplicable and disturbed. Again, a sense of not belonging, of being where I shouldn't. Old houses emanated, certain trees warded me off, a ghost gum (white gums – wandoos – not the ghost gum from the eastern states) would often 'spook' me, and bizarre lights appeared over dams and swampy areas.

But I was a young scientist, and refused to let these things go without explanation. One of my greatest apprehensions was around drinking wells – portals to a connectedness to all hidden water when the surface was so dry. I have written a novel about subterranean waterways, and poems about strange eels that swim between farm wells. When I was a child I believed snakes travelled the subterranean ways between wells on the farm, on Wheatlands … I felt compelled to climb into wells to find out. And I did. And I struggled to get *back out*. I built up my fear levels. Apprehension was discovery, and pushing my body and psyche was experiment. I remember thinking the first time I read Mary Shelley's *Frankenstein* as a thirteen-year-old that science could be pushed too far into the realm of 'mystery'. Poetry seemed the only way out of this conundrum. One of the most uncanny experiences I had on Wheatlands farm came in my mid-twenties, when I was looking after the farm for a couple of weeks with my former partner – I saw a distinctive plinth on the horizon of the farm. I knew the distant fence line and paddock very well. It was stubble and red-grey dirt. No sheep in it at that time. I took a photo of this plinth shining in the sun. I had the film developed and there was no sign of it at all. Of course there are logical explanations, but the point for me is the performative nature of mystery and what compels us to investigate it, to make art of it. As always, it's an anxiety of presence – of belonging and unbelonging and being unable to find one's way home. I applied logic to the situation and found my logic, rather than the situation, wanting.

On that same visit, we had two friends come up who were into the 'weird'. To them, every sheep skull was a contact with the other side, and they somewhat creeped us out. The translation of their gothness into the landscape (they were very urban people) was a distraction from presence, but also, maybe, an appropriate way of seeing and encountering the death that makes the 'life' of such farming. A couple of years before their visit I'd written my poem 'Wheatbelt Gothic', about the displaced way of seeing in the crepuscular light of apprehension and warping of what is actually there, to make it seem as if what's been implanted 'belongs' – the removal of vegetation and culture and replacing it with an architecture of Western utility and (spiritual–material) control: churches, chapels, graveyards, machine sheds, engine sheds, stone houses with pitched roofs and all-round verandahs, shacks, asbestos … boustrophedon … palms, chimneys, Metters stoves, chicken coops, milking sheds, sheep ramps … And yet the goth couple, who were heavily into the occult, which we definitively were not (for all the fundamentalism of my then partner's upbringing, she had turned against all forms of spiritually controlling forces), walking along firebreaks and climbing fences in their city goth clothes, pancake white faces with dark mascara, working against gender (which was to be celebrated, especially out in the wheatbelt!), added a different inflection to wheatbelt gothic, and one that ironised its very imagined existence.

I have seen this 'strangeness' with the Wyeth houses in fields in the rural Midwest of America. All constructs, all remodellings as if hoping to incite new mystery, new fallibilities of spiritual presence and absence. But one who was never absent, is not absent, and can't be pretended into absence. Again, the nature of the colonial/frontier desiring for permanence it cannot have, and should not have. And as for the space race, the Cold War politics made anodyne by diagrams of the hardware and the flight path to the moon, which I cut out and collected in scrapbooks, might not have found expression in the wheatbelt as such, or in the fields of Ohio if I'd grown up there, but the fear they masked and also produced was evident in the ufology that lurked on the edges of every farmhouse's feeble generator shed supplied 32-volt lighting, and even that faltering as the juice runs out or the spark plug carbons up. A cold war of later colonialism.

~

The direct wars of colonialism in the so-called wheatbelt of Western Australia are simply covered up by the term 'settlement'. But it was a systematic construct of clearing land for wheat, sheep and cattle farming, with land ownership most often in the hands of British colonials, but from the end of the First World War in particular, a lot of the labour for clearing scrub was carried out by southern and middle European workers. Soldier resettlement schemes and land grants contingent on the deletion of native bushland and the creation of 'working properties' meant that Crown land was redistributed for such purposes on a large scale.

Tracy's mother's family were wheatbelt 'pioneers' of the early twentieth century, following a migratory path from colonial India and Australia House (where her grandmother worked recording the Australian war dead, though she was English) to join other family members in the Carnamah-Winchester area, where even her grandfather's studies in agriculture overseas served him ill for the Australian conditions. The imposition of European farming methods led to the damaging of land to such an extent that salinity was the inevitable result.

Tracy has letters from her great-grandmother lamenting the fact that if only they could clear more land, the farm would succeed. It didn't and couldn't. These letters, sent to another colonial daughter in South Africa, are littered with familiar stories of infant death, children with fly-affected eyes, failed crops and drought, and the complexities of courting and communicating over distance. Aboriginal people were not considered relevant to their 'making a go of it' (as the saying here goes). They are barely mentioned in the letters, though it was their land being cleared. The story of the family's twenties 'failure' – a large family basically birthed to work the land, left without a means of support, travelling hundreds of miles south to the small city of Perth in the hope of surviving – is a common one.

Tracy's resulting upbringing generations later was basically fringe-urban, but with a lot of time spent in the forest areas around the hills above Kelmscott and Armadale – ironically not far from that vast forestry area known as 'Kinsella'.

When my great-grandfather Ned Kinsella and his eldest son returned from the army at the end of the First World War, his wife refused to go back to the bush with him. He went with his older sons anyway, and became a Group Settlement leader back on familiar country in the karri forests around Karridale, where certain Kinsellas are buried. These settlement schemes were brutal on the land – tearing down the tall karri trees (some of the tallest in the world) to feed the timber mills, and 'opening' the land for dairy farming. Perversely, Ned was a renowned bushman with a lot of 'bush lore' – and yet the forests he so loved, he in no small way dispatched to their annihilation.

This blending of development with an infusion of the 'native' is a key to the success of the colonial machine – it convinces itself it possesses a conscience about a relationship to the land it is consuming. Ned and his forester son Claude, my paternal grandfather, would never have perceived themselves as belonging – living or dead – anywhere but the place they were born. They saw it as their belonging, as well as their home. Ireland remade in south-west Australia, still struggling with the British yoke, but one with more 'opportunities' for them. One needs to understand this in order to build a picture of the contradictions of colonial-migratory presence.

One of the most disturbing aspects of my colonial heritage – such a deadly word in this context is 'heritage' – concerns the signing of a petition by my great-great-grandfather, Edward

Pat Kinsella, the Irish Gaelic speaker who 'bettered himself' by mastering the language of his oppressors, serving them on their big land grants, eventually getting his own small farm among the tall tuart trees at Ludlow on the south-west coast, and also becoming a (Catholic) schoolteacher (in English). He is a significant figure in the history of the region (but what of Anne, his wife? – surely as 'significant'), who was unusual for being an Irish 'pioneer' rather than a disenfranchised labourer, and this is signified in the most disturbing way. And this 'disturbance' is, at least in part, to do with the fact that his signature turned up on a petition to exonerate a colonial white who had murdered an Aboriginal man in the north of the state. The news reports and other records of the time are absolutely clear: it was a case of murder, over the use of a saddle, and anyone who signed the petition was valuing a white man's fate over that of the Aboriginal victim. It was an appalling petition and on it was the name 'Edward Kinsella, of Ludlow'. This 1870s crime eventually received insignificant punishment.

I wrote a radio play for the BBC and the ABC entitled 'Petition at Ludlow', in which I looked into the reasons for such a signing, and issues of collective colonial culpability and responsibility. What Tracy and I *seem* to have found in our research – without excusing Edward in any way – was that Irish settlers experienced undue pressure and ostracism if they did not toe the line/s of their English overlords. It was a colony of class and division, and oppression was divvied out according to status. In the play I also examined the ongoing betrayals of Noongar people in the south-west– the exploitation of the remaining forests and of the land through sand mining, the ongoing failure to create a treaty and to return country. The petition is still, in a sense, being signed by all non-Indigenous inhabitants of the place in their ongoing acquiescence to such injustice. The play shifts between the late nineteenth century and the early twenty-first century, with the main drive being a pair of dialogues of self-scrutiny and 'confession' – Edward Pat with his wife, Anne, while I talk with Tracy (also of Irish heritage) in the present day. Heritage is always loaded, and always carries consequences. It's how we scrutinise and critique and interact with our heritage that matters, surely?

At JTG, heritage is the residue of responsibility met or unmet. Wrongs of the past can be confronted and rectified, and the present is always about learning and adjustment. We are not better than the past, but the past is there for us to learn from, to be aware through. Tracy and I spend our lives in conversation about all things. Every day, in our relative isolation, we discuss the events of the world, our communications with others, and what we are working on. Further, along with Tim – who is the main 'see-er' of what goes on in the locale – we discuss bird and animal sightings, how they compare (or don't) with similar sightings from previous years. Weather changes and topographical variables also feed into the matrix, and we keep a fluxive picture of what 'here' is at any given time. To understand what's happening in the greater world, we feel a deep need to understand what's happening at 'home'. The white-winged triller's altered song (mating?) and the different movement of weebills and yellow-rumped thornbills and silvereyes as they do their 'stations' across the block and the neighbouring reserve – these things are vital for us to note and discuss, because they are key gauges of not only the health of their own lives, but that of the biosphere. Jam Tree Gully is as much a window to the world as New York, Paris, Delhi, Beijing, Moscow, Nairobi, London …

Last night we launched Tracy's new novel, *We are Not Most People*, in a city bookshop. Tony Hughes-d'Aeth, a friend of ours with whom I sometimes travel into the deeper wheatbelt (talking over the land and its situation as we go), gave the launch speech, which carefully considered how very different origins and experiences can segue, and how the socially alienated and isolated can find comfort in each other. It was a fascinating evening in so many ways, acting as a nexus between country and city. Many people either travelled down from the wheatbelt (especially York) for the occasion, or had wheatbelt histories – including Alan who owns the Crow bookshop, and who grew up on a large farm 400 k's north.

Quite a few people came from far away for the occasion, including Stephen and his wife, Dzu. Stephen had been shearing and Dzu working on the wool sorting table at Eneabba, two hours south of their home in Geraldton, and four hours north of Perth. Stephen said, Well, we were almost there anyway, so we drove straight from work. The next morning they were working in Mingenew, the town where I worked the wheatbins as a youth – four hours further inland from Perth. Unless you are a wheatbelt person, it's hard to get a grip on travelling such distances 'just for work'. And as is the case with most of the agricultural underpinnings of the wheatbelt, it obviously comes at a cost in terms of the environmental impact of transportation – but vast broadacre farming produces a large chunk of the world's wheat output, and inevitably has serious consequences for environmental and animal health. As Stephen is the first to say, there are other ways of doing things with far less impact. We have to environmentally reform the entire wheatbelt. He is an inside outsider – he knows from working the hard way. It's said that a shearer's job is the toughest physical labour in the world, and that's true for humans and sheep.

Stephen has been a shearer for thirty-five years and can shear sheep without cutting them, and often does special jobs for people shearing one or two 'pet sheep' using his portable plant. His trajectory inside and outside the industry has been unique – for being vegan for many years and later vegetarian, in his care for sheep and advocacy of their rights, while garnering much respect from farmers and team owners for his reliability and honesty, seen by plenty of his fellow shearers as a 'good bloke'. The shearing world has a low tolerance for bullshit and is its own monitor. That there is an ethics of a sliding scale at work around sheep shearing is not widely known. From the sheep bashers to those such as Stephen who respect the animals.

Stephen believes that shearing is what keeps some sheep at least from being slaughtered, and he is right in this. But increasingly sheep are being bred that shed their wool and are only being raised for meat or breeding stock. Once their 'usefulness' is reduced to this, they have no possibility of a life without slaughter at the end, as is the fate for many wool-bearing sheep too, of course. As a vegan I do not use wool, and am not a supporter of the farming of animals, but having said this, I know Stephen's humane shearing and his desire to look after sheep and keep them alive, and living good lives, is admirable. Sometimes these are complex pictures all we animal rights people should take on board.

I admire sheep, and Stephen admires them every bit as much. He truly gets to know their characters, often shearing the same flocks year in, year out. Sheep are highly individuated creatures. When they make their desire lines across paddocks from feed places to water troughs, from dams to firebreaks, they do so with a knowledge of mapping and topography. They create sophisticated codes of presence that can be read, but also altered.

A wether (a castrated ram – and I am convinced it suffers and knows what it has lost, what it has been denied, what is done to force its character and destiny) that decides it is the 'leader' is an incredible creature to encounter. Deeply intelligent and often fierce, it watches over a flock in a way that is beyond human comprehension. Wethers are also dexterous – hooves are far more subtle than they look, and they can be very 'mouthy'; I have seen a wether, a ram, and many ewes actually chew through binder twine to open gates. These forced colonials, these slaves of the colonisers and the post-colonisers (who still use the machinery of the colonial), will do all they can to outwit the human oppressor. I have witnessed remarkable decision-making, distinct evasions, and radical reworkings of desire lines (those sheep trails) to confuse their 'owners'. Ask a shearer about 'big ugly wethers' and who is or isn't in control at the moment of catching, dragging and shearing.

~

We visit nature reserves quite often and always stick to the trails. These often small, fragile and exclusive places, set aside among seas of cleared ground, are all that remain as semi-intact ecosystems in the region. Gathercole outside Wongan Hills is probably our 'regular', but at different times there have been others. Gathercole, like many wheatbelt reserves, exists because of a large granite outcropping, which made it impossible to clear. Having said this, much granite outcropping has been cleared for no obvious reason, and other granite areas with their remarkable patches of rock bush have been degraded by grazing sheep and cattle, and by their use as water-catchment surfaces.

Of course, granites were (and are) traditional water-collecting places for Aboriginal people. Gnamma holes – openings in the granite often expanded using fire, rock and sticks – were human-made water-storage places located such that they caught the sheeting run-off of rainfall. They were rich food places and very often of massive cultural and spiritual significance, being intrinsic parts of songlines and Dreaming. When we visit these places, we do so as unobtrusively and respectfully as we can, though it is heart-rending to witness the constant damage by visitors: those broken ledges of rock where rock dragons and pseudo-scorpions live, the filling-in of depressions in the rock where after the rains tadpoles thrive. In the warmer months after the colder time, flies are in mass profusion, and they keep some impatient and easily tormented visitors away. I consider the flies part of the rocks' protective consciousness, a force field against opportunistic intrusion. Surrounded by farming land, the rocks are a beacon of spirit and hope.

We visit nature reserves to acquire knowledge, and in those nature reserves I have taught my children about flora and fauna, about the ways of the land outside farming, as far as I can know outside appropriation. But in those nature reserves we have often encountered dumped asbestos-ridden building products, the remains of intentionally lit fires, hunters illegally picking off the last remaining roos and wallabies, and the residues and paraphernalia of drug use – small dope plantations wreck the environment as much or more than anything else. As Tracy always says, It's tragic and disgusting that so many people in the region seem to think of nature reserves as 'waste space' – as space that's not being 'used', and thus a repository for their material wastes and their spiritual indifference.

Yenyenning Lakes, between Beverley and Brookton, in the Avon River valley, epitomise and feed the catastrophe of the colonial. This lake system empties into the Avon River, and as it has become incredibly saline due to land clearing and an absurd damming of the main lake to service a local (*inland*) speedboating community, its fate is the fate of the river system itself. The bushland surrounding the lakes is a nature reserve now, but many of the trees of these wetlands are dead from rising salinity. Mum once used a red filter on a photo of the splinters of deadwood bone that make up this hellscape, to show what agriculture has done to this magnificent place. I have set hellish stories there, overlooked by County Peak with its struggles, asbestos sheeting residues strewn about, dampiera growing between the rocks. Shooting abounds. Duck shooting was long popular, but the reserve status was designed to protect ducks. Go for a walk along the white sands of the lake system and you'll find lots of shotgun shells, salinity eventually encrusting them. You'll find bullet holes through the ski club's tin shelters, you'll find 'dead marines' (beer bottles) poking their heads up from the mud and silt. You'll also see exquisite mulga parrots and many other birds, a vast array of reptiles and occasionally an echidna, but for most of us the whole scene will be apocalyptic. The infernal salt machine is poisoning the river.

I once took Lee Ranaldo from Sonic Youth out there, and he took a series of photos that capture the grotesque weirdness of the place. I think he felt he was at the interface of something, and he surely was. 'Uncanny' is too much a colonial imposition to deploy, and 'weird melancholy' too colonial and too wistful – this is brutal, disturbing and dangerous.

When Tim was a very small boy, I took him and our daughter for a winter outing to Yenyenning. It's a long drive along a gravel road from the bitumenised York–Beverley–Brookton road, and once at the lakes there was a rough track ('improved' slightly now) to the shores of the main lake. On this track I got bogged. No mobile phone, and no one there on a weekday in winter. With a toddler and a young girl who grew quickly anxious, I had to work out how to extract myself. It was a job for a tractor, but the nearest farmhouse was kilometres away and it was too far to take small children. I found a picnic blanket in the boot, inserted it under the front wheels and jammed it with wood and debris and rock I accrued from around the place. I built a platform and managed to drive the car back out of the quagmire.

It was a salutary lesson about accessing degradation – the wetlands reclaiming, rejecting the interloper. Interestingly, and probably as a deferral or sublimation of the stress and anxiety that grew around being bogged in an isolated space and realising that something was different and amiss – young Tim developed a fascination for bogged things. Months later, when Guru was working to unbog a vehicle below Walwalinj, young Tim watched on, clapping his hands and singing 'bogged unbogged bogged unbogged'. I wrote a refrain poem, 'bogged, no traction', out of it.

Tim was and still is a person who, once he settles on something, keeps at it. His imaginary world of Iting is a massive island surrounded by many small islands, a place of forests and human settlements that are extensions of the organic world, all joined by walking trails, with species of birds and animals found nowhere else on the planet flourishing and sharing the space with humans. Its possibilities are always growing and the protections of the environment always increasing because he has a mind to detail. It would have to be one of the most mapped (with animal trails, bird flight paths, and human movement patterns) and detailed paracosms I have encountered. He gets bogged down in detail, but only so he can unbog it and progress to the next bit of the narrative. Remarkable commitment.

In telling this tale of being bogged in a relatively isolated place, I have intentionally suppressed the drama of it – but the tension and worry were extremely high. We were isolated with no form of communication. I had told my family roughly where I was going, but not specifically. I never made that mistake again; I am always very specific now. This event had a dramatic effect on my poetry and my poetic sensibility. My attempt to 'describe' the event and to convey the strangeness of time having such significant consequences (to still be stuck at nightfall would have been catastrophic, and bad weather was closing in), and the damaged nature of a place we also found so beautiful, made me think in terms of curved rather than linear space. It was not a matter of straight lines. When I came to write of this, I wrote in terms of the Gaussian, of theories of space and time, of mathematics. This is the beginning of the poem:

Imitation spatialogue

'I shall not defend Rowleys Pastoral: its merit can stand its own defence –'
—T. Chatterton, To Horace Walpole, 14 April 1769 (First draft)

Some months have passed since the Yenyenning track
proved impassable and I was lucky to get the car
and the kids out of the salty sludge;
                                                returning,
the ski-boat fraternity has turned out in force,
        and one of the original reasons
for the damnation of the Avon –
                                                the saline

choke-out of Yenyenning –
was reiterated.
Tailgating us in their four-wheel drives,
their inland dry speedboat travesties homed in
on the main lake.
Aim: to rip it up, drink beer.
Depth is not great
but enough to ski
and certainly resplendent to waterbirds
even if the bush in the surrounding reserve
is a villainy of the dead
where polemics accumulate
and some enjoy global warming;
looping
straight back out of there,
also to get the kids out (less so the car), we –
us this time –
want to avoid
confrontation with the vandals
when they've set their scene,
created their combat zone;
the issue
of the lake –
vestigially inherent
but forced into shape
by damming and manipulation,
is one of intrinsic curvature –
otherwise known as Gaussian curvature:
ostensibly,
I feel the strength of *their* –
the skiers and drinkers

and bush bashers –
harnessing the waters of the lake
lies in their confidence
that it is curved in the shape of a bowl,
that the product K
(intrinsic curvature)
is positive
because k1 and k2
share a negative sign;
I sense they are wrong,
and that a heavy winter
means the bowl has buckled,
that the floor of the lake has saddled
along the lines of k1+, k2-; K-,
or, even more extremely
with a monstrousness
actively preparing
to rise up
on the balmy late spring day –
a subscription of agency
to the much maligned and abused lake itself –
+N upwards, k1-, k2+; K-;
of course,
I have the visual representation
in my mind's eye,
or, if needs be,
in Graham Nerlich's *The Shape of Space,*
to fall back on:

And on it goes. I was desperate to find a system for working through the contradictions of presence, of time and space and catastrophe and catastrophising, of the failure of modernity and the consequences of colonial modes and modalities of presence. So I tried to come up with a different 'kind' of poetry – one which critiqued 'landscape' decoration (exterior design!) in poetry, in receiving experience as something to be turned into 'art' as consumable. Further, I started thinking more in terms of what the European notion of the sublime was trying to do as a control device – rendering all confronting experience as an intense feeling that can be translated into art. I had always questioned art, but this seemingly 'so what' experience became pivotal for me. We've all been through something similar – but that's the point; I have had many more dramatic experiences in life, such as having a gun held to my head or being in a horrendous bus crash in the Himalayas, where life and death decisions had to be made, and which still haunts me most weeks thirty-three years later. But such incidents without fanfare can mean an epiphanic shift in what art can and possibly should be (at least for me).

The book that the experience and the resulting poem became part of was templated on Edmund Burke's *A Philosophical Enquiry into the Origin of our Ideas of the Sublime and Beautiful with Several Other Additions*, and was entitled *Shades of the Sublime and Beautiful.* I have often tormented myself over why I find such beauty in salinity and damaged places – not their ongoing damage, but their attempts to heal themselves – and I began to realise it's because they demand restoration, healing and recovery. Of being left to themselves and what they are, of seeing and experiencing and letting be. If these places are one's home, it is more imperative; if they're not, then one takes such notions 'home' and looks to take the learning to the preservation and respect of *those* places, too.

I have always been interested in the creative abstractions of mathematics. I should add that specificities and the quantifiable and 'solvable' have also interested me, especially as they pertain to constructing a poem, or listening to music, but I am devoted to working out of deviations from the standard. My particular interest of the last decades has been in and around spirals. From around late 2005 after getting back from Ohio, where the testing of the tornado siren invoked a deep sense of apprehension and disturbance interfused with a desire to understand circumstances and consequences, I began to think about the smaller funnels, willy-willies or dust devils that swirled through my childhood. These small twisters, which come and go quickly, I used to try and insert myself into as a child, to be 'drawn up like Dorothy', to end up knocked over and covered in dust and stubble and dried leaves and whatever else the willy-willy was eating. They are a common feature of life in the wheatbelt, working the damaged areas like a moral vacuum cleaner that dumps what it has collected with abandon. For me, they were always specific. I wrote poems about them on the farm from my early teens on.

Then one day, driving well north of York towards Tammin, Tracy and I saw a massive funnel – a twister, which one never really thinks of in Western Australia, where the north is threatened by cyclones every northern wet season (southern summer), and which I have experienced in a variety of terrifying ways as they moved south on their 'paths of destruction', but tornadoes of such magnitude are not common in the south. This funnel was a classic American Midwest twister shape, and making a blood-red and filthy spiral spewing garbage into the sky. We tracked it till it diminished minutes later. Back home, I rang the Bureau of Meteorology and they told me it had been recorded and had knocked over a shed (I think). We discussed the rarity but not the 'unknown' qualities of the event.

Spirals truly had me. A year later I photographed a large (strong?) willy-willy near Quairading heading east. I listened to John Coltrane's 'Spiral', I examined the artist Richard Long's spiralling installations, I considered the spiritual histories of spirals. I wrote a book called *Spiralling*. Once something has hold of me, it is part of me. Learning can never stop.

~

My Uncle Gerry sometimes brings a bag of mandarins from their trees when he and my auntie visit my mother and Guru. He always asks that I be given some when we're next over – we are usually there for Sunday lunch, even though it's a 180-k round journey through the valley. Because of damage I did to my stomach through heavy drinking, I cannot eat a lot of citrus these days, though I still love it. In fact, I love citrus so much that once in Cambridge, about two years after I 'got straight', I started drinking vast amounts of orange juice. One night, after I'd drunk about 3 litres of 100 per cent juice, I went into spasms. A doctor was called and apparently I'd OD'd on vitamin C. Old habits in a healthy regime? Too much of a good thing? Oh, by 'got straight', I mean got off the grog and substances – a common rehab expression. I am not talking 'straight' genderwise or in terms of sexual orientation. In fact, I have questioned gender categories since my teen years and spoke of fluidity long before it became an accepted term of referencing non-fixedness … I identify as I need to identify at any given time, and though I cannot deny my male privilege, and won't, there is much in masculinity that appals me, and always has … and I was beaten and sexually assaulted by other kids as a child as a response to my not identifying in ways they clearly thought I should. It's something I feel quite strongly about.

Digressions on digressions, but I wheel back to the point. Mandarins. So we take a couple home and I might eat a few segments while Tim eats the rest. I sample them because mandarins have a special meaning between me and my uncle. As Dad was largely absent from my childhood outside holidays once a year, I connected strongly with my uncle as a 'father figure'. He had three boys and was always comfortable with one or two extra trailing along behind him as he did farm work. He taught me to drive at eight or nine years of age and I managed to crash the car into a fence. I learnt to feed and water the sheep and pigs. And to milk Princess the cow – and yes, I did the teat-firing-hot-milk at people trick, I am ashamed to say.

This was childhood, before I was vegan. With my cousins, but trained by my uncle, I collected eggs from weird places (hessian sacks up in pepper trees – chooks can get into semi-high places if they feel driven), or laid near the dangerous big pregnant and just farrowed sows in the pigsty. I also learnt to fence, to shoot, to talk to the working dogs, and to drive a tractor and plough. And it was with regard to the last that mandarins entered the picture.

When I was about nineteen, my uncle needed help getting the crops in – wheat, barley and oats. My cousins who would usually do this were elsewhere and I was asked, and needing the money stepped up to the plate (the plough disc – I have always loved them as pieces of art). For a couple of weeks he and I ploughed in heavy weather working in shifts. I have written many poems about this period of *really* learning how to crop. Of being out on the tractor in low temperatures late at night and being mesmerised by the stars while trying to keep the lead wheel of the disc plough in the groove set by the previous run of the paddock. Of how to figure-eight a corner out, of how to fuel and maintain the tractor and machinery, and later how to load the seed boxes and the fertiliser boxes and set the equipment. Anyway, every shift I took a meal or two with me, usually prepared by my auntie, but always including two or three mandarins, which my uncle made a point of indicating were off the farm trees (as the grapefruits for breakfast and all the fruits of the jam spreads were, too), and as such had *special* health properties. Though a large amount of spray was used on the crops (a practice my cousin, who still farms part of the old farm, now avoids 'as much as possible'), none was used on the fruit. My uncle knew what spray could do, though he did plenty of spraying. So those mandarins spoke across generations, dislocations of organics and poisons, across familial relationships, and between mentor and mentored.

Now, thirty-seven years later, from trees grown from cuttings of those same trees and planted in soil below Wongborel (Mount Brown – across the other side of the valley from Walwalinj, Mount Bakewell, being two lovers separated by their tribes for breaking a taboo), where my auntie and uncle retired, I am reminded of that special learning time together. And when we're visiting their place, Avonlea, with Tracy and Tim, Uncle makes a point of picking mandarins and handing them to me, saying, Do you still remember? I do.

Also at Avonlea are the ashes of three generations of family disinterred from the Wheatlands farm grave plot, which was down near the great flooded gum so often shot at and holding back the salt at its bottleneck. I have written on the irony of removing ashes from land that contains hundreds and hundreds of generations of Noongar people, whose graves were bothered and disrespected by colonists, and *still are* by developers and 'users' of the land. It's a difficult conversation, and one I make in my poems. My auntie understands the pain, and the ironies, as, I think, does my uncle. We have to articulate these contradictions – it helps no one to pretend they're not the case.

When the Meckering quake hit in 1968 and my mother grabbed my arm as the metronome did its dance across the piano top, Auntie Elsie's house under the Needlings split in half. She had to abandon the farm she'd run with the help of her brothers for many years and move into town. One of my earliest poems was about this spinster sister of my uncle – I had found it a shock as a child to know that after her fiancé had died of pneumonia, she'd never had another boyfriend, never married, never had children, never gone out with anyone else. I didn't really understand anything about that at the time, but as I grew older I did, and it shook me in ways I can't quite explain – it seemed such an absence, but I am not really sure why.

Maybe it so bothered me because she had been going to marry, then was destroyed by the physical loss and with an idea of love linked to time and place and a perpetuity of a possible ideal. I liked her a lot, and she liked me, I think. I wrote an elegy for her when she passed, but what I most remember is the vivid image of her covering her arms in nylon stockings when she worked outside or even hung washing out under the summer sun, to keep her skin white and freckle-free. *Undamaged.* Now, given the devastation skin cancers have wrought in Australia, there seems an ultimate wisdom in this. When I was a young child we were unaware of this: we all went around as exposed as our gender would allow. I was always barefoot and shirtless, my feet so tough they resisted all prickles other than doublegees. I would later suffer from many basal cell carcinomas. Tracy's father was afflicted by melanoma.

When Auntie Elsie was covering her arms it was more about the 'whiteness' of her skin, her skin untouched by a lover, the skin of aloneness, and the colonial skin under the Needlings on Noongar land, with the old stone outbuildings built in the middle of the nineteenth century with their gun slits. I tried to render that in a poem when I was sixteen or so, and did, I think. I revised it staying on the farm when I was eighteen as part of a series about 'characters', about people I knew around the district interacting with the land. Of course, it was a narrow view, but it was an attempt to understand something about presence and absence, and about dispossession and what 'home' might or might not be.

~

Tracy just made a remarkable discovery – a batch of emails she sent when we first arrived in Gambier, Ohio, in January 2001, which she'd thought had been lost many years ago. She has given me permission to include some here, which I do because it jolts me back to that time and place, not just as 'setting', but in the intensity of making a new life away from the old, while always looking back to Western Australia. The jolt is in the connecting with a new place and realising how much we tried to understand it through the template of where we'd come from. This is never easy, and always brings misreadings of place, but we all need starting points in making new journeys.

I do not use the word 'setting' here in the somewhat diminishing 'picturesque' sense of the word, or as the artificial construct of a framed photo that captures the moment of 'visiting', but as part of a broader conversation of trying to make a new home. I think of a photographer like John D'Alton from Schull, West Cork, and his intense photographs of that region. This sense of immanence in the photograph, so compelled by the oneness of light and surface, the way form influences light, and light influences form, makes it a poem, a novel, an essay, a painting, a song, a musical interlude all at once. In the photograph we have a moment that can never be again, and yet is *there*, now. Photographs for us to observe and reflect over again and again, to submerge ourselves in that moment in the context of our own immediate surroundings and lives. Locality is the key to D'Alton's photography of the rocky, boggy and rain-swept places of the south-west of Ireland – a patient submergence into the place that over time reveals it to him, and that he finds points of entry to observe and 'record'. His photographs of West Cork don't come rapidly, and aren't a series of rapidly taken snaps, but slow plein-air encounters with the world he inhabits. And in the same way, Tracy's remarkable emails are this, too. Here is one, addressed to my mother, to whom Tracy is very close:

> On Mon, 15/1/01, Tracy Ryan wrote:
>
> Hi – we're so glad the parcel got there, and we *knew* you would like that book … I have forwarded your email on to John's Kenyon address as he'll be pleased to read it too – also the anti-virus question is more something he will know about. He's just headed off to the office. Classes don't start till tomorrow but there are some articles and poems to be copied for handouts, as well as some translation work he has to finish. It's lovely to see him head off with his armful of things all organised – I know the students will really enjoy his course as it's absolutely his area, it's what he knows backwards … Also it's great that he works so close to home, and yet we're not 'in' the college as we were in England. He's going to have an orange juice with Wendy S today but then come home for lunch before heading back.

[Our daughter] just came in and asked for a second slice of tofu cheesecake (which she is having for breakfast! a bit decadent, but she has had such a sore throat and been so off her food that I figure anything she eats is good!) – I found it a bit bland and fine-textured myself, but she & John love it. It's incredible how it bakes and sets just like a conventional baked cheesecake. Earth Market in Subiaco does something similar but they put a layer of jellied fruit (with agar agar jelly) on top & I think that would be better. I can't take much that has a baby-foodish texture but if they like it, it's just as well, as the mixture made 2 pies and they have heaps of it to eat their way through!!!

Well, John sat down with [our daughter] yesterday evening and they worked out a chocolate chip mining method for her design & technology project! They called it the hook'n'pick (capitalists! they even have a brand name). Very clever indeed. Made out of a paperclip stretched out.

The snow has melted a little and you can see some patches of green, but we're definitely in for more as the sky has that dense white look. It's certainly a heavenly place though I read letters in the Columbus paper where people talk about not being able to afford their heating bills (one woman died recently in a kerosene fire because she was trying to avoid using the proper central heating) and I realise that we are very lucky to have it all provided for – like most places, it's a lovely place to live if you are looked after, but this sort of cold could really wear people down if they didn't have a good house. Gambier, because it's a small college town, doesn't really have a poorer side and you could easily believe life in America was all smooth. As [a friend] said to me on the phone recently, 'I adore book-loving educated Americans', & while that's typical [of the friend] I know what he means, different in other parts of America, but here in Gambier it's as if you have the best of the English culture with a MUCH more open & friendly people. Americans talk to you all the time.

Tell Stephen I found an old guitar down in the basement and was thinking I might practise on it – but one of the strings (the D string) is entirely wrong. It's flat and you can't sharpen it because it's either too short or too tightly wound or something. I used to be able to string a guitar but I can't remember much about it (maybe this is why they left it in the basement). Tell John A. he would love the basement as it's full of old discarded things that he could make stuff out of. Literally – old gadgets and containers and machinery. It's also a combination of laundry and workshop (tools and so on). There's an attic as well, in the gabled part of the house, with a little staircase leading up there but I've only been up in the semi-dark so I don't know what's in there.

Here and there are ladybirds in the house (must have got trapped! – very strange) and the birdlife seems to increase every day.

Well, that's me for the day. Lots of love to all of you,

Tracy, John & [our daughter]. xxx

What might seem relatively benign to others is devastating to us. As we got to know the county and the region better, we saw how the poor were separated off from conversation and from the reality of the comparatively moneyed. Well-off students would do fundraising for the poor, and make donations, and visit 'folk down by the river', but there was a separation that could not be resolved. As time went on, we found ourselves connecting more and more with 'town', and finding that our own backgrounds correlated with those of workers and farmers, no matter how much we politically disagreed. We had far more in common in 'book ways' with fellow teachers, but maybe more so socially and demographically with the very people who would see us as a threat to their patriotic values – not by way of violence, but by way of belief.

This is a gap one cannot easily reconcile or emerge from. Where we were lucky was that we became part of a circle of liberal-minded teachers at Kenyon who could get what we were on about, and understand what this gap meant. This next email shows this, and for me reflects the nature of making home as well as community, with the support of others who have very different life experiences from one's own. For people to embrace both our cultural difference and also our veganism, which wanot as common back then in Western societies, was remarkable and gratefully received.

What's fascinating to me as the emails go on (finding this batch is like reinstated memories for us – and memory is something we both accept is desirably changeable and shifts and remakes, so this is all quite confronting, as I've said) is how the bird species get names, and how the analysis of bird behaviours evolves and becomes more specific – for example, the language of chickadees and their being interpreted and interpreting the 'speech' of other birds by way of foraging, warning and so on. The generics become specifics as we build up time of presence, make for associations with others, learn more about the history of the place, interact with students from all over America (in a geographic sense, if not so much demographically, though to some extent) and all of them so different from each other working together to decide what their own communities are or are not, and we negotiate the difficulties and rewards of schooling and functioning in a place that is both familiar in some ways, and very different in others.

A second of Tracy's emails from early 2001 shows a thread in life not taken. Tracy and I had discussed leaving academia and running a vegan tearoom – not as a small-business capitalist longing, but as a way of showing people that a vegan, organic, culturally respectful, rural 'way of life' was viable, even in the destructive world of Western capitalism.

> 25th Jan 2001
>
> Hi Wendy, I guess you will be back from the airport soon and probably not likely to be on the email while you have a guest! I hope you all have a really good time together! We are both very tired after a long day of working at bits and pieces, and John has his long day of classes tomorrow too. He's still not feeling 100 per cent, but managing okay. He asks me to ask you whether you think it's worth him/us giving Stephen a ring to say hello? In any case, you might mention to him that we are making plans (imaginative ones, but good ones) for maybe running a small business from York one day when we are back there, you know the tea rooms idea, and side lines like vegan soap and candles – I am even doing some intensive reading on how you go about this. (Maybe if we do veggie meals we can use produce from Stephen's organic garden? If he would be our supplier, and that would be another source of income for him.) I will tell you more about these ideas in another email; we are hoping finally to settle back there, information just for family and not for general broadcast, by the middle of next year! (By the way, that work I mentioned I was offered is looking more feasible re the

dates, I am only now having to wait till mid-Feb to get info on the exact pay...). So we would be back then, and then back for good next year, if all goes well. John may have to make occasional excursions overseas for work, but we would be basing ourselves entirely in York. This may all sound like fantasy but we are pretty determined to put money aside and achieve it, step by step.

Yes, [our daughter] enjoyed her outing to the historical society and she's now also about to join something called 'Kangaroos', which is an after-school club run by Kenyon students for the primary school kids, they do craft and things for an hour or so after school on Tuesdays and Thursdays. So she's keeping busy. She had bookclub again today. Also she's been reading novels about Amish families and finding them very interesting.

I'll write more again soon but it's getting late here now so I'll sign off. Love to all, Tracy (and John, and [our daughter] who is asleep). xxx

Kangaroos! And here's another email addressed to a Cambridge friend from a couple of years later, not long after our son was born:

Thursday, 20 February, 2003, 10:50 AM

Dear [...]

Sorry it's taken me a little while to get this note to you, but I wanted to say thank you for your good wishes and for the _beautiful_ quilt, which has been in constant use since it arrived – Timothy likes to lie on it listening to his musical duck (!) and it is very lovely. ... yes, we have seen many Amish quilts because one or two Amish buggies come into our village every Saturday (weather permitting, which it doesn't, at the moment – we are all but snowed in, a foot or more deep) and the occupants hang up their quilts and set out their baskets to sell in the centre of the village. ([Our daughter] admires the quilts, and quilting in general, greatly.)

[Our daughter] is just getting over a nasty flu, but otherwise ok; Timothy has fortunately managed to avoid it. He's already a few pounds heavier than in the photos you were sent – I can't believe how fast he is growing – and he is beginning (5 weeks old now, tonight) to coo and make odd little sounds that are his 'words' – all vowels and strange facial expressions, but lots of smiles too. I've forgotten so much of this sort of thing because of the long gap between babyhoods, but it's wonderful rediscovering it all. And he's not too bad a sleeper at all – only wakes for his feeds and goes straight back to sleep at night, which is a boon. A bit colicky, but we've been through that before and it will end eventually. (Though they do say only one baby in 5 gets it, so ours have been statistically unlucky.)

We are really looking forward to the spring – normally I'm quite happy with snow but it means keeping baby indoors – so it will be good when we are able to take him out for a walk/pram ride. There is a great walking track here called the Kokosing Gap Trail, which is a former railway line converted for community use (a pity they discontinued the trains, but at least it's been put to good use) – a little bit like walking in Wandlebury [Woods, just outside Cambridge] or somewhere like that, except that you're going in a more or less straight line, and the trees and birds are not the same if you look closely! (what they call a robin here is a huge thing bigger than a blackbird, and its red breast is a different shade.) Anyway, I can't wait for the thaw. Till then we are shovelling our way out every couple of days only when we have to, for supplies!

I'd better go now as Timothy has gone off to sleep and I want to get some too before his first waking! It was so lovely to hear from you, and good of you to send the gift. Thanks from all of us,

Tracy. x

What I find so interesting in this email is the use of 'our village', for by then we had certainly come to see Gambier (and later Mount Vernon) as 'home'. What changed all this? The second Gulf War, some health issues, and the complexities of belonging/unbelonging. We always unbelonged, as we did (and do/don't) in Australia, and in Cambridge and so on. Constantly self-displacing, but for unresolvable reasons. Tim was an American under American law, but what does that actually mean? He is a person of a specific location and communities, but also a person of the world. We still discuss these things constantly. What we spoke through, ultimately, was rurality. Tracy was born on the urban fringes of Perth, but always close to paddocks with horses, orchards and the forest. She writes of urban spaces, often, but has lived nearly all her life with me in rural spaces. Rural is how I think – not just as non-urban, but also as zones of damage, intrusion and toxicity, but offset with nurturing, growth, providing, and great possibility of repair and community. It's not a simple binary – it's a complex picture whose 'settings' are constantly in flux. The rural is the medium, but no set piece.

~

Over the last couple of years I have been conducting peace readings, and on some occasions people have videoed them. I have done them in Cambridge, London, Rotterdam, Perth, and even to the birds, insects, sun skinks and vegetation of Jam Tree Gully. For me, the basic building block of the human interface with the biosphere, with the planet, is peace. In trying to stop the production and sale of weapons, I do so because I believe that without weapons there is less likelihood of damage. If humans have a weapon within reach to connect with when they are angry, they often will do so. A poet has a job to do – art in itself is meaningless if it does not jolt us into self and collective reflection. I say this over and over. Those bits of AK-47s welded into a sculpture in the British Museum are telling and horrifying in so many ways – even their display in one of the epicentres of colonial note-taking is ironic to the point of agony. The artist knows this. The artwork jolts one out of apathy, if not out of complicity.

I did a peace reading in a small room in a pub in Cambridge, along with a group of folk musos. It wasn't well attended, but there were enough devoted people to make a statement. It was run by a woman and her two children, who were Muslim and thus already outside Cambridge's Christian structures, and who were strong advocates for refugee rights. It was an evening of cultural sharing and of resistance. It was peace through music and poetry, and through not being intimidated. As I was walking back to college after the event, I cut across Jesus Green as I often do, and a couple of homeless blokes were setting up on a bench for the night. I might have given them some coin, or said hello, but what interested me was that they were setting themselves up for security – cardboard and a few possessions were being positioned as a kind of fortress. In the background (or maybe their own foreground!) were blackbirds, working the darkness. It wasn't a particularly cold night, being on the edge of summer, but it was drizzling and there were groups of young people across the park drinking and yelling at passers-by. The homeless guys weren't bothering anyone, but they obviously knew vulnerability, and knew that they could be in for a kicking from the drunken young fellas. They were looking across, and commenting. Peace.

Once I was sleeping rough with a couple of other guys I'd met on the street in Fremantle, who said, We've got a place to crash for the night, you can come along. We were sleeping under a car port (they assured me the people who owned the house had no car and didn't mind) under sheets of packing-case cardboard, when some blokes pushed open the metal gate, rushed in and started kicking us. Before we could even lift ourselves they'd gone. Hit and run. I ached for weeks. If they'd had access to weapons, they likely would have killed us. Or at least the chances of a fatality would have increased had they had access.

~

One of my favourite places on the farm as a child was the shadehouse up from the house. It was made from wandoo and tea-tree walling and roofing, and in it were two hammocks among the plants and always a couple of waterbags, cooling despite the heat. Canvas waterbags are a brilliant conception. My cousins and my brother and I would take shifts sleeping in the hammocks on hot nights and talking about all things – but mostly about what we'd do the next day. We too had our trails and lines across the farm and the district, and would wander them, and map them. In talking of these routes, of the points of repair around the place, we integrated that place into our gyroscopes. A colonial act, an act with consequences, but also a process of verbalising the exterior world, of internalising it.

But there was more to it than this. While my brother and our youngest cousin planned nature excursions, another cousin and I planned our hunting and 'military' expeditions. Armed, and equipped with army surplus canteens, webbing belts, jackets, 'ammo pouches', gun belts and even fold-up shovels, we mapped our campaigns across a thousand acres. As a strategy gamer, I thought of the ground in term of hexagons, of lines of sight, and what would later evolve into a fusion of landscape theory (of prospect – what you can see and how you can be seen, and refuge – how to remain hidden and not be seen) and rendering of place into a 2D conceptual space in the mind. When you fuse this with poetry, you actually unwittingly develop the matrix of colonial-settler poets, using their Old World ways of seeing against a backdrop of half-understood images, camouflage scenery and surprise appearances of quasi-mythical creatures – in the same way the kangaroo was reconstructed as a Euro quasi-mythical entity in poems like Barron Field's early nineteenth-century 'The Kangaroo'. This is reductive and ultimately disrespectful of place and the knowledges of its peoples, and of all flora and fauna and dirt, but it was also the means via which I enhanced an ability to *start* to *read* place. Morphed with my brother's and other cousin's sensitivity to the natural world, and with my own inherent love of place and nature, and with a growing ethical awareness of consequence, strangely via this strategic orienteering I was able to leave behind at least some of the aggressive and colonial apparatus.

So, again, what we come from is not a clear indicator at any point of who and what we are. In the same way, I have met soldiers and particularly sailors who have abhorred violence, and who on leaving the military have dedicated themselves to peace and the environment. I recall once when in Fremantle, after I'd been protesting American nuclear warships being in Cockburn Sound, I encountered an American sailor at a local pub. He and I got drinking and talking and we found our politics were strangely similar outside the military – he had joined up as a pathway to feeding his family, to decolonising his own family's oppressions in a white-ruled America. And yet, as I said to him, and he agreed, in serving the military he was serving the core structure of that oppression. That was a paradox he couldn't resolve.

~

Kangaroos. I didn't have a teddy as a small child, I had a Kanga – a red kangaroo I doted on. It hopped through the dirt, across buffalo grass, and dug in grey sand and unearthed a sandgroper. I cannot remember how Kanga found me, or I found it. I don't remember its gender, though it had a pouch. But having a pouch didn't mean it was female, did it? I have always been fascinated by nests, but I don't put them to the use that Gaston Bachelard does. And pouches are safety but also prisons when the hunters close in. Though I have seen doe kangaroos 'cramming' in their young, which are no longer joeys and too large for the pouch, to try and carry them away from hunters.

~

The first time I saw a sheep being killed and 'dressed', it not only altered my sense of security but also compelled me to poetry. Along with the silk stockings on Auntie Elsie's arms, and Uncle

Jack (Uncle Gerry's older brother) describing weekend hobby farmers as 'make-believe famers' – 'their sheep without water and flyblown' – it became an indelible point of reference of the paradoxes and confrontations of rural life. The people I saw kill sheep were in no way 'cruel', and believed no animal should suffer, but the killing was very direct. They took a sheep into the 'killing paddock', chased it down, brought it to the ground, and slit its throat. Its body was then dragged to the shed, the hooks inserted between the sinew and bone of its hind legs, and it was hauled up over a wheelbarrow, where its belly was slit open and its insides were 'plopped' out. It was beheaded and bled, and 'dressed'.

As kids, we wheeled the guts away and fed them to the pigs. I was shocked when one kid removed the bladder, throwing it so it burst, and on another occasion popping it with a stick. When the guts arrived, the pigs emerged from their pollard feeders, from their dusty or muddy diggings, their rubbing against (and ringbarking) the wandoos in their quite large yard, even out of the low-slung shed with its straw bedding. They went frantic, snuffling and eating the insides of the sheep. I was warned that if I went down on the ground when they were in such a frenzy, they might tear me apart.

This haunted me all my childhood, and later, when I had to look after the pigs (only feeding them kitchen scraps and pollard and pigfeed), I always trod aware, with the big sows and boars in clear sight. Pigs are genius creatures, and if they want to sort you out, they can. And when I accidentally got between a piglet and its mother once, I barely escaped with my life, leaping over an internal wall in the sty. When the pigs went, I helped plant and reticulate the avocado trees on the moonscaped ground of their ex-prison domain – but a territorial domain it was, only visited by crows and parrots and humans and the odd fox. That bladder, that killing, was in my first cycle of poems – a differentiator between the kids who were around it always and the kids who saw it on holidays.

So many farmers I have known (outside family) defend the shooting and poisoning of cats – not to protect the native fauna, but because they are extraneous and unwanted. The native fauna is often part of the justification, but it's infrequently the primary reason on massively over-cleared farms. Killing for a living becomes killing to retain a sense of the land as farmed. It's often a contradictory state of being: the colonisers fighting the introduced colonisers.

On the big farm outside Mullewa that my father managed (hundreds of k's north of Wheatlands and Jam Tree Gully), he was very 'farm conscious' – a side of my father I had never really seen before. The farm seemed to bring out the mercenary, the disconnected side of him. It's what's expected of me – my responsibility, he would say. He was methodical and reliable. He ensured the codes of farming presence were maintained on a massive scale.

The contradictions of the colonial machine are kept 'functional' by efficient or relentless maintenance, and my father was a superb mechanic who kept even the biggest machinery rolling out to do its bidding, its duty. When he'd been in 'Nashos' – doing his national service – he'd taken it very seriously. His sense of nation and patriotism underwrote his commitment to work, to getting a job done, because that's what, to his mind, 'made Australia great – the best place to live'.

~

With the wind howling I thought of sheltering under upturned boats on St Georges Beach in Geraldton, camping out so we could dive in the still of the early morning. The sea fusing with the sandplain farming areas, sand dunes trying to keep them separate. I saw a wooden figurehead bobbing in the sea off Sunset Beach once, a bare-breasted mermaid of cracked and warped wood dressed in foam, dragged back by breakers. On the islands of the Houtman Abrolhos, about 80 k's west, was where the Dutch ship *Batavia* was wrecked and there followed one of the most brutal recorded events in maritime history – at the time, I wondered if it was connected with this incident! A sea littered with wrecks and points of contact with Yamaji people across hundreds of years. Champion Bay, where the invaders came in force, and now the great mineral and grain and container ships in their waiting rows. I nearly boarded one of those ships, *The Helen,* at seventeen, and headed off 'to sea'. Another story. I wanted away from the bullying, from living on the seams where I was not wanted. Diving, I connected with the world under the reefs, the crayfish feelers in arrays that tracked my intrusions, the snapper and the reef cod. Once I got trapped under an overhang and thought I'd die, the silty water swirling around me; another time a yellow-bellied sea snake oared past me, a few centimetres from my mask as I surfaced. Out there I was nowhere, and yet I had connection with what makes the planet. I felt this was what the Yamaji kids must feel all the time, and on dry land as well, in the rivers, climbing the Chapman Valley hills. Now there is an American listening base near Geraldton, and its array of feelers is a kind of doom in the ancientness of the place. An ultimate exploitation of world power colonialism – the coldest war.

Once, with a friend and his father, and two other erstwhile friends who were plotting my humiliation (which they would later succeed in implementing) we motored out on a boat past Africa Reef and became caught in a storm. Massive waves, the like of which I have rarely seen (despite being in storms in large vessels, though not as high as the massive land-eating waves off the Mizen we saw during the St Jude's Day storm in Ireland). Out at sea, with no land to reference, these were swallowers of boats. We got through by keeping the bow to the waves and the motor holding out – it's when I am best, in a crisis, when things are as dismal as I often felt then. Already alcoholic, with a Dantean view of humans' cruelty to humans and the planet, I felt alive helping keep others alive. My bullies puked their guts out; I didn't, and they hated me with a passion after that. But I was as scared as they were, and was as pathetic as I ever was – nothing heroic in it. Just an oversensitised numbness that made do – if you know what I mean, which you probably don't, and don't have to. There's nothing special, nothing unique, and nothing to learn from. Just the early days of a long endgame that would take me to the door of death in Fremantle Hospital in my early thirties, and Tracy being told I had died. I was only alive because another social reject, not very brave either, told the doctors what to do to bring me back to life. I am in a second or third life, and am grateful. The water has consumed friends of mine, and I have almost been consumed by water, but it has also shown me that there are different states we can exist in at any given time. I remember nothing from when I 'died' from an OD, but though I was on dry land when I came through, I thought I'd been swimming.

A poet friend once said to me as I was writing poems of the sea, But you're an inland rural poet! And I said, Yes, but I am also a poet of the rural edges with the sea. And the most inland poet is obsessed with water. Tracy has written of the anxiety of trying to exist with a lack of water, and the deep effect water has on her though she lives in a dry place, especially when she makes contact with the sea, or swims (which she loves). Such strong juxtapositions make poetry. Geraldton and Schull are both places of the sea, but also of rural hinterland. In Ohio and the fens of England, it was the river and fens places, the rivers and forests, the liminal spaces of possibility that fascinated us. Tim was born by a river, and that matters. When I am on the edge of the desert, water is deep below, I am sure – flooding the mines. Water will come when a cyclone sends a low pressure system inland. One day the dry lakebed will flood and the birds will come back. One day the inland sea will rush back in and change everything, for good and bad. When the British unleashed their atomic weapons at Maralinga and Emu Plains in South Australia, they filled the psychic inland sea with an eternal toxicity that all the 'cleaning-up' in the world can't erase. They granted a legacy of cancer to the peoples whose land it is. They also added to the collective and cumulative contamination of the biosphere. With Australian government collusion, we share their 'science'.

Travelling across Australia on the Indian Pacific train, coming into the radiation zone is always the moment on the trip that shifts my psyche and no doubt alters my biochemistry in some way. Only 40 k's away from the edge of the zone – not technically in the zone, but we know nothing keeps to such artificial boundaries. Wedge-tailed eagles soar through the radiation zones and travel over the train. The bare places are emanating. Below the Nullarbor's karst limestone plain are many caves of fresh water – in that treeless, waterless place. Many rumours of UFOs abound in the region where colonialists like to assure us that not even Aboriginal people went traditionally because of the lack of water. As if it's up for grabs, as if a psyche of presence didn't extend beyond the edges. The railway line cuts across the bottom of Australia inland through Cook, while the Eyre–Wylie highway inclines towards the coast and the Great Australian

Bight. To avoid flying, we often travel across as a family, and standing looking out over the Bight towards Antarctica, we know the weight and force of the sea those hundreds of feet below the cliffs, and that they hold all the dry and flatness in place, keep the world's curve flowing.

~

I often conceptually drift into other places – place where I am not *physically*, not literally, but where I have strong associations and a strong personal history. Just now, I drifted into a Cambridge summer with the effusion of pollens and seeds from hedges and meadow plants, the cow parsley along the backs, the bumble bees lightly heavy. Walking up towards Madingley I constrain all I see and feel and hear into a mnemonic, into a memorable verse form, and drum it into my memory. I need these moments where the damage and pollution are momentarily pushed aside, and the intensity of life overwhelms. I call on them as binding, as message bundles to keep me going, to fuel my activism of preservation.

One of the earliest memories I have of a Cambridge winter is seeing a fallen leaf encased in black ice – an encounter that would bring me crashing down to the ground, and yet so pristine! Near that same place one summer, listening to a performance of *A Midsummer's Night Dream*, I leant back and crunched a leaf below my hand – a leaf that had been severed by a bird or a gust of wind, and not part of its autumn falling, which was some way off. It had separated from the flow of nutrients, the flow of sap, before its time – it was no longer part of photosynthesis and transpiration and guttation. It was separate but reconnected as fertiliser of its own source, its own origin. But it would likely be raked up and placed in a college compost heap and become part of a garden bed next spring. But close by. Thinking of this now, I reconstruct my thoughts of the time – Titania was speaking … yes, and I was wondering what type of leaf it was. I knew then; I can't recall now. But if I looked up the history of trees in that garden, I could probably work it out. If I needed to.

~

The year is measured by responsibilities and chores. If we get summer rains, within a few weeks there will be a caltrop problem – and pulling them out can mean the destruction of hands (this introduced prickle is named after a landmine!). A little later, the nightshade is rising with its globular dead-planet fruits which, though toxic, some have been known to turn into a jam – they kill animals! These introduced plants, like the wild oats, rule the calendar, and with the impact of climate change have gained traction – they have proved themselves adaptable. I have no disrespect for these introduced species, but try and keep them under control for the health of the environment. They have become naturalised, and have rights of presence, too, but too much and they choke out all else. This ecology has been so devastated and so changed, I accept it cannot be 'pristine', but there must be a balance of life and a zone in which all life is valued. It's not a simple equation – again, it's complex. There's no stepping back and leaving it, not yet, and 'management' to try and bring health back is part of it. But a colonial control mentality expressed as largesse and sensitivity is often extremely blind to the importance of life itself. Nothing is learnt by ticking off the requirements of a script of recovery, while exploiting the planet elsewhere (and maybe even locally) in every way possible. We cannot separate off one place from another – each is reliant on the health of the other. It is all interconnected. Pulling weeds by hand is our way.

Every day at JTG is full of 'natural' action, or an interface between different modes of being that is either fulfilling or concerning (the boys down the road firing their homemade cannon at crows is not a healthy interface!). Take Tim collecting small pieces of quartz. (He leaves large ones alone, as creatures may be living under them – as indeed they might be with small pieces, but he can at least see more clearly with these if anything of a size the eye can fix is using it as a shelter or an egg-laying zone.) We get all sorts, from milky and smoky quartz to white and apricot and even rose quartz – and line them up on the fence rail outside the lounge room window and watch each day as the same crow (Australian raven) comes and knocks a single piece off to the ground. Next day, the same. There are reasons for such an action, and we like to think about what they might be – and, in Tim's case, he reads extensively in books on bird behaviour to find clues, but also to come to his own conclusions. There's a synthesis in presence.

I don't use a lot of 'equipment' around the block outside a whipper snipper, pumps and Maun fencing pliers (to remove fencing, not install it – removing the electric fences was one of the primary resistances against the electric colonial I wanted to implement; cruel controls they are), along with hand equipment such as shovels, rakes, hoes and the like. In the warmer months, one has to be careful of equipment because of sparks and fire. By working with hand tools we reduce that risk. Often in my labours, I come across bobtails – blue-tongued skinks ('shinglebacks' and other names apply). These remarkable creatures live for years in the same territory, and have complex family groups that work the area. They brumate (though climate change is disrupting this), and appear from their refuges famished with the warmer weather, hissing and extending their triangular blue tongues in warning at potential 'predators'. Sadly, they die in vast numbers, especially after their emergence, as they sun themselves on roads and are run over. They appear to be slow-moving, waddling on short legs with stumpy bodies, their 'bobbed' tail used to store fat for sustenance during their sleeping time, but when roused they can move extremely quickly. I have been bitten by bobtails – when we were kids, my brother used to keep ones that had been driven out of areas of cleared urban-fringe bushland – and they do, as the saying goes, latch on and don't let go. They have flat ridges of teeth and can inflict a nasty wound. But other than infection, there's nothing to worry about (though people sometimes say the wounds don't heal). Throughout my childhood and adult life I have removed ticks from them, using a hot needle, as they cluster around their earholes and under their thick scales. But unless it's a life-or-death case I no longer do this, as I have no desire to hurt a tick either. Live and let live.

If you've ever lived around an extended family of bobtails, you'll be aware that a certain kind of interaction and spatiality of coexistence evolves. Having seen young born, having watched the young grow and work out their use of the family territory, of the crossing paths of the parent couple who largely stay together over decades, you see in them yourselves, whether you want to or not. We have had one of the family hit by a mower above the block, which was a trauma for them and us, with the gravel ants quickly dismantling the flesh and leaving a skeleton which has now fallen apart; others have been taken by cats or foxes or large birds of prey, but the core family unit is still intact, foraging, feeding, trying to make sense of the dramatically shifting seasonal structure which is outside anything they have experienced across their thirty or forty or fifty years of life. Climate change deniers like to talk of rural Australia in terms of cycles – and those cycles and patterns of flood and drought do exist – but those very cycles are being impinged upon and altered by extreme temperatures and changes in vegetation. Do not forget that tens and tens of thousands of hectares of remaining native vegetation in Australia are being stripped away each year for mines, pastoral leases and development. It is a catastrophe on the level of the destruction of the forests of the Amazon basin.

And now the pastoralists have their eyes on the Great Western Woodlands, one of the largest and most naturally diverse regions in continuous connection still left on the planet. Farmers and their backers in the Great Southern shire, especially centred around Esperance, are talking of clearing 400,000 hectares for farming that will be low yield and significantly contribute to climate change through the loss of vegetation and diversity. Like Adani's Carmichael coalmine in Queensland, which means the devastation of numerous habitats, including the Great Barrier Reef, and the production of yet more coal to bleed hothouse gases into the atmosphere, this is something that doesn't need to happen.

To simply say *How terrible!* is useless. People need to be on site, protesting and stopping the bulldozers with their very bodies, and, most importantly, they need to deny markets to the destroyers, to cut off their profits, to stop consuming in such pleasure- and leisure-seeking ways. The new colonialism is one in which even those who have suffered colonial ravages utilise the colonial machinery to extend their own wealth-making and control, under a smokescreen of 'it's our time'. Colonialism has been the blight of humanity, and the tools of colonialism will dismantle its last vestiges by any other name.

I am always thinking over the paradox of my ancestors' famine migration to Australia, the extractions and insertions of a colonial immobilising that prompts mobility, an 'escape' of the displaced, colonialism's victims and their becoming the displacers, the victimisers, and the displacement of Noongar people in the making of presence in the 'new country'. It's a disturbing irony I must constantly return to, and it feeds back on itself in a world disrupted by climate change (the most virulent and pervasive colonial outcome). In essence, climate change has brought a new form of potato famine to Ireland. This doesn't mean that the murderous policies of Trevelyan in the mid-nineteenth century, with his manipulations and denial of foodstocks to serve English profiteering costing millions of Irish people their lives – colonial acts which drove a newer colonialism in abreaction – are to be seen as anything but the acts of a colonial power. But in failing to act on climate in any meaningful way, like the rest of the world's nation-states, the Irish are actually contributing to their own destruction. The new colonialism is one of progress without fetters, of going 'forwards' without learning from what has happened in the past, of blurring science and development. We are all accountable as we consume and participate in the invasive economics of the globalised world. Wrong will always be wrong.

~

I walk around the block with my journal and vegan pastels. I often take impressions of what I see, and write over them – words mingling with colour interest me. Something across the valley shines, and I take it as a warning. Something is shifting. How to record this? What will it mean? I am being followed by a male red-capped robin. It's not curiosity: my steps must be stirring up insects – gnats, maybe. What does this mean? I draw shapes on the pages. Representations of positions and activities. Signs of certainty entangled with uncertainty. Paradoxes, oxymoronisms, tautologies, contradictions – this is my uneasy presence even here, where I know as well as I can know.

And now there are feathers and now a carcass. A male bronzewing pigeon? The glinting bronze-green? Such wary birds. And that stench – a tomcat's piss. Its taking over the territory will mean mass destruction for native wildlife, and for introduced creatures as well. What does it mean? Do I come out at night when I hear it snarling warnings as it searches for females to impregnate? Do I emerge from the house and make a racket every time I hear it to ward it off, move it on? To where? I will likely do this out of concern for all that I know here, but it's shifting the issue. (Not the 'problem', but rather, the issue.) I am not scapegoating for the ongoing workings of the colonial machine – destroying habitat and native creatures like the carnivorous woylies and thousands of species of birds, mammals, insects, then blaming the cats they themselves introduced. No, it's not that easy. It's just not. But I will go out and make a racket and it will move on.

Burton's legless lizard outside the front door – shovel nosing towards prey. Remarkable. A summer memory. Inside, Sonic Youth's *Washing Machine* is playing and Tracy is translating Rilke and Tim is making a list of birds he has seen over the day and I am calling to come and look …

~

My Grade One and Two teacher in primary school made me stand in a rubbish bin because I could read, and because I wouldn't do the strange little dance she expected of me – all this being an extension of her moral disapproval of my family situation. I often wonder if I could have found the strength not to hide in the back seat as Auntie Jackie drove us past the school in her old grey car, maintained in immaculate condition, though she had very little money. My mum was putting herself through university then, at a time when mature-age students were rare, and because she 'lived at home' she was granted a mere $28 a week. (Actually, that car now would be a significant collector's item, a piece of Australian manufacturing history – ironies on irony!). Auntie Jackie drove us to school on wet days, and came on some other days to collect me because it was a known fact I'd be surrounded by bikes and bullies and harassed and 'smashed'. I was proud of her, really, and I did a lot of outdoor things with her – we built stuff, we went into the bush together, and she and I often went fishing. I now look back in trauma on my fish-killing, but I remember the bonding with joy, especially sitting together as the sun came up over Cockburn Sound. But I hid on the back seat of the old car so that the other kids couldn't see me, so that the teachers wouldn't comment on my 'lack of a father', on separation and divorce and our 'different' family. That was the late sixties and early seventies. It's almost impossible to explain it to people now. If it's difficult now, it was beyond words back then. And it shouldn't have been – I am only grateful for the life I had. I remember my mum playing tape recordings of Thucydides's *Peloponnesian War* preparing for exams. I remember Auntie Jackie saying, Come outside and we'll kick the footy. And we did, even though she was a Pom with little understanding of Aussie rules footy. I remember living a life that did not accord with the conservative family propaganda of the day regarding 'single-parent families', 'latchkey kids', and so on. But it was the safe and secure house of that very same propaganda. Jackie was always there if Mum couldn't be, and did a superb job of parenting and looking after us, as did Mum. Both of them were proud that there was always a fire and afternoon tea to come home to. Mum says, Because of a lack of a dad, people will assume what they will, but adds that they have no right, no idea, and that circumstances were such that it was really helpful for both of them. It was a good long-term interaction. It was a sharing that worked well for the kids.

~

Yeats is my mother's favourite poet – I grew up with recitations of his work and have memorised many of his poems, as has Tracy. And Danny from the drug and alcohol centre next door to us on Bailey Street in Geraldton went to Mum's literature class and recited Yeats off the top of his head. He did the same for me on a jetty in Carnarvon in 1980 on the same night a Golden Gloves boxer, a Yamaji guy of my own age, stood up for me and my brother when white bastards were going to show us what they do with unwanted interlopers in 'their town'. That town where our father then lived, that town where we saw the iron bar over the bar of 'Iron Bar' Tuckey, that town then described as the 'most racist town in Australia'. Yeats that night, and blood, and water. An Anglo-Irish poet who embodied Irish liberty but also Irish colonialism. A paradox. Our paradox, too?

~

Walking out of the Tower I come across police arresting someone. They lift – no, they drag – an Aboriginal woman from a bench and slam her head into the pavement and then handcuff her. Does it matter that the arresting officers are all white, that the woman doing the cuffing and the slamming is large and blonde? Is this a colour-coding of power? I stand to make witness, and other cops gather. The arrested woman and her partner, who is sitting back and watching on, clearly waiting to see what will happen to her and to him, clearly indicate this is a situation of playing things down, not up. That calm is the best way out of it, and not to disrupt. I follow his eyes and his lead. I go away and ten minutes later walk back. The woman is sitting up, and her partner is watching the cops go through their things. I see him again and he sees me. It's okay, he says with his eyes, but he also says, clearly, Witness. Let the world know, mate. They are treating us like shit and it's our country! I am doing so. I am letting people know.

Never forget that for all its multiculturalism, Australia is a deeply racist country with an apartheid against its First Peoples. As the Whadjuk patrol circles Midland keeping an eye out for Aboriginal people in need, it knows it needs to get there and help out before the cops arrive on the scene. What does it mean when most people who aren't Indigenous walk past and put their heads down and pretend not to see anything? The denial of this event in this racist place was a multicultural one. One understands that intersectionality means many people who would respond are in less and less privileged positions of response and suffer greater and greater consequences, but no matter who you are, when you see such an 'event' you should intervene in the best way possible. Normally, I would have yelled at the cops to stop, and likely been arrested. The partner of the woman clearly indicated to me *not* to intervene, as it would have made it worse for the woman and himself. But his look didn't say, Remain silent – it said, Act when we are as safe as we can be. But act! Silence is strategic and only temporary. Then be bloody loud about it!

Of course, it can never be safe for Aboriginal people around white cops, and what might happen to the woman in the lock-up is deeply disturbing. In the Fremantle lock-up thirty or so years ago, I saw police throw a young Aboriginal man around a circle, laughing their ghoulish laugh and saying, You aren't so tough now, are you? I yelled and screamed and cried and then got smashed bloody in the cells. When I complained to the judge the next day he overtly said that if I continued he would have me locked up and throw away the key. It wasn't to be mentioned – none of it had happened. I could not find out what had become of the young bloke, the victim. His story was suppressed. I can only tell what I witnessed.

This is the reality of colonialism notching up into the next gear, a gear that works as in a syncromesh gearbox – gear matching shaft rotation, doing the work of adjustment to the conditions. Machines can be as brutal as their users. In Australia, racism is rampant, but the most concerted institutional racism is against Aboriginal peoples because they are the great threat to the capitalist machine of colonialism. It is their land that's been stolen, and that theft needs to be protected by the institutions and multinationals and associated edifices and their minions in any way they can.

How do I discuss 'home' in the context of this dispossession? How do I discuss a belonging even in the context of a desire for correction, for justice? Ultimately I can't, and shouldn't, because my descriptors of home potentially become forms of erasure, even if I wish them not to be. I acknowledge this. In some ways, the illness of the body I have struggled with over the last decades becomes personally symptomatic of the irony of my condition of writing place and recognising the contradictions implicit in this. I write myself towards silence in an agitated, often febrile body and state of mind. It constantly risks self-indulgence yet it is also a declaration of culpability and a responsibility to record. It is not an affirming self-portrait of presence, but it is a record. I am made up of bits and pieces of worlds I have fragmented in my presence. I am not trying to find a unified self, I am trying to find a way of speaking place without laying claim to ownership. Home is a marker of presence, not of certainty or security.

~

With one of the main markers of my time – our time – at Jam Tree Gully being my thyrotoxicosis through Graves' Disease, it is probably not really strange to note that it has made its physical mark on the house itself. In extending and remaking the house to suit our working needs, so the house inevitably reflects and absorbs the signs and characteristics of its inhabitants. The house can be, indeed, a living entity – and if you have ever experienced the expansion and contraction of a house shifting from the lowest temperature of the day at dawn through to the extremities of a wheatbelt summer, you'll know what I mean.

In fact, so severe can such shifts be, and so sensitive is even the most bespoke house to such change, that concrete and fibre planks (not asbestos) and gyprock panels can crack and literally be torn apart. The house groans not as an animal, but as a house laden with the expectations of its inhabitants. There are plenty of niches made for ghosts to inhabit when they are ready. As the creatures and vegetation of the block and environs register climate change – some vanishing for good, others arriving to try and maintain conditions they've been used to elsewhere, wandering to find an appropriate dwelling – so does the house, which is part of the problem of impact on the land in greater and lesser ways.

(We have tried to reduce impacts to make it lesser ways, but it is still relying on a history of manufacturing, transportation and so on.) It marks dramatic changes in the familiar – as soon as it 'settles' into its role of presence, its discomfort is expressed in sudden dramatic shifts – the hottest summer, the driest run, the worst storms. Its response to extremes, coming thick and fast, is wounds and scarring – as we all wound the bush, the land, the planet, that which we have made registers the wounding as well.

In the case of my Graves, I spent much of four months in bed and often leaning with my head against the clay-painted board wall, reading once my mind could focus enough. A characteristic of thyrotoxicosis is extreme sweating as a result of overheating; I was struck down in high summer, and the combination was dire. Very quickly, the bedsheets would stain with sweating, and my head left a shadow in the green clay paint. Sheets can be changed, but walls not so easily. So deep did the sweat go that even repainting cannot heal the sign – it changed the nature of the board itself. So whenever I walk into the room, whenever I go to bed, or read, I do so within the echo of my own halo of mortality – sure, survival, but also a constant reminder of how tenuous life is, even that of a house.

A quid pro quo? And so the house registers the minutiae of our own lives in so many ways – how we make it work for us through renovation or modification, and how our illnesses mark and sign.

One of the most horrifying things about those four months in bed at Jam Tree Gully, with occasional visits to the specialist, was an endogenous depression I wasn't familiar with – so extreme that the sight of a tree that once brought me untold joy, a tree I felt pain for in every way if it was threatened, made me feel like death. As my thyroxin levels stabilised, the joy I have in seeing a tree or any other living thing came back to its fullest, if not more. But the sense that I could feel such a loathing or indifference even under such extreme 'chemical' conditions marked me as much as the wall had been marked. I understood something about people and the way they treat ecologies – indifferent, even loathing.

In my case, the loathing came from a feeling that I couldn't do anything for any tree – that I was useless. Mostly, I am out there trying to do something for the environment, or I am trying to cut back on consuming and usage to lessen my impact. But relying entirely on Tracy and medical staff, and on medication to get things stable, I had to adjust to a different reality. The positive was that when I came out the other end, I found a new way of writing the complexity of contradictory and troubled presence, and that became part of the *Jam Tree Gully* poetry book. Art, music, learning, activism morphed not only in the outside pragmatic world of 'doing things', but also in a conceptual space of almost stasis. A doctor had advised me to go back to music in a big way, and I did. I began to see music interacting with my activism and the texts I was reading, and I drew pictures of what I couldn't see outside. I imagined its change. My ears became highly attuned to kangaroos hopping past, to every birdsong. And when I got up and looked out of windows, I drank in all that could be seen, but also saw what might come with the passing of the hours, and days.

Not prophetic, but an urge to the preventative as well as the witnessing. William Blake's poetry and art filled my head again. I wanted to write poems full of what I term 'anchor points' – solid observable and measurable points of reference – and 'error zones', those places where meaning slips to become a point of wonder that makes us reflect on what and why we are reading, and the consequences of where and how we are reading. I'd developed this theory while living in Ohio, and had often used it with my students when we went out on field trips – wandering outside, even looking out a window, visiting Mohican State Park in Ashland County and thinking about the night sky as seen from the Kenyon Observatory.

I wanted to develop a theory of poetry in which what was 'real' wasn't devalued, but what was 'doubtful' was equally relevant and valued. And bedbound, and longing to walk the block and the reserve, to encounter all those creatures I knew and that probably knew me, I created a world in my head that adapted and adjusted to the change humans were enforcing. When I eventually emerged, I was ready to become a different kind of activist – one who sought to prevent damage even before it turned up on planning maps or in shire council minutes, before it was reported in a paper, even before the destroyers thought of destroying. I wanted to pre-empt the damage to stop the damage. Preventative holistic medicine. A poetics that became the Jam Tree Gully poetry cycle. In my illness, not only did Jam Tree Gully become clarified from the inside out, but our 'home' of Ohio began to inform how I could better respect and understand my part in the colonial dispossession of my birth home. How belonging and unbelonging need to be in tension and conversation to allow persistence; how the shadow on the wall need not be erased, but recognised and offered as a marker of presence and a guide to the future, a future of reconciliation and restitution to the land and its people and all people.

~

I often look back at our years in Ohio not only to help understand the pattern of our own lives, but as a way of understanding Jam

Tree Gully and the Western Australian wheatbelt. The stark differences and the sometimes surprising similarities in issues of 'presence' help me better understand and clarify my ongoing torment of belonging/unbelonging.

I have an imprinting, visual memory, and as I think of Knox County, Ohio, this comes into play – overlaying images with those from Jam Tree Gully and even the Cambridgeshire fens, but also producing what seem very specific 'seeings' and moments. I taught Tim this technique years ago (and discussed the problems with using it – it's a kind of capturing and curating, of taking the 'scene' as if it is one's own to take and preserve … something archly conscious that goes beyond mere casual memorising) – how to look at a painting or a scene, use one's eyes as a camera eye/shutter, and pyrograph the image onto the mind. When I use this process to take in something visual, it tends to stay. Further, this eidetic disposition is how I make poems. I see the poems written on the screen of the mind, and transcribe them from there into speech or written text.

In thinking back to our years in Ohio, I have a collection of visual images gathered in this way. Many of them are of birds, trees, vistas, unusual natural phenomena, and some objects (an old rail bridge across the Kokosing River, the houses we lived in, municipal buildings in the centre of Mount Vernon, and buildings of Kenyon College), but not nearly as many as 'natural' scenes or moments. And few people – I tend not to imprint with people because I find it an intrusive act. A gravestone of John Crow Ransom stands out more than people I was close to. Having said this, I have a deeply figurative portraiture of those people, which is about character more than scenes or looks. Just because I didn't imprint them in the eidetic way doesn't mean I didn't respect or interact with them. It's just a different ideation of connection.

So my visual memory is very particular. In being shown where a groundhog snapped a branch of a tree at the bottom of the yard of a friend, who was also colleague and our immediate neighbour, what I recall so vividly is the walk across the meadow, the lines of trees dividing yard and meadow, the wood pile, and the tree with the broken branch. After winter, with the thaw long past and the budding branches reworking the light and shade, I marvelled that this unusual event was also a specific event – all the more for the telling and the showing, the introduction of it into social discourse. This was an extension of friendship through the medium of a 'natural' (if unusual) event our neighbour knew would interest us. All of us poets together, all of us with different ways of seeing and writing.

~

In my distress of whiteness, Gambier's whiteness was always a problem. Don't get me wrong, I am not suggesting communities should have quotas of heritage or ethnicity, but I always feel that if they're constructively open, then people of all backgrounds and heritages will find a way of belonging, of sharing presence. Colonial histories are too often 'officially' constructed for school consumption in order to delete histories that challenge their outcomes, and so often are only inclusive when it serves the needs of labour and profit. If Johnny Appleseed, say, is a self-contained capitalist-aspirational mythology of the colonial, then an abused and rights-less labour force is less likely or less able to work through or against it to serve its own ends. How does one enter a post-history of segregation and exploitation and pretend it's not the case?

It's easy to make assumptions, it's easy to expect an underground railroad town like Mount Vernon to inherently continue to be that, as the painted-lady Civil War munitions-fortune houses still shine as history, as the Rolls Royce factory produces parts for a globalised industry, but it's a jigsaw puzzle an outsider-insider can't make work, or is not 'allowed' to express. This is not unique to mid-Ohio.

As I learnt when visiting Richmond, Virginia, there really are 'white folk' out there who believe in a white nation, as there are in Australia, with its various patriotic groups. These must be resisted, and owning up to our own naiveties is part of this. For me, we are all people with the common cause of justice in mind, working for equality and fairness. As one who celebrates diversity and cultural difference, whose main concern outside these underpinning coordinates is the health and intactness and agency of the non-human environment, I can too easily take it for granted that what I say will be interpreted within this framework. Of course that is arrogance and hubris, and I have tried to become more sensitive to the fact that no user of words owns words – and that words are in constant flux. I enjoy a good laugh as much as the next person (as they say), but I think humour, even self-deprecating humour, can be very destructive if it doesn't constantly adapt to the environment in which it's used. A white comedian who ridicules their own position via routines that show their own foolishness in making assumptions about non-whites is still exploiting that dynamic to extract a laugh. I find this deplorable. Humour dates because people move on – old jokes that once brought self-scrutiny now all too often don't allow self-scrutiny and just inflict damage. It's almost as if humour can only live in its moment, then should vanish – but even then, the hurt of humour in any form can wittingly or unwittingly leave scars on others well beyond our remembering that we inflicted them. Humour does not often culturally translate. Web capitalism, with its making of the 'all-humanity' marketplace, might suggest it's possible, but it's not – difference and regionality will always define at least part of who we are.

~

When Tim was due we were anxious that if we had to make the run to Columbus in the middle of the night the snow plough might not have gone through. A winter baby. To give birth in a reflecting and prismatic landscape was disorientating but exhilarating for Tracy, and by proxy, me. Travelling through the snow with corn stover poking through, I was always wondering why it hadn't been used as silage. A road travelled often is never the same. On that road I picked up a deer tick while pissing under a small pine tree – we discovered it embedded in my scalp later one night. On that road, we saw a horse resist going into a trailer and bolt and jump a fence into the woods. On that road we wondered about converting our international driver's licences into local Mount Vernon licences. On that road we hit black ice and slid and slid, out of control. Tracy wrote a story about potholes being portals to other worlds. We stopped behind the yellow school buses and swerved to miss deer. We rushed visiting family to the hospital in Columbus. We drove back after weaving our way past the Ohio State stadium the day the fans ran amok, turning over cars, smashing things. We frequently drove past the museum and went in once to see the mannequins performing their heritage history roles – the fact that the clothes, the catalogue and almanac materials had simulated existences. A road, there and back, full of implications, and hitting the highway, the massive Peterbilt trucks, the trailers laden with PCBs, the wastes of modernity going somewhere.

And clapboard house after clapboard house of greater or lesser size, with more or less space around them, with flagpole holders empty or more often full, bristling. This is a difference with Australia – Australian flags are flown, most likely on small rural properties outside cities or towns, but they are frequently a sign of right-wing politics and xenophobia, whereas in America they can also be about a broader inclusiveness, the migrational dream of oneness of America: the melting pot, as it's called, for all creeds, beliefs and 'colours'. I've never bought into this, as to melt people down into sameness is to lessen rights, not share them out and increase them. To coexist with difference is the challenge for me, and one I think desirable. Flags symbolise the ironing-out, the common cause over difference, and inevitably lead to an othering of difference which becomes perceived as a threat to the status quo.

So the flag in America might be left or right, and it might be an affirmation of an idea rather than a demographic, but it is still about 'in' or 'out'. Trump's wall as flag in its full regalia – keeping out. Australia is flagging its allegiances more and more as anti-Muslim bigotry gets hold of more and more people. Flag means the old ways, flag means compliance to the White Australia Policy, the first enactment of the Australian federal parliament in 1901, and though no longer policy, it's a residue that defines 'in' and 'out'. One doesn't have to be white to be 'in', but being in under the flag still means compliance to those old colonial values in certain ways, whether one agrees with them or not. It needs dismantling on all levels. Flags are the shrouds of 'nation' and its policies of inclusion and exclusion.

The core of Gambier is the 'three-sided plateau walk' of Middle Path. We do not have many photos of our years in Gambier, but there is a wonderful photo of my mother standing on a snowbound Middle Path, snow sitting in beautiful temporality on the scaffolding of bare trees. I have since learnt that many of these trees have been removed because they were considered diseased or unhealthy (caused by chemicals, salt laid down for de-icing, poor drainage and the like), and this is crushing to me, to us. Though these trees are a construct in a place where there were once vast woods, and though it was bare when hacked out, a joiner between buildings and desires for learning, the trees speak across eras and across difference. They are an embodiment of the best hopes for a liberal arts education, for fairness and environmental respect even within human-damaged and remade environments. In their replanting, one hopes that care to prevent future damage will be an intrinsic part of their nurturing, and that they will be granted the agency they deserve – not just decoration, not just symbol, but essence. Poor soil quality and poor drainage are local issues of concern in the restoration, but so is the entire biosphere. I have just seen a satellite map of Ireland and it is brown.

One of Japan's island's has just recorded its highest temperature since records began, and the figures of cataclysmic climate shift are rolling in by the hour, minute, second. Restoration at Gambier – even of the human-constructed 'natural' – and restoration at Jam Tree Gully (of the cleared and grazed land) align in this. Jam Tree Gully speaks to Gambier, and Gambier speaks to Jam Tree Gully. They are not mutually exclusive. All rugged up as she is in that photo, my mother is shading her eyes against the glare, against the winter sign as it is reworked by the crystals of ice. Like being out on the salt scalds of the wheatbelt induced by farming, or out on the natural salt lakes of the wheatbelt, one shades one's eyes because of the reflection. Light is alive, light is what we live off, and yet the light heats the world we are smothering with greenhouse gases. In that photo taken maybe a few days before

Tim was born – ice baby, snow baby – is the glare of life and a future we all want to sustain.

⁓

One of the strong attractions I have always had to 'America' (not as nation, but as a collective of communities and a geography that intertwines with this) is the 'freedom of faith'. The irony is that faith is one of the most dividing and bigoted issues one encounters in many parts of the US. In central Ohio, Protestant religions still hold sway, though even over our years there we were pleased to find an increasing diversity and increasingly open discussions about difference in faith. As Ohio promo literature will often point out, Native Americans built mounds and these were likely associated with faith, but this is discussed in very loose and noncommittal ways. A lot of the time, general discussions in supermarkets and at social occasions centre more on the 'absence' of Native Americans in a particular area at the time of 'moving west' than on acceptances of such presence and related spirituality.

Interestingly, the residue of a belief that belief is implicit in presence (and prior and likely ongoing claims to land) might be found in such names as the local social service Moundbuilders, an important help zone in Knox County for locals who cannot afford private mental or social health care. The divides caused by disparate levels of health insurance are one of the most shocking things for the newcomer to the US, especially coming out of the Australian system where there is basic universal health care, no matter how much conservative governments try to diminish it.

Faith and mental and social health are so entwined in that part of Ohio that secular help is difficult to find outside the wealthier sectors of society. Churches offer support that is accommodated within their belief practice but doesn't reach beyond as much as some might like to think, especially where it's not proselytising. As someone who was brought up Anglican – and who is married to an ex-Catholic (very much having left all church now) – and who seriously wanted to convert (and was committed) to Judaism in his teenage years, who earlier thought he had a vocation because when he was due to be confirmed a warm yellow light shone through a chapel window and lit his face, who then politically denied all religion while deeply believing in the right of all religions, whose brother converted to marry a Muslim who is very liberal-minded in her way of seeing, any form of exclusionism is disturbing. I find exclusionism unfathomable, or at least difficult to fathom.

And such exclusionism we came across in central Ohio when in middle school our daughter would not join lunchtime Christian groups (at a secular school), and where a couple of years after she left, a Jewish student was allegedly branded with the shape of a crucifix by a creationist teacher using a tesla coil. (There was a long trial covered by *The New York Times* – the teacher was sacked by the school for teaching creationism, the case continuing for many years on appeal.) Probably most disturbingly, many deeply religious locals – literally waving the Bible – defended the teacher's position, saying he was, to paraphrase, teaching what the parents wanted. There *is* increasing tolerance, but demarcation lines of 'deliverance' go deep. It reminds me of the time I was at the supermarket and a pick-up pulled up with a dead deer flopping out the back (I saw variations on this many times), and I made some remark about respecting the dead, and for a moment I thought I was going to be shot.

Just after Hurricane Katrina, when weapon sales had soared, I was walking by a bayou just outside Monroe, Louisiana. I was dressed only in black (as I have since 1997), tall and lanky and white-haired ('like Andy Warhol') and carrying a book of poetry. A pick-up truck with the proverbial Movietone gun rack in the back pulled up alongside me and the passenger yelled out, Hey, or Oy, or the like. I looked up and said, Yes? My accent must have thrown them because they burnt off out of sight. But a short while later they were back and parked facing me, revving their engine. I walked past without looking – custody of the gaze, as many women know to keep when they certainly should not have to keep it. But I was being challenged. Dead deer, odd maleness, difference – all challenges particularly emphasised and emphatic in the rural or small-town world, or on the fringes of cities. And moving back to faith, because I am sure all of the people above were deep believers in something, I have seen the same enthusiasm for exclusion all over the world, the same denial of difference as denial of climate change. They are linked.

What I do know is that people who have spent a life in Knox Country are unlikely to recognise this 'version' of presence I am painting. It's what we take to an experience, how familiar we are with patterns of being and belonging, and what we take away – but all presences (even temporary ones, such as a student's three or four years at college) are part of a place and are not to be excluded, to my mind. We are all *polysituated*, and we learn to respect where we are by understanding where others are, why they arrive, why they leave, why they visit, why they try to make a home regardless of how they do or don't 'fit'.

~

It's no doubt clear by now that the way I especially connect to a place is through its flora and fauna and topography. Sometimes I write to people in Gambier to hear about what's around. I just wrote to the manager of the Brown Family Environmental Center at Kenyon College to see what's happening as July turns to August, and I hear back from her:

here's the short list …

birds – the usual suspects: cardinals, jays, bluebirds, field sparrows, tree swallows, wrens, woodpeckers

other wildlife – green frogs are very active right now, tons of dragonflies, tiger swallowtails, sulfurs, monarchs, spicebush swallowtails

flowers – bee balm, black-eyed susans, brown-eyed coneflower, purple coneflower, joe pye-weed, and lots of other stuff

You should come down to see it first hand!

Such communiques are important to me. I look at a photo of out 'last American house' in Mount Vernon – on High Street, not far up from Main Street and the public square. It's the pileated woodpecker that used to work the oak and walnut trees around the house that I most strongly recall, along with the mirror-busting pileated woodpecker at Louis and Patsy's house, where we first lived in Gambier for the first six months of 2001. I guess many living there would most remember the incredible array of architectural styles of this town 'founded' in 1805, all proudly listed on the Knox County Historical Society pages – including Queen Anne, Gothic Revival, Second Empire, Greek Revival – or they might remember the incredible houses on Vine, the churches, or the solid public buildings. I do remember them, too, but I more remember the water treatment plant by the Kokosing River and my concerns over its workings, or on the celebratory side, the track between Gambier and Mount Vernon, while worrying about rubbish being dumped in its shallow and reasonably fast-flowing water. Though we had a car (we always share a car to reduce our imprint, usually a four-cylinder vehicle – in this case, the ubiquitous Dodge Neon), we preferred to walk where possible. I often took visiting writers, especially from Australia, on walks around the village, town and district. One friend wrote recently and said he remembered us walking and discussing 'steamboat Gothic'. This makes me think of Cincinnati, and again, it's the birds I recall, and, of course, the mighty river. And the bridges. I am always fascinated by crossings, especially from one state to another – literal or otherwise. I have been re-reading James Wright's poetry and making translations leaps across Ohio from Martins Ferry, and am reminded of a sadness that transfers in part to Mount Vernon, often called (when I was there) the 'most Republication town in America'. As a pacifist, walking down High Street to the square, I couldn't help but bring 'history' into it, as history is imprint as well, and think of Clement L. Vallandigham giving his anti-war speech in 1863, asking myself what 'anti-war' actually meant for the Copperheads and their anti-abolitionist stance, their inevitable pro-slavery, and their occasional stirrings or considerations of violence to stop the war. This was not anti-war per se, it was anti *that* war and what it represented. This would seem to be a moral conundrum but it's not, as it was never about pacifism, but about control. I am thinking of how to write a poem of this with regard to the oldest trees, to the lineage of birds and spicebush swallowtails, the purple coneflower staking its claim on a vacant block, here there.

I guess I am so fascinated by woodpeckers because there are none here in Western Australia. Walking around Cambridge, as I often do, I am always on the lookout for woodpeckers. One morning I had the great fortune to see a rare lesser-spotted woodpecker up near the American (War) Cemetery near Madingley. I wrote to the Royal Society for the Protection of Birds about the sighting. To contribute to the wellbeing of a place by reporting a sighting that might lead to conservation is a positive thing, yet it can have negative consequences. After reported sightings of the Australian night parrot, which had been believed extinct, people began invading habitat and disturbing the few survivors, so their lives and hopes for recovery were at risk of being destroyed.

In such a built-up environment as that around Cambridge, it seems a reported sighting can be helpful in a way that one made in the vaster spatialities of Australia might not. I often see rare and endangered species along the edges of Madingley Wood (used by the university for 'research', which is always a concern) and the American War Cemetery as I take the walkway between the two. The living and the dead all part of the now. Strangely, in that place of quiet and respect, away from the vast amounts of toxins dumped on the lawns to keep them shining, there is 'room' for animal, bird and human interaction. I cherish such things. But I also know there are spaces one should not venture into, or even look into, and I don't. Not all space is available to all of us.

Footpath between Madingley Ancient Woodland and the American War Cemetery

The path is shaded in later summer
and moisture clings in the lean tunnel
even in dry weather – exposed to the east
side of the forest with its more recent growth –
elm, elm suckers, ash, blackthorn,

and an understorey that has made its
appearance and diminished: dog's mercury
and bluebells, though always the residual moss.
On the west side, well away from the path,
the most ancient woodland with its oak

and hazel, ash and sawflies, its blue tits
and hummingbird hawk-moths. They venture
throughout, of course, but you feel their origins.
On the left side, the American war cemetery.
The dead with their origins, eternally here.

The soldier-surgeon's deathcall: 'to you
from failing hands we throw/ the torch'
proclaimed from the base of the flagpole
wavers over chalky boulder clay
and drops away into the glare

of mowed lawns and pristine white
crosses: 3809 headstones and the remains
of 3812 men. It's clean and impressive.
It makes you remember or wonder.
Each tree reaches deep with nurture.

Sun breaks into the tunnel, over
the path, infused with smog stuck over
the county, and on the edge of transplantings
a gardener places a poison spray pack
in a garden shed. Nesting boxes

hang along the edge of the wood,
and outside the recruitment call, I sense
a flitting across the leaf litter into the green;
before the branches are laid bare and the wood's
soul is revealed, in part at least. The absence

of poppies an adjustment come with time,
the specificities of locale and its bequest.

These places I have inhabited for long periods, with my immediate family, not only become part of me in an osmotic memorialised and remembering sense, but also bring with them a responsibility for cross-referencing, to meld them into myself. We absorb experiences, events, 'sightings' and presences, and they make us how we are, but they also leave marks and traces, and we must be conscious of this. Even when I piss on a tree, or on the side of a country road, I realise that I am chemically altering that place, that my wastes are part of its presence, its fertility and also toxicity. We carry responsibility in so many ways. When one travels or moves under duress (dislocation through war, injustice, economics, and so on), one is inevitably less concerned with this, and less capable of doing anything about what one leaves behind – the residues of passing through, of dwelling short term – and that must always be understood and appreciated by the longer-term inhabitants of those places (it could also happen to them). But if we wish to understand how best to respect the land, we need seek out as much knowledge as we can, to remain in a state of heightened sensitivity and know that for every action there is an equal and opposite reaction, metaphorically at least. And metaphors matter because they have consequences for how we communicate with each other. And understanding across the cultural and linguistic gaps is always essential, and cannot be achieved by Google as mediator.

~

When I look at a photograph of the Mount Vernon High Street house, I think of the hole in the wood box that went through to hell, and the drop through the bathroom into the sewers. I think about the frozen pipes and no working stove when we moved in. But I also think about the history of the house, its simple ornamentation, its way of having family spaces in proximity to each other, but private – that American family and individual dynamic – and the public exposure of yard and presence. Porch swing. Decking. A corner block, its pillars said welcome and separation at once. It's a psychology that takes some getting used to. As does the privatised garbage collection and privatised everything else. Where the town corporation begins and private industry begins and ends is always slightly bemusing to a newcomer. But the sidewalk outside the house and running the length of High Street was wonderful in its consistent irregularity. The house was so orderly, and the shade trees with their abundant birdlife in the warm months (and also in the winter) spaced in such a precise manner, and yet the sidewalk was out of kilter, just a little. My daughter and I loved to walk it, just to be there in the street and watch the squirrels running in and out of their tree hollows. The always-mowed brighter-than-green lawns, the always-freshly-painted houses – the ones that weren't were visibly frowned on, and one could sense a desire to enforce a middle class in a 'classless' society'.

But wealth *is* class, and travelling across the 'big road' to the other side of town, where much smaller houses, many or most equally as neat as the larger houses, spoke aspirational values of pride. A neighbourhood values system. And then neighbourhoods with car wrecks and paint peeling and clear poverty, where such policing was less effective because it had no way of being effective. There's no way of hiding inequality. My politics of wealth distribution are slant to this, and yet I might not be welcome at all in the rough side of town, though it's where I feel I belonged. Not welcome because my reason for being there would be questioned in a way it's not, say, back 'home' in Australia. And when the subprime mortgage crisis hit, and I was back visiting, so many of the 'better-off' houses throughout the county, the state, the country, were on the market for 'a song'. Wealth is a fickle thing, and belonging and connection to a place should not be so vulnerable to the manipulations and vagaries of money, banking and markets. When I see the places we lived in, I see the gifts of welcome and inclusion, with all the problems such offerings bring (someone will be denied something because of it), and not material comfort or social 'success'. Both Tracy and I read Thorstein Veblen's *The Theory of the Leisure Class* when we lived there (in a 'thrift edition'). As one would?

~

When I was eighteen I tried to obtain a Red Cross passport so I would have no nation. Of course, Red Cross passports were only available to people who had had nation taken from them. And I respect that. But I am trying to convey how from a very young age I felt no kinship with 'flag', but rather with land and community and the natural environment. I knew the flag was a sign of too many conflicted things, and that in seeking to resolve these conflicts and disjunctions and mould them into a unity, it actually created an oppressive machine that would destroy you if you were an outsider or (even peacefully) opposed it. Opposition within the rules of the structure might be permissible, but not challenging the structure itself. I was never one who looked to other countries as being 'better' – they're not. *All* nation-states are a problem; any nation as an exclusive and empowered entity is oppressive, or is likely to become oppressive once it is militarised in any way.

But land and community do not have to be oppressive, and can be just and respectful. Maybe one of the reasons I have kept moving around the world – where it has allowed me to go – is because of all this. But in the end, I am always drawn back to the wheatbelt, to Jam Tree Gully, where restoration of damaged land is an ongoing process, and where presence might be able to be part of a restoration of land, conversation and rights. And looking out across the valley in my mind's eye, as I can do from wherever I am located, even when the blood moon vanishes behind cloud, the eclipse a slow shutter photographing the state of the world, the kangaroos passing through Jam Tree Gully on their desiring lines, I know that I can speak for nobody else but myself, and sometimes, with their permission, for Tracy and Tim, because we are a community. But I know damage when I see it, and damage is to be prevented, resisted, denied.

~

We are all pining for Jam Tree Gully. I have been back each week to make sure all is okay, but Tim and Tracy have been stuck in the city. We'll be back there full-time soon. But on the weekend I took Tim up with me, and he felt liberated. I wonder if this is how 'weekender' ruralists feel, going to their properties when they can manage it? I don't connect with that thinking, and I don't agree with 'property', but I can respect the feeling of connection and encounter. Tim's entire world view has been formed by living away from cities, surrounded by trees, birds, reptiles, mammals and insects.

As we approached the northern end of the loop, we saw a rolled utility in a paddock. I slowed to ensure no one was trapped in the vehicle, which had clearly flown off the bend, crashed through the barbed-wire fence, clipped a flooded gum, and rolled. Tim pointed out that two of the wheels were missing – it was already being stripped by people driving past, who saw the wreck and grabbed what parts they could. I wondered about the fate of the driver – the cabin was crunched pretty badly. No grass was growing into it, and forage grows fast at this time of year if it's been raining, and it had. So it had crashed within the last week – since I had last driven this road. These are dangerous roads.

When we arrived, Tim was ecstatic – maybe a displacement of the distress of seeing the wreck, and of escaping from the concrete and electricity of the city. Euphoric. Because within minutes we had seen a juvenile goshawk circling overhead, and were investigating auras, clusters and halos of leaves beneath overhanging York gum branches that had been nibbled off and dropped. I had seen this when I was up after the big winter storms and assumed it to be the result of the weather, or possibly a possum, but these were fresh and had occurred since the bad weather. We examined the fall of leaves carefully and observed a pattern. We examined the chewed ends of stalks, the fact that leaves but none of the fruits – the small nuts – of the York gums (which had just finished their cold months' flowering) were evident. We both said, Cockatoos!, and honestly, literally, at that very moment four or five magnificent Carnaby's cockatoos flew past just up the hill. We had seen them at JTG before, of course, as it's on their route as they move towards nesting trees, but as more and more of these old feeding and nesting trees (with nesting hollows) are erased, the more the birds come to rely on other food sources. Neither of us had ever seen a Carnaby's cockatoo eating York gum nuts, but the pattern of stripping and the leaf dispersal and, yes, the evidence of manure (washed into its whiteness against the clay, laterite soil and gravel driveway) confirmed it. They *are* known (rarely, it seems) to nest in old York gum hollows. So much of the hakea and dryandra and other preferred food plants around this entire region have been cleared, but they feed on a *variety* of eucalypts as well. The weeping-wee cry of the Carnaby's cockatoo is the most contradictory celebratory and mournful sound, and one which lifts us from chairs, draws our eyes towards the sound, no matter what we're doing. So few left, and under such stress. We fear for them flying past the area, as there are a number of blokes around who would shoot them with glee – though it is risking jail to shoot endangered wildlife.

So we were sad to see they were resorting to old York gums, which have no nesting hollows large enough (they're more suited to nightjars, smaller parrots and other smaller hollow-nesting birds – though York gums get large and thick and termite-hollowed, they don't generally form those deep, high, solid hollows of, say, wandoos), but also glad the cockatoos were feeling safe enough at JTG to feed and take refuge. And indeed, having been away for a month, Tim remarked that nowhere else in the world he has been had he ever heard so many different birds singing at once. His knowledge of birds is profound, and Jam Tree Gully has been the epicentre of his understanding.

My suggestion that it could be a possum weren't entirely off the mark. We checked under the possum's tree near the house, and indeed there were scattered (and vaguely chewed) leaves and possum scats. That tree is still one of its stopovers as it moves over its territory. Reassuring.

I emptied 8.5 millimetres out of the rain gauge, and noted that the lucerne trees planted along the northern firebreaks were coming into blossom. Yes, and I did hear the splendid blue wren calling to its mate. And yes, I did see the silvereyes flying out from the geranium by the front verandah where silvereyes or brown honeyeaters nest every year, though rarely succeed in raising their chicks – 'nest failure' is common due to storms, cats and birds of prey. Tim is sure the silvereyes will succeed this year.

Most vitally, the mungart (the Ballardong Noongar name),

Acacia acuminata or raspberry jam tree is just coming into flower. Those yellow rolls – tight cylinders, as botanical books call them, or yellow-lashed rollers, as I often call them – are appearing one or two or three, here or there. Soon the entire block and the reserve will be a dusky enlivening yellow. It's the vitality of the year, of the ground itself that nurtures them. We have one that sources water and nutrients from the septic, no doubt, which is a good 15 metres high – way beyond its design specs. That tree is much valued by birds of prey, which watch surrounding lower and clustered jam trees for the songbirds that so favour them. With the mistletoe that attaches to most jam trees, thornbills build their incredible nests of 'deception' – false-chambered in an attempt to fool the cuckoos. The red-capped robins make their lichen-encrusted swirls of grass in the forks of branches, so camouflaged that it takes Tim's sharp long-distance eyesight to spot most of them. Jam tree saplings are often nibbled down by kangaroos, but they always come back with enthusiasm – they are in tune with each other. The seeds of the jam tree – out of those bunches of pods that curl and crackle in the hot months – are a favoured flour source for Ballardong Noongar people (it's never a case of 'was'; they still are, should Ballardong Noongar people wish them to be – nothing can be erased, no matter how hard the colonial machinery of survey, clearing and property tries), and the underpinning of life in the region. These trees last through tough summers and can be used on the edge of saline lands – they are not overly salt-tolerant, but enough so for the second round of reclamation, at least. Essential.

Jam tree wood was once used in vast quantities for fence posts, as it is extremely hard, and stinks when it is burnt. In a sad reality of now, people in the district looking for a hallucinogenic high have been known to strip the bark from hundreds of jam trees and 'cook it up' to extract a drug. So many trees are required for a dose that whole reserves have been stripped bare. This is not traditional medicinal usage, but exploitation for pleasure and false visions. This remarkable tree, which yields a gum often considered a confection by many Noongar people, is treated by exploiters as being without agency or spirit. Tim shakes with upset when these trees are hurt. He feels it, as the birds feel it, as the sun skinks and monitors feel it. I think about this as I take Tim to a bus stop on the edge of the city so he can journey up into the Hills for the day – so far from our home – and explain to him that the small plastic ziplock bags strewn around the seat and shelter are methamphetamine deal bags. Disposable plastic bags are going to be around for a time yet.

In a couple of weeks, a group of concerned rural dwellers in the town of Moora, deep in the wheatbelt, are going to stage a 'last stand' – a desperate plea to stop the damage to the remaining bush, to the land. Road-widening, land clearing and sheer bloody-mindedness are reducing the remaining 3 per cent of pre-settler bushland to half that. People travel to Western Australia during wildflower season to drive the roads and see the incredible display of everlastings, dampiera, wattle, leschenaultia, bottlebrush, grevilleas, and the list goes on and on … and yet this growth of the roadside – the 'long paddock' – is being keelhauled out of existence. The first clearings, then the follow-up clearings. And as salinity consumes the bare land, caused by removing the trees and the water table rising as a consequence (the ironies of a dry, low place) and hauling millions of years of salt deposit (brought in by winds from the oceans) to the surface, making salt scalds – crystalline cities of beautiful waste (who says political poetry isn't aesthetic, whether we want it to be or not!), such last stands really are just that. This is what I have written for the occasion – a celebration of the jam tree.

Euphoria

for the' Last Stand' resistance and for a 'moderately' salt-tolerant wattle

The first jam tree blossom has arrived at Jam Tree Gully.
Getting inside the blossom and dowsing in pollen
without causing damage, that's the euphoria – to carry
the legacy and increase the bounty, to share with insects
and the infrastructure of thornbills who each year nest
around mistletoe (subletting). Euphoria! As the eating-
away-at-edges accumulations merge with the wholesale
fire-sale clearances, the emergence of those yellow-lashed rollers
is cause for transformation. Fast-growing, nipped in early days
by roos but coming back unassisted, the basis of eternity
is built out of their temporariness. Euphoria! My childhood
of salinity is not just a memory, it is an object lesson
in bringing back from the brink – rellies who knew
that jam tree and needlebush are part of the comeback,
that hell can at least be partially unravelled and restitution
made – a rain of pollen and seeds and lichen overalls,
the work of restoration as driven – more driven –
than the lazy fantasy of clearing, the sweat built up from erasure.
But euphoria is preventative and a restorative medicament!
It takes you out there to see a prospect is worth nothing
in soul or flesh when forced, without interruption – tree lines,
stands of bush, are vision! In the rush to maximise
the quota of wheat, the mutuality of coexistence
and sharing is lost, as, in the not-so-long run, is the wheat.
This country knows better, knows best.
Its people will tell you, if you listen. Euphoria
can be staying who you are and tuning in to the blossoming –

even the depilation of blossom onto ground and windows
and machinery and fur and feathers and skin is a counteractive
depilation you might learn from. Two-way mirror of the
    wheatbelt,
the euphoria of jam tree blossoming. Yes! Yes! Learn
from mungart, from *Acacia acuminata*, the mantra the chant
the tree's own euphoria – a guide away from despoliation.

~

Early this morning I received this message from Mum:

> Dear John,
>
> You would have been interested to be here last night – the most tremendous bang! I rang Lorraine and she said their doors rattled and they thought it was just outside their place. It was really scary because we thought it might be the start of an earthquake. Anyway, it seems there was a meteor over the city then this loud bang over York-Northam area. They think it was a meteor but are not sure.
>
> Love,
>
> Mum.xx

I had been reading about it. I had been looking out the Tower window at the time, to see what was happening with a car having the shit revved out of its engine in the car park below. I was looking in the right direction to see the meteor pass over the city, over the hills, towards York, but I didn't.

We will be in York on Saturday to have lunch with Mum and Guru, and to attend the York Agricultural Show (that time of year again), as we usually do. I have felt many tremors in York –

we get few over at Jam Tree Gully, though we get the earthshake tremors of the Bindoon firing range 30 k's away. But York is on a fault line and it is said by Noongar people that when the warrior Walwalinj and his taboo lover Wongborel – the mountain and the hill across the river valley – come together, it will be the end of time. Another echo, another reiteration, another refrain. This memoir is only a series of murmurs and stories.

No doubt we will talk much about the 'event' on Saturday. It will be the buzz of the show. In a region known for its UFO sightings, this will add grist to the mill. For me, it's a yearning to be where the meteorite declared itself – out where I know how best to dwell, to understand the questioning of my presence. A poem about the frustration of distraction, unseeing and absence:

Meteor

Like to think a native metal
sources the green glee fields
        the paddocks flush
        with green or yellow
flowering canola all lit up at night
the sun reversing and coming back
        to undo the wrongs
        committed below its
watch of the valley as ablation sets
the tools machining and a spectacle
        is shedding burn
        and the sonic burst
coming in low a chunk to pick up.
This fall this hit this illumination
        triggering call after call

to verify a UFO, to make
merry with so much footage in this age
of citizen surveillance a variable
with many impacts.
Curve fast high slow
down enough to leave a product to leave
a source of knowledge the scare of all
down around our ears,
earthshake or deliverance,
apocalypse which is not too light a word
for the targeted haphazard chance
what are the odds,
crater on the curve
of body earth. Reading a little less than
enough can still leave a spirit, room for
spectres to swap stories:
where were you-we?
Where was the gap in foresight looking
out from the tower at the precise time
as the light-roar was
ending the earth as
we know it and you-I saw stuff-
all, saw city lights burning fast
against the end, a car
revving in the car park,
so loud it distracted or sucked phenomena
into its obsessions, its addictions, its fury.
Meteor's impact métier.
Dazzle of earthed quakery.
So easy to dismiss what you can't personally
verify when those you love assure you've missed it.

~

The meteorite has become the talk of the state, the country. My cousin Ken watched it approach York and heard the sonic boom. It likely landed somewhere nearby – what managed to journey through the atmosphere. As kids, we'd often see shooting stars when we were camping out on the farm. Ken runs a spread in the corner of the old farm – his inheritance. He has revegetated the old salt scalds over a lifetime and has created bushland. It is remarkable – a healing. Walking under full stars, we would work each other up with stories of UFOs and alien abductions, in that zone where such stories buzzed about, where hauntings and odd occurrences were part of the isolation of farmhouses, and likely the guilt of presence even if that wasn't completely understood or articulated. The truth of the ground is never far away. It speaks in the rocks, the trees, the marking, the gun slits in old stone buildings. And Auntie Elsie's house below the Needlings was, after all, split and tilted with the Meckering quake. The fault lines are restless.

The media are filming in the main street of York town, emphasising 'the oldest inland town' of Western Australia – 'town' as thought of by colonial 'civilising'. Dwelling in Aboriginal communities had its landmarks and buildings as well, but not the permanent structures of Western desiring. Or is this really the case? Maybe they are in places if non-Aboriginal people learn how to look? Maybe there were in fact many permanent structures? How many meteorites seen and tracked and located by Aboriginal communities over millennia? How many stories of their arrival? A cosmology woven through all being. A science and an ontology, working together. I have anxiety about not being with family – with Mum and Guru – when the house shook.

Tracy, Tim and I all feel the same. We should have been there at that moment. Maybe they'll find a fragment of the meteorite on the land once collectively called Wheatlands during that interval of and in presence. But it seems its flight path was otherwise.

Of course, the conversation around the lunch table, under the eye of Walwalinj, was about the meteorite. The house shook like a bomb had gone off, said Guru. Some years back when his work shed had caught fire, some compressed air tanks had exploded, and it was like that. After it happened, Mum and Guru had gone outside with torches and checked around the house and the surrounding area to see what had happened. Mum judged this year's photography entries for the York show, and sitting at the judges' table with judges from other areas of general competition – the best vegetables, the best flowers, the best canola set, the bed wheat sheaf, the best artworks across the different age categories, the best jams, the best appliqué, and so on – the only talk, once judging was done, was of the meteor. Many had seen it, all had heard it. It was guessed to have hit the earth the size of a football, which meant before it burnt up in the atmosphere it must have been pretty big. Some were saying that it had been seen and heard as far away as Tammin. And others that it must have come down nearby but that no one would ever find it. Some knew of windows being shattered, and all had thought it was another Big Quake – after all, Meckering, the centre of the biggest quake in living memory, had received three strong tremors (and probably many weaker ones) only in the last week. The atmosphere was, well, electric. Tracy, Tim and I could only say how odd we felt being away from the wheatbelt, down in the city, when it happened. How disconnected and frustrated we felt. People in the wheatbelt understand such feelings.

The show itself was buzzing with attendance and activity.

Sideshow alley was bigger than usual, and there (at fifteen) Tim located himself to contemplate and then try out the more intense rides. He was a little disappointed that this year I wouldn't be riding (reminding me of my various poems regarding the Cobra, the Twister and so on), as these moderated exposures to physical risk had always been part of our bonding. But I have been a little unwell recently, and thought it prudent I give them a miss this year. I can barely believe I am saying this – a life of risk has defined me in so many ways. So as Tim sported on the machines, Tracy and I wandered the displays, confirmed Mum's choices of photographs in the various categories (Tim rushed in later to have a quick look, but his main interest, along with the rides, is to talk birds and animals with people), and I spent an age examining the entries and winners of the various grain and crop categories. What was especially interesting was the display of Federation Wheat, being 'brought back' as a milling grain in a kind of historic re-envisioning of early broadacre farming. The worrying nationalistic and colonial undertones aside, it's actually a less manipulated grain than most, so it is of interest to me. But it's still, of course, a product of crossing and selective growth. William Farrer, touted as a 'pioneer' of Australian plant genetics, developed the strain by crossing Purple Straw and Yandilla varieties, producing a high-yielding and relatively rust-resistant wheat. The National Museum of Australia has a feature on Farrer and his work that connects with the pragmatics and the mythos of Australian farming. It quotes Farrer:

> In a new country like this, where the climate is so widely different and in many respects the very opposite of that of the country which, only a short time ago, was the home of the vast majority of our farmers … the traditional practices of the

> old country have to be unlearnt, in addition to entirely new ones learnt.
> [http://www.nma.gov.au/online_features/defining_moments/featured/federation-wheat]

This quote is not questioned or challenged, but it does work as an entry point into understanding the inherent damage to the land that comes with European-style broadacre farming in Australia. The 'unlearning' needed to extend (as it still does) to the whole notion of broadacre farming, to working often infertile soils to death, of clearing so that the hydraulics and functionality of the land are irreparably damaged, so the salt starts to rise. When I was working on the wheatbins as a protein sampler, I thought a great deal about wheat varieties – their yields, the hardness of the grain, the amount of protein, their susceptibility to disease, their responses to pesticides, herbicides and fungicides, their 'vulnerability' (or appeal!) to introduced and native insects. I also thought about hybridisation and experimented a little with grain growing. The creation of reliable strains of grain outside genetic modification is a process of trial and error. It was this thinking (and some tinkering) that led me to think, later, further about genetic modification and its risks, its hubris, and its bad science in terms of the health of the planet. GM cropping didn't get a foothold in Australia until relatively late in the new imperialism of seeds – Monsanto and other companies redefining the colonial by yoking growth with poison, resistance to threats and a creation of new (often undetermined) threats. I consider GM a farming of paradoxes and a paradox of farming. In the end, it is pure capitalist greed – food stocks vulnerable to profiteering, and the natural environment the expendable factor.

Agricultural shows in Western Australia attract political

parties, where they tout with the best and the worst of the show people. They too are a travelling sideshow. Seeing a deeply conservative government minister's posse of young men all dressed the same and walking as a unit was quite intimidating, an unwitting symbol of the rise of the far right in Australia. We avoided them. Even further out on the far-right margins, which in Australia are rapidly becoming a new centre, was the 'fringe' party with embittered 'Aussie battlers' touting anti-left conspiracy theories and displaying signs quoting Prince Philip as saying, 'Cull the human herd' … which, though a paraphrase, is actually along the lines of what Prince Philip did say. This frightening undercurrent of misanthropy is built around far-right bigotries that are very familiar to us further down the Avon Valley. York, being the 'oldest inland town' (it's said again and again and again) and one of the spokes from which the wheatbelt emanates, is largely conservative farming in its underpinning. As properties break up and get smaller, that conservatism sometimes segues into a fortress-bunker attitude: driving past you can see the Australian and Eureka flags. On the big farms the homesteads are often too far from the road for anyone to see the flags, or for the nationalists to bother displaying them.

Consider what these shows would look like if Aboriginal people were coordinating them (entirely), and maybe teaching others how to use the land without damaging it further. I find it distressing how little acknowledgement is made of whose land this is. But Aboriginal people are present and attend and tolerate the absurdities of an agricultural fertility rite that has meant destruction and dispossession for them. Noongar people are culturally generous.

But though the right and far right are always present at such shows, and function with impunity, different ways of seeing the land and belonging/unbelonging are also evident. The tree and plant stand, encouraging the replanting of damaged land with native species. The various community welfare groups. Even the Salvation Army guy who always (year in, year out) stands by the gate shaking his bucket for donations for the disadvantaged. Yes, that's there, too. A show is more complex than the sum of its parts, than the displays of farming machinery and the preservation of 'settler' ways.

As Tracy and I stood close to a camel, trying to read its expression, to understand what it was saying with its intense watching of us, I exchanged breath with it. It was breathing hard from carting people around the show. The show is full of the exploitation of animals – in many ways it's the basis of the event. Birds in small cages, sheep being rounded up by a sheep dog through the crowd, and the strangest and most anomalous animal–person interaction of all: the gymkhana. Horses and girls are still a powerful combination and conversation in the wheatbelt. Horse floats hauled by big pick-ups, usually by the 'horse women' mums of girls who travel from event to event over the year. The horses we watched were incredibly 'well-kept', and their riders clearly devoted to them (doting, actually). There was even a deep and obvious rapport between human and horse in most cases (not all – one rider and her 'skittish' horse were in obvious disagreement). However, as you'd expect, I have deep problems with the use of animals by humans in this fashion, though I fully acknowledge that many horse people care as much about 'their' horses as they do themselves. I have had family and friends for whom horses have been, to their minds, people. My brother rescued a horse once.

The breaking and use of horses has underwritten human 'advancement' and sustained human existence in many places in the world in such an extreme way that one might talk of human–horse civilisations rather than human civilisations. My uncle and cousins were horse people. As was my auntie, but it was my uncle who was a real 'horse man' – he went to his bush school in a horse and cart. They attended gymkhanas and kept a few horses on the farm. They truly loved their horses. Horses were omnipresent at Wheatlands. As a young girl visiting her sister on the farm, my mother would ride occasionally.

I admire and respect horses. I have felt intense closeness to horses at various times – not as a keeper or rider of horses (though I did ride them here and there when I was younger), but as someone encountering a horse and spending a few moments, or a short while, conversing with them. They converse with people, when they choose, as any horse lover will tell you.

I see horses in the district every day – I can interact with them in passing without having to 'own' them. Jam Tree Gully, before we arrived, was a horse property – now the arena is covered with trees. But my most intense interactions with ideas of horses have come about through the work of various students I've taught over the years. One, Siobhan Hodge, has recently published a book of poetry about human mistreatment of horses, and about her love and care for ill-treated survivors of the racing industry. On the night I launched that book, we drove from Jam Tree Gully to a city bookshop, and in doing so passed the 'glue works' where horses are boiled down. The knackery was 'cooking' horses that night and the stink spread from what had until a few years ago been the fringe of the city into its heartland.

We reconnect with Tim and go to leave. We have seen fewer people we know than usual – family members are actually over at Northam for this year's showtime hockey match – and the crowds are thick, but a cousin won the under-eighteen art competition, and other relatives have won this cropping award or that craft award. And we had one radical encounter – a poet-activist of the region who dwells on an abstracted spiritual plain was generous enough to come up and introduce himself and say how much he respected all our environmental activisms, and what we are trying to do. It was generous of him.

Walking back we passed a nexus of York gum, wire fence, and long sprayed-dead grass, where earlier zebra finches had been cavorting. Tim was disappointed to see they'd moved on, but we picked up our chat on when we'd last seen zebra finches over at Jam Tree Gully – always up the top of the block, never in the lower reaches. Finches were the bird which showed me that the salt wasn't the bitter end. Out beyond the tamarisks my cousins had planted to reclaim the damage there was a patch of needlebush, and in that protected realm the zebra finches nested, zipping back and forth (as I wrote in an early poem of mine) like apparitions. I would crawl into the centre of the clump of needlebush trees, cut up by the sharp leaves, and sit for hours listening to and watching these intense small birds with their black and white checked tails ('zebra' – the colonial transference of descriptor says it all) and orange-red triangular scoop beaks. I thought their quickness a sign of intense thinking, of working to make sure all was safe and okay. They taught me how to write poetry, out on an island in the salt, far from any other human. I went in there without a rifle, and without thoughts of hunting or survival. I went to learn, and those birds – having to recall me after long gaps of absence – would be cautious at first, then flit around me. I thought of it as acceptance, whether it was or not. My imagination flared and lit, but without bringing a conflagration. I kept it burning inside my head, and left them alone. I watched nesting, I saw chicks being fed. And translating this aloneness of watching those 'wild' finches is how I find connection with people – to value their company and remain who I am inside, too. Community and the self and peace – equally important, and the core of my anarchism.

~

Tim and I walked from the Tower up to Woodbridge and back along the 'middle' Swan River on the eastern bank yesterday, towards the Scarp. We spotted numerous bird species, including little cormorants, magpies, pink and grey galahs, corellas, pelicans, striated pardalotes, red wattlebirds, black ducks, wood ducks, a straw-necked ibis among six or seven sacred ibis, an egret, a white-cheeked honeyeater, spotted doves, singing honeyeaters, brown honeyeaters, rainbow lorikeets, twenty-eight parrots, willie wagtails, and 'feral' pigeons. One of the most disturbing sights was of a pigeon head sitting on its own on the path as we emerged from the river walk back into the suburbs that are increasingly closing in on the river. Nearby, there were feathers strewn around – probably a cat. The eye looked intensely at us, living in death. It was traumatic, especially for Tim.

The Helena River walk we do – usually seeing a mob of feral goats, which have got to know us quite well – is less formalised as a walk than the Swan River walk. The two rivers converge opposite Point Reserve in Guildford, a couple of kilometres downriver from where we started our walk on the Swan yesterday. These colonial namings stick in my craw, but I use them to avoid appropriating Noongar names. (Sometimes I do use the Noongar names, but only where I have obtained permission from elders.) Interestingly, when we were standing at Woodbridge watching the river flowing rapidly past (it was the end of the rain season), an Aboriginal elder was explaining to some visitors how if you keep moving against the run of water it will take you up into the Hills where the Swan becomes the Avon River, and if you go with the water it will take you down to the sea at Fremantle. The other branch of this system of rivers is the Canning (another colonial requisitioning), upon which both Tracy and I spent much of our childhoods, at different points on the river – she was at a thin part of the river; I was at a broader part. Together, these rivers form the lifeblood of the region, and yet they have suffered so much through development. Only last week one of the rare and unique Swan River dolphins died – a mother whose calf (as I write) has not been sighted since. This dolphin was found dead on Como beach (a thin strip of river sand) entangled with fishing tackle and trailing plastic bags. I have not told Tim yet, though I will.

For Tim, the river is also the way home, in a figurative sense. The waters it carries also come from Jam Tree Gully – sliding down the hill into Bird Gully, flowing through the gully down into the valley and down into Toodyay Brook, and on into the Avon, the Swan, to where we were yesterday, looking across at the old colonial vineyards with their sprayed banks, and the encroaching housing estates. The river system needs to breathe, and closing it in with houses is not helping anyone. Thirty or so years ago I joined Aboriginal protesters and others trying to stop the redevelopment of the brewery on the Swan River below Kings Park – a place know to the Whadjuk people as Goonininup, a place strongly associated with the sacred snake, the Wagyl (which made the river and all around it), and a powerful Dreamtime place. The struggle was lost and the government of the time, despite union opposition, pushed ahead and built luxury apartments overlooking the river. The then state premier later became a friend of mine and she would now surely oppose any such development. She works passionately for the environment and Aboriginal rights. This, for me, is a further illustration of how power always leads to wrong decisions, and always leads to ethical compromises. I have been friends with a number of politicians over the years, often opposing their policies, but finding the people they are outside the structures of government (and industry) power are very different. I oppose the structures of power because they are the vehicles for oppression. The Wagyl is to be respected in all ways. There are places on the Avon River near Northam where one should only go if a handful of riverbank sand is thrown into the river to appease the Wagyl, and there are sacred places a Wadjula like me shouldn't go at all, and I don't. I have been shown the channels the Wagyl grooved in Mount Matilda outside York as it made its way down to form the river, and I respect the spirituality and geology of this. I respect the cosmology.

Soon we will all be back home at Jam Tree Gully! None of us can cope away from it for too long. It's as if we've reset an internal compass as well as a clock to work with the rhythms and influences of granite and light there. Nesting season for many birds will be in full swing, and reptiles will be stirring. And the grass will be growing long. And the firebreaks will soon need doing. And though there has been more rain than average these last two months, we will still be watching our water supply because it's very possible that next year will bring drought, and excessive use now will mean difficulty, even suffering, later. One must always keep an eye to the future – protect it, respect it, and give it a chance to be what it would be without more human-induced damage. But I keep going back for regular check-up visits, to see how things are faring in our extended absence.

~

Arrived at JTG and the phone line was dead. It might sound funny to most people in Australia, or the US, or the UK, but we're on a landline out where we are, and there's little or no mobile phone reception. That's a good thing, but the landline is how we communicate with the world – to send these drafts to the publisher, to converse with like minds. We're on a priority line because of my Graves issues, so I hope it will be fixed soon. It's the most basic technology, but it's still technology. And as we plan to convert the house to entirely self-contained solar power, and make another step away from the grid, the phone line will remain until they forcibly cut it off because old copper-wire landlines are being phased out. But nestled in the hills on the edge of the plains, reception is difficult anyway, so maybe we'll be one of the few who retain a landline. We hope so. Slower speeds, but so what? It was only a couple of years ago we were able to go off dial-up internet – an internet so slow that most web pages wouldn't load and emails over a couple of megabytes were impossible to send (and even a couple of megabytes took an age to go through). But this is how we choose to live. Jam Tree Gully is about a technology of ideas, not a heavy footprint of energy use and consumerism. It is about a refuge and a non-violent resistance, but also an awareness of the world. We keep informed, we read about technology so we can understand what it is we're choosing to deny. The old landline has been out a couple of times over recent years – usually caused by strong rains flooding the connector box up on the main road and shorting the line. A fault on the line, as they say. Always strange when they say, Give us a call if it's not fixed, as we can't call anyone! It seems our absence brings problems.

It also seems as if we have a purpose for being at JTG – keeping an eye on things, ensuring the animals and plants are watched over. I say this because all around JTG the little and big clearings gather pace, and people literally cross borders to push back vegetation. We have to be vigilant. But one good thing – though the entire roadside has been poisoned (the annual Roundup-ing of the district), the shire workers have respected our request for them not to spray the northern edge of JTG. No, we don't think in terms of fences and borders in terms of property, but we do think in terms of zones of protection and respect – porous, yes, liminal, yes, but not open to abuse and yet another colonisation within the colonisation … subsets of occupation.

Jam Tree Gully is now in expansive and intense flowering mode. The jam trees are an explosive yellow, pollen dispersing across the valley in clouds. Bees are electric with the abundance. Birds are wound up with nesting, and the cross-talk is exciting and also haunting. All the fears we have of raising children in a world we are ecologically destroying are also felt on behalf of the next generation of birds. But like our children, they are also part of the healing, the resistance to the damage. Having been staying in the Tower in the city of sirens, as Tracy calls it, we more and more realise how essential it is that the resistance that is Jam Tree Gully is maintained. I come home to the mass flowering, and see that even the flat-topped yates planted only five or six years ago are now in bloom, and fruits are already visible. This is the first year they've fully flowered, and what's exciting is that though they prefer swampier ground, the micro-system that's been created between the lucerne trees along the firebreaks and the stands of York gum has created a suitable habitat. Blue wrens, willie wagtails, silvereyes, red-capped robins are working the insects and flowerings, and knitting their trajectories to the cascading trajectories of life on the block. It is exciting.

We all yearn so much for this place we share that it pains me to have to leave. We will be back full-time in a couple of weeks. It gets closer. We'll be back as the days get much warmer, heading towards heat. The heat that dominates all. The dry that will come and could go on and on. To the evergreen world of vegetation that contains its own haunting – a dying-back from excessive heat, hot winds, lack of water. There is lush growth from so much rain (the most in August for fifty years), but that fast growth can be vulnerable when the drying-out comes, and though we have no salt at JTG, surrounding lands affected by salinity will be waterlogged and summer will bring the growth of white crystalline cities of death. And with the waterlogging and salinity, the trees, even fairly salt-tolerant trees, will be laid bare as skeletons in the heat of December and January and on and on. They are on the verge of premature death, brought on by land clearing and climate change. Despite their apparent hardiness and durability, the evergreens are vulnerable – when leaf loss comes, it usually signals the loss of life. But sometimes, back from the rootstock, new growth … and we always pin hope on that. Never give in. Even when we are told human-induced climate change is irreversible we refuse to give in. It's too easy to give in – too many people want to resign themselves to a dying planet. We don't. The green flourishing of JTG contains its own ghosts, and the ground the spirits of many whose land was taken from them. We owe them all respect, we owe it to them to repair. This is their land. To emerge from this constructed refuge we've made is reason for rhapsody. The pain is the pain and can never be glossed over, but birds and roos and echidnas and reptiles and trees are portals to decolonisation.

A few things from the check-up on the state of being at JTG. Large roo scats in chunks suggest a big boomer is around, and paths through the long green wild oats show a mob has been laying down new routes around the block. I say 'new' as they are outside their usual patterns, working a way through to the best grazing areas. They enjoy moving from treed shelter during the day to open grassed areas in the evening through to dawn. As I look around the block, I find myself staring at the heavily lichened granites clustered around old York gums just north-west of the house – or rather, the old York gums that have emerged over the decades from the granite outcrop. I rarely go up there because it's a favourite echidna haunt, and I don't like disturbing them (we see them rarely). Sadly, driving up, I saw a large, mature echidna recently hit in the middle of the road – crossing near the falls where we pick Tim up from the school bus. I study those granites long and hard, and feel there's something I've missed about them over many years. The looking hard and not seeing interests me, but I won't climb up to them – I will leave them be. I note the great tank's water levels, judging by the crazed seams of constrained leaks and their dressing of algae, which relies on the water cohesion to stay 'submerged' on the outside curve of the concrete, fusing light and water and plantae … the excitement of twin chlorophylls and 'open air' all in tension. Even on a cool day, the concrete curve of the tank feels warm to touch, and warmer where there's no water – my usual method of testing levels. But it's full now, and a tepidness informs touch with ambiguity, a fuzzy logic of situating our future vis-à-vis water supply. I am still thinking about the scabs of lichen on the granite flaking as new plates form. The precise points of rock changing, its old radiation worked by the fungus and algal fusion, their conversation of branching and increase.

But it's not that, not entirely – it's the gap between the rocks, the underneath where the echidnas dwell, rest – there's something else I detect. A small marsupial? It's a hunch. Just the other day, at his school in the hills, Tim came face to face with a possum in a tree fork – they stared at each other for thirty seconds. I am looking up at the outcrop, staring at something I can't see, and shouldn't see.

Jam Tree Gully is no paragon, but it has to stand for a different way of doing things across the board. Not just ecologically, but also socially and politically. A different way of considering presence. We are part of it – it is not a reflection of us. Indeed, as water rushes down the hill, and as the sun dries stalks to glassiness, the reflective surfaces are fleeting, temporary. Driving behind a large SUV, I read the stickers 'Want More Grunt? Then Root More Pigs' ('root' in Australia being a slang word for sexual intercourse), and 'Unlock More Snatch', printed above a bolted shackle. The guy had his arm hanging out the driver's window, tatts bulging – his body language and the face watching me in his side mirror said, Come on, try overtaking me! There is furious sexist racist anti-environmental rage out there – it's real, and not to try and understand its presence is to consign all efforts towards a healing to oblivion. The resentment is linked to an aggressive form of fear, a desire to strike out at what's not understood and what seems a threat to a 'way of life'. Australia doesn't have an equivalent to the Second Amendment, but it has the psychology of one. What is under threat is ambiguous, but in the end it comes down to 'sovereignty' and 'property'. These people want to occupy the land and pre-empt any (perceived) threats to their control of space. But unless you can talk with them, they will stop you talking. It's as if language is something to be mistrusted, and yet it's in language we might find a way through.

I believe poetry can speak to all, and not dilute its impact in doing so. To write only one type of poetry is to deny language to people who might participate if given a choice. There's a way through this. There's a way to lessen the violence and dampen the latent violence. Sometimes, having a yarn with a neighbour who hates what you represent can save more trees and animals (and humans!) than almost anything else.

~

This week Tim is doing work experience in the York library and staying with my mother and Guru, in the shadow of Walwalinj mountain. It's an important reconnection for him with a town and an area that are pivotal to his understanding of the world, and which he loves. York, Ohio, Cambridge, Schull – these are the places in which his sense of land and nature are confirmed. A couple of days ago, he and I went for a walk in the Brixton Street Wetlands Nature reserve, down in the city, in an effort to support the protests to stop damage of peripheral wetlands. In a long-planned 'development' of an adjoining area, with its old stands of marri gums so needed by endangered red-tailed black cockatoos for food and roosting places, the wholesale flattening of a large slice of land into an industrial park means issues with hydrology as well as removal of remaining habitat. Even an area of river gums, not native to this area but planted decades ago, is an issue, because they've been adopted as a roost by the cockatoos. In writing a poem of support for the campaign, I tried to talk about how in the absence of native trees, these old stands have become important. And the clearing of majestic old-growth marri trees is a disgrace. Just the other day, down in Gelorup, near the small coastal city of Bunbury, a four-hundred-year-old giant jarrah was cut down in the night by vandals. (Developers are trying to get permission to build a road through there and were having to find a slightly different route.) Gelorup is where my 'pioneer' great-grandfather, one of my foresting ancestors, died.

The wetlands are one of the most biodiverse places left on the planet, even though there's little left, and a massive traffic bridge has been built through the middle of them. Surrounded by houses, shops and light industry, they persist. There are more carnivorous plants in those few square kilometres than in all of Europe, we are told, and it is one of the few places the robin redbreast bush (a melaleuca) still has a strong grip, drinking from pools and the wet ground. Quenda (a marsupial) live in the wetlands, as do numerous other creatures. They bristle with life. Tracy once lived on the edges of those wetlands, in a run-down house after her family fell on hard times. It's where she originally got asthma, but she loved the swamp, and tells the story of walking past the reeds and hearing a 'whoo-whoo' and running home to her mum to tell her there were people hiding in the reeds, and her mum laughing and telling her it was the frogs. In fact, moaning frogs. And Tim and I heard squelching frogs while we were there (sign-bearing froglets). The next day, Tim was in York. One of our strict policies in moving between bush habitats is to ensure we have clean shoes – dieback pathogens and other bio-contaminants can be transferred so easily from one environment to another. It's why we never walk in heavily dieback-affected forest, and we have asked people who have come from such areas not to bring their vehicles (or bike, on one occasion) down from the top road to Jam Tree Gully – we do not want dieback there, or anywhere. I will send Tim the poem I have written for the protest.

In the watery zone the trees speak life force

In the watery zone the trees speak life force
against the loss, especially when the dry comes.
Fruits of marri trees stock the skies, but the red
and orange tail flashes of cockatoos coming in to roost
are short-circuited by the sudden, brutal absence.

And so many years ago stands of river gums were planted,
having grown and added to the slimmed pickings, to add body
to spaces hacked up, providing refuge for these long-lived birds.
Now to be felled and fibred – a mockery. Trees that take the
watery force
into birdsleep between sky and earth, raucous and vibrant.

'Reshaped', it won't grow fast enough as the canopy world
is deleted across the coastal plain. And developers don't *get*
the interlinked destinies of wet ground and vegetation, of Yule
and Crystal Brooks and precinct and vicinity – nor consequence.
The edge of the wetlands is still the wetlands and the buffer

is each step you take over what was, because it still *is*, and connects.
Today, walking the edges of the Brixton Street Nature reserve,
not wanting
to go too deep in because quenda and bobtails, native bees and
butcherbirds,
need places beyond our steps given what's left, we knew the
silent drinking
of the redbreast bush, and the wodjalok sliding from marri
branch down fast

to yellow wattle bloom, while the passed-cold-wet-months of sign-bearing
froglets'
prime time, and yellow buttercups tracking the light for suggestions
of flower-loving insects, were cross-talked by dragonfly angles, abrupt
over the buff waters of pools tuned by melaleucas, nymphs of other cycles
close to the surface which something sprints across into shadow,

a native grass tree offering fresh flower spikes – the kind of sustainable
development the wetlands know about. Bobtail eating flowers to glow
from the inside out is a joy no heavy earthmoving equipment can recognise,
nor the drawers of precinct maps – not really. We can live within this moment
remaining from before the exploitation – we can cross, too, if we're careful.

We all need somewhere to land, to eat, to deliberate and envision lives,
but not where the cockatoos eat and sleep, not where carnivorous plants thrive.

~

As the third point of the triangulation of the last few days, Tracy and I went from dropping Tim at York across to Jam Tree Gully. We will be back home proper in a week. But all focus for us comes back to Jam Tree Gully, and through its lens we see and understand the world better. Guru had been over, mowing the paddocks, which have been heavily replanted with trees, and in which, fantastically, many self-sown saplings have taken root over the last year. I was pleased to see he'd managed to detect them all, and hadn't mowed over any. When I say 'paddocks', it's a little misleading, as it's really all one zone now – all the internal fences have been removed, other than one on the edge of the house bank which stops people slipping down the hill (and is easily got around by native animals). There are still corner posts from five or six paddock divisions from the previous tenant, because they're steel and set in concrete and hard to remove. Trees grow next to them now.

As I walked around I saw how close Guru had come to the beehive in the hollow of the largest York gum down low on the block – he said they'd chased him out. Many years ago I was also chased by bees from this hive, and got four or five stings and tore my calf muscle as I clambered across a pile of rocks and fallen branches to escape. We leave them in peace. The mowing marks went right up to the hive, then abruptly stopped! The markers of incident! The strange dynamic between intrusion and withdrawal, mapping and unmapping. The signs of Jam Tree Gully. I reconnected by walking, as I always do, listening to the nesting encodings of weebills, thornbills, red-capped robins, wrens, twenty-eight parrots, magpies, crows, silvereyes, grey shrike-thrushes (a pair followed me for a while, watching me with tilted heads and one eye each, speaking to each other to share the vision of reappearance). As a kid, I would have been walking all over in bare feet, but now I was reconnecting through shoes, though the muscles did similar work. Later, talking over the wrench it takes to leave again, if only for a week, Tracy started discussing Gerard Manley Hopkins's lines in 'God's Grandeur' – 'And wears man's smudge and shares man's smell: the soil / Is bare now, nor can foot feel, being shod' – in the context of consumer-fetishised humanity too often losing contact with the land through their accoutrements, through being 'shod'. And though we agree that in many ways it's not relevant to apply Hopkins to wheatbelt Western Australia, it's also strangely resonant and apposite – he understood the deep loss of connection with what matters through such a buffering, such a disconnection from the earth, the land, the dirt we walk on. It's something Yamaji poet Charmaine Papertalk Green captures so brilliantly and constantly in her poems of feet, walking, and contact with her country. Both she and I wrote poems in which we talk of doublegees – those violent expressions of colonialism in their 'attack' on bare feet – and how we might overcome them, and keep walking, our feet touching the land. Charmaine's land, and the land I walk by invitation, or hoping for permission.

~

Mowing. Guru was in a vehicle rollover last night after leaving Jam Tree Gully – he'd just been mowing our top paddocks between the trees. He was run off a gravel road and the utility with the mower on the back caught a culvert as he pulled over to avoid a collision and the ute went through a fence and rolled. The oncoming driver who caused it didn't stop but fortunately someone found him a short while later (and it's a very isolated gravel road so he was lucky) and he is in hospital down in the city – Tracy is driving my mum down now. He's okay, but has twenty-two staples in his head where his toolbox connected in the somersault. And the seatbelt caused injury, though it also saved him. This is the pastoral reality. *Mowing.* We were all in trauma and shock last night, and Mum was so distressed. But there's something to be said about rural people when the 'chips are down' – the guy who found him rang his wife and she came out from a farmhouse with towels (Guru was covered in blood from head to foot) and they cleaned him up and looked after him. Out in the 'middle of nowhere'. And they were kind to Mum.

I step outside and smell the cut grass from Guru's mowing yesterday, and see a juvenile black-headed monitor rush from some leaf litter along the side of the house, and the smell bites deep, bitter-sweet. Jam Tree Gully is both temporary and always, belonging and unbelonging, intrusive and representing hope for restitution, and Guru is alive. Those pastoral traditions I write against haunt me, always.

Mowing reality

This utterance does
not fit a long tradition
and there's nothing
pastoral about it –

the mowing
was done, then
the mower loaded
onto the utility

vehicle, then
the vehicle
was driven off
the edge

of a gravel road
into a culvert,
twisting through a fence,
so it rolled on its top

then upright again
in a field of darkness.
The driver was injured,
the mower destroyed –

the mowing machine,
not the mower –
the machine's
operator.

And when someone
found the mower (human)
and the mower (machine)
he rang his wife

to come with towels,
to mop up the blood
but not the oil – the machine
wrecked beyond

repair, on Mokine Road
which is a gravelly
nightmare, as some of you –
few of you – might know.

And now I look out
at the moved lines
where capeweed flowers
spring against the cut –

interstellar smiles –
but the high grass
is gone and songbirds
are too full-mouthed

to sing about revelation,
bonanza, the fruits
of fall. The mower,
the mower, the mowed.

But as with Ohio, as with Schull, as with Cambridge, the rural, for all its social complexity and the damage done, is capable of coming through with the most intense sharing and care for others' wellbeing. This is a generic statement, but one with personal inflections. We are now two days after the accident and Tracy receives this email from Mum, and it says much, and embeds the hope we all might have in the world's repair.

Dear Tracy,

Just got back from inspecting the crash. Marvellous people – the farmer said he would fix the fence and he took all the valuable stuff back to the farm homestead. Really big place. We just collected most of it. We have to decide what to do about getting the mower here but they said it can stay there until we decide, then they will take a vehicle down to load it on to (probably G's) ute for us. Anyway, we just got back and need something to eat as we only had half our breakfast. The crash site is extremely dangerous and the farmer rang the shire to complain (again!). If John had gone off the crumbly edge into the deep gully he would have had no chance. You can't see the vehicles coming in the opposite direction because of a hill. Will send photos when I have had a cup of tea etc.

Love,
Wendy.

p.s. His wife is absolutely lovely and knows L. I judged her photo best exhibit at the show. When the dust settles I will have her round for a cup of tea to talk travel and photography as she loves both. Much younger than me but that doesn't matter.

And we are almost home, almost back at Jam Tree Gully.

~

Heat is the silent underpinning of this rural memoir, as is drought. This year's was a wet winter, but there have been numerous dry years and a severe drought some years back. It is hot now as I write – always 4 or 5 degrees hotter up here than in the city, especially when a heat ridge forms. Dust isn't a cliché, it's what rules our dwelling. In preparing the firebreaks a few weeks ago, I was so covered in, saturated with dry red dust – the dust merging with my mucous membranes, filling the inside of my body as sludge, an internal bleeding and clotting – that my clothes (also festooned with oat seeds and cut wild oat stalk fragments) were beyond repair, beyond cleaning. I was the raddle man of the block, always conscious of the firebreak as an act of erosion as well as protection.

And in the humidity of summers in Ohio and the fens of Cambridgeshire, dryness and moisture have equivocal relationships as storms or rain events maintain a basal metabolic greenness. But here, when the storms come, even where they bring an eruption of green, a dryness rapidly sweeps back in, eviscerating, crackling lichen across the granite boulders. The humidity making its dirt-sweat patterns across skin, quickly gasps and is gone and a dryness you struggle to breath dominates again. For six months of the year at least, this is the reality. And that dryness, taken over the years, is dramatically increasing.

This year, preparation for the fire season has been difficult because of late and heavy spring rains. Don't get me wrong, we delight in the extra water, which will keep us fluid for at least three or four more weeks than last year, but the regrowth after grass-cutting, the green tinge of forlorn hope, comes out of the deeper wet of the soil – the same wet that will keep the trees alive if rain doesn't come for longer than usual, which is likely the case – and has to be cut again. So it's work, and it's stressful against deadlines, but it's much much better as a sign.

After days of cutting and raking firebreaks (trying to avoid more heavy machinery work), we are ready enough. More to be done, but the essentials are in place. I think of the waterbag hanging in the shadehouse in those eviscerating seventies summers when global warming really got its hooks in, riding up on the residues from the Industrial Revolution to the present day, and I think of Eunice Newton Foote working in the US in the 1850s and her work largely ignored. That waterbag sweating to cool – we loved it. As we did waterbags hanging from roo bars on the front of utes. The insect-spattered hessian belied the cool water inside. It's disturbing for me to look back on, but I can taste the water.

Sunstroke, the doctor over me a haze, a delusion, a hallucination after such long exposure out on the salt as a child. Enveloped by the crystalline whiteness of expeditioning with rifle and pack, mapping and talking to space, to myself. And the summer sun. Treated for sunstroke; verbs and adjectives come into their own and the nouns of encounter are lost. This colonising of catastrophe, this risk of death in a space of death-making.

Two days ago Tracy and I went down to the remnants of the roost in Edward Street, Kenwick – one of the four remaining great roosts for endangered red-tailed black cockatoos. It was a disaster area – the brutality of Linc Property and the Gosnells city council and the McGowan government of Western Australia, and the failure of the federal government to intervene (no surprises there), and the magnificent marri tree (up to one hundred years old) where Nev had gone to his platform in the canopy as protector now cut to a stump, a stump Nev's mum said had marked her hand with its blood when she placed it on the cut line. And in the heat, I yelled poems and spoke in sadness and anger, and the sun burnt its mark of crisis into me.

Nev's tree is now a bloody stump

No form can contain the grief of this poem
this elegy which is residue of a shattered tree,

a marri, brought down with cuts and bruises,
dismembered. Sounds gory, doesn't it? – it bloody

well *is*, people! It is a slaughter, it is disrespect

of ontogenesis on a massive scale – small, big,

an eternity to construct. Battered in a moment.
Not treated with the pride bestowed on the big steel

sheds and concrete aprons, the sump to catch
the creek that still flows out of the wastes,

forlorn and sclerotherapised, so beloved
and then forgotten by the planners

and their mates in cahoots with the profiteers'
endgame. Nev's mum said she put her hand

on the dying stump and it bled an imprint,
her hand lifted to show the blood of world.

Her pain is all our pain – she has the pattern
of the shattered tree inside her now

and carries it around so we can remember.
How many other lives will we let down?

Jiddy jiddy flies manic, wondering where
it *is* now, where what was has gone, where

it will land to contemplate its moods.
It catches a fly, and lets it go. Lost.

That evening, both Tracy and I were sick with tension and heat exposure, covered in the white limestone dust of the developer's road-making, their concreting and stealing of habitat. A drive to Perth from Jam Tree Gully is case after case of this – every day, the remaining great trees going. Science consoles itself and desires science fiction to be made real. They should read Ursula Le Guin.

The heat is here, among us, cooking, drying out, extracting what moisture it can to feed the vacuum. 'Nature abhors a vacuum'? Plant that here, in this ground hardening with the drying, ground that will become so hard it won't be broken. And if they do break it, which they will, it will be for extraction, not growth, not the vegetal renewal of the here. The now.

So I call in the heat of my life. The beach sunburns, the dehydrations, the heatstroke, the sunstroke, the skin cancers burnt and cut out. The writing against listlessness, the working outdoors in hat and in shade where possible – struggling to protect the shade trees. Of working not to spark, not to strike a rock with metal which will ignite and rewrite the pattern, against the natural cycles of fire and germination. The burn-off people burn and burn and burn and species vanish – don't grow with the germination, the cracking open of seed by fire, because they are burnt before they can properly seed themselves. But in this heat everything will burn – fences, houses, machine sheds … and the burning-offs that get out of hand, as earlier this year, when the warnings went out for high winds and still the authorities burnt the bushland and catastrophe came of it. Heat and drying are the volatility encouraged by more clearing, more deforestation. The forests burn more and more intensely because all the pressure is on them and the mass clearing has made the world tinder. Conserve to survive. Reduce imprint to survive.

It is so hot now sweat is occluding my vision and my ability to write from memory, of how to configure the page and even how to form letters. My body works to keep my brain cool enough to function, to transcribe the words I hear-see inside. Heat works to prevent the writing – the stimulus is the paradox. Embalmed in the volatile oil of the York gums – eucalyptus reassurance, the odour that is the trail through life, a thermometer, a broken thermostat. Rufous whistler – thunderbird – calls out from its high point in the York gum outside this window, its russet chest deflecting the glare off the surface array, calls out because it can hear heavy machinery across the valley … machinery, remover of perches, builder/s of heat. Running hot.

Cicadas. Will they be always? Always be? I sit in the extreme heat waiting for Tim's bus. Late afternoon and the cicadas are bursting out of the shadows along the creek that runs alongside Toodyay Road on its way to the polished granite faces of Noble Falls. The withering shade – almost all the flooded gums are dying, cicadas clinging to the bark, clicking away the time of shorter lives vis-à-vis these ancient trees. Even the younger trees, with cicadas' moulted skins, are dying. It's the same all the way up to Toodyay along waterways – this sad refrain of agricultural run-off, of herbicides to kill off the weed growth, of the confused water table. Cicadas are a childhood of wherever Tracy was in Kelmscott or around the base of the Scarp, wherever I was near the Canning River or in the banksia woodlands or up at the farm under the haunting wandoo and salmon gums arched over gravel roads, in the jam tree and York gum woodlands. Even out on the salt, that burnt-out eye, cicadas in the evening among the needlebushes. How did they emerge through the silty mud, the crystalline scalds? Cicadas counting down time, and counting back to converse with those whose land it is past, present, future, beyond any conception of time colonials have imposed on it. This is not romantic, this is the hard science of country. This is the truth cicadas speak because they carry the knowledge, the cosmology, speaking across day to night, from down here to up there, emanating. I recall that mantra from when I first understood speech: It's stinking hot … it's going to be a stinker today. But most finding comfort in the cicadas without articulating why … or maybe they did and I didn't listen or understand what I was hearing?

Thirty-nine degrees today. Mid-November. We hear that last night dry lightning strikes took out thousands of hectares of about to be harvested wheat crops in Wubin, Buntine, Dalwallinu, Kalannie, Pithara – the towns we pass through as we drive to Geraldton to see Stephen and Dzu. The crops are just starting to be taken off around here – headers in the paddocks, plumes of dust, water trucks sitting on the firebreaks, anxious.

~

Back in Schull and walking the lower reaches of the copper-seamed mountain, Mount Gabriel, down to the Colla Heights, looking out over Long Island Bay and Long Island to Fastnet Rock and the lighthouse. Here, the rural is a matter of angles – those small farms, even smaller home blocks, and then the holiday homes. Many machines grinding into rock, to chip away at the old red sandstone, to level it out for the pad of a new postmodern cottage that will look out past the Teardrop of Ireland, to the eternal desiring for America. In another new build, angled away from the rising rock of the peninsula, a fake dog or fake pig will appear at the feature window, always sun-hungry in this mostly overcast place, looking out over the islands of the bay, islands where one or two families live and where before the famine many lived under difficult conditions, farming.

Farming here is sheep and cows. Pasture can be lush with slurry and rain, but the meagre soils over rock hold little outside the grip of winter-lit gorse, soon burnt back against advice because it's the traditional way. I walk and talk with farmers. I always do. Disagreeing about everything, but interested enough to catch their interest, or their curiosity. Hay-cutting and baling fascinate me, though I disagree with the ends to which the hay and silage are put. And this time, *back*, we are delighted if slightly astonished that there are Go Vegan billboards alongside major roads – 'Dairy takes babies from their mothers' with a huge picture of a cow and a calf. Andy Warhol with purpose. I wonder how one would fare down the back roads, so narrow a car can barely pull aside if another approaches, and tractors make their own rights of way, casting pads of mud that shape and reshape under boot, runner, car tyre, the fields spread onto the macadam, building up a bed for a grass layer running down the centre.

Rurality here is changing, as it is in many if not most places around the world (slowly or rapidly) – *and who would have thought it possible!* That's more than rhetorical – the meat and dairy industries here are entrenched in a manipulation of cultural identity built around the slaughter of cows, around a rootedness in stone and tribe. *The Táin*, epic myth of 'identity', I've tried to rewrite from blowback and post-colonial residuality. I can't succeed, but I can see Christmas dinners care of Moodley Manor – a meat chef who went vegan years ago, whom we used to support with purchases of his vegan foodstuffs. Purchasing is not a power, but to not purchase meat is an empowerment of animals and their rights. And today Tracy saw an article in an Irish magazine called *Stellar* about one in five young people here believing the entire world would become vegan by 2030. This energy is more than a trend, more than a social media proliferation of connectivity and defining against tradition, it is a shared ethical awareness. And now the Taoiseach has upset right-wingers by saying he's going to eat less meat to reduce his carbon footprint. It happens not because of social media (the sell social media companies and hardware manufacturer destroyers of the planet would have us believe), but in spite of it. It happens because biospheric collapse is imminent and young people can see this. And when phone and other fetishised consumer technologies are called out and abandoned, and linked with animal and biospheric rights, we will have a change that will tip things back in favour of life – all life! And the rural shifts, the tolerance for new ways of 'farming' that aren't abusive and damaging in multiplicitous ways, are where it has to begin and stick. And if it can happen in traditional and 'isolated' spaces, it will thwart the factory farmers and mass marketeers of abuse and damage, of suffering. This is a slow and bloodless revolution.

Last time I did this 16-k walk, an infection in my foot got the better of me. It was said back then that I might lose my foot, even my leg. But through good care I got through, writing small poems of limited syllable count in bed. In bed, my politics of unbelonging came as unstuck as the sheets when I was feverish – I *was* of there where I last walked, and of the cottage bedroom where I was bound, because sickness (and the kind treatment of medicos and Tracy) made it so. So walking it again today in winter sunshine, the first day in almost three weeks in which the sun has properly shone, was a rewriting of fate, a reconnecting with an absolute of presence, being here, 'enforced' belonging.

So, here I am. Again. Walking, gathering, collating. I write a poem in my head as I go, accruing data, and remapping the familiar map because even one's own internal (de)mapping wants to remain the same when it can't and it shouldn't. I see an albino dove and I am thinking of its issues of connection and belonging – cherished or denied, or is its state of *difference* irrelevant? I think of the modes of greeting others walking, of touching a cap or not. Some people, certainly the mail person doing the back roads in a little van, remember me. We all smile at each other, or just nod.

I search a tormented hawthorn tree on the edge of a boggy area for signs of the twine that dead ravens had been suspended from – all traces gone. But a *dead car* under a few trees that survived recent Storm Ophelia, encased in moss, is still there. And everywhere tossed bags of Beef Improver, and the 180-degree movements of shedded cows looking out over the bars and through the bars over the threads of hay to the sea, to islands, maybe thinking of the 6.5-second intervals between flashes of the great and foreboding Fastnet lighthouse, on its rock hurled by a giant out to sea. We have been here during storms that have sent waves reaching up high towards the lantern. Once, an earlier version of the lighthouse was swept away. The coast around here is full of shipwrecks, and as the migrant ships passed the Mizen on their way to America, coffin ships and those slightly better off, the rocks of the island drew them, it is much attested. And at Crookhaven on the same peninsula, Marconi triangulating radio signals with Fastnet and a ship at sea heralding the doom of our age: the communications revolution whereby we announce the end we have made.

But in the cow fields is not the answer. The cows are unfree, and the methane rises. It is early January and a steady 10 degrees day and night, and the fuchsia hedges are flowering, along with roses and hibiscuses in winter gardens. This is more than the Gulf Stream flowing by and more than an anomalous year – the shift here is as dramatic as the misreading of cordyline 'palms' as tropical, which they're not, but they are introduced from the cooler coastal regions of New Zealand. The garden of Rosewood is fed by a stream that runs down from Mount

Gabriel with its twin domes of navigation, of sky routes, now lit up at night and jokily prompting UFO sightings from visitors. On that old mountain where the last wolf was hunted out in the late eighteenth century, and where Neolithic copper mines lure those desperate to connect with something past the past. And when the year is thin at Halloween, *something* crosses over here and maybe on Knockaphuca. Messages from different parts of Australia tell us it's hotter than ever before. *Communications technology* – charge your device from mid-air, making contact with a surface. Energy drain.

The walk, composed and jotted down on the way, this rural immersion outside the holiday season, the 'winter let' that brightens faces of locals even if you are inimical, vegan and hardcore – the same 'back home' in the bush, where smiles are even fewer.

Colla Heights reprise two years later – first walk this route since foot infection

Sun copper-catch
Deeper seeming
Wild wren sermon
Quick enigmas

Hedge tunnellers
Emergent fed
Back without rhyme –
Climb-crawl rhythm

Stereo dumped
In blanked hawthorn,
Magpie startled
By bay deflects

Flight failure, flecked.
Fuchsias flower
January,
Albino dove.

But the talk is
Beast from the East
Will come again,
Remodulate.

Freshly toxic
Power poles on heights;
Fastnet leaping
Sea swan over

Long Island stretched
Flush to water –
Odour of dead
Posts makes different;

Each so many
Metres – bracken
And bramble
Underpinning

Seahills rise per
Demi cliff face
Steps robin names
Sound carriers

Beef Improver sacks
Strewn and football
Face on football
Still against wall

Two years after
Last walk when
Infection took hold
Legless sober

Future, and now
On point under
Heights new builds
Busting up stone

Mud on closed roads
To thwart expansion,
Tractors dragging
Trade against cow

Liberation bill
Boards in my head.
Return with farm
Chaptering farm

Around Colla
Rocks and nearer
The sea, over-
Looking Carraig-

Lea; kelp beds raise
Higher than tide
And a strand shapes
An otter biting

Down on thin foam.
Graves Roses shed
Is called into
Bog, a mansion

Rises with tall
Windows to take
Islands and bay –
Decorative pig

Sniffing the view.
Seabird that calls
Subwoofer to top
Range mate sails

The channel, way
Markers, the route
Unseasonal
Spectral disrupt-

Or – where so few
Trees so many
Down and sliced, stacked:
Ophelia?

And the smell of peat burning in hearths as smoke blurs the over-warm air, and the stench of treated power poles – replacements for those snapped off during 9 October's Storm Ophelia – and the peaks and troughs of gorts ('fields' in English) *claimed* from rock and bog. Houses in clusters like cluster flies, which find attics and the spaces inside walls to hibernate in, then get stimulated by central heating or just 'unseasonal weather' taking rooms above 12 degrees and bringing them out as spring. Houses in cow fields with roads running past emit waste into ditches – garden refuse dumped … red plants still in plastic pots, which will run away if they can take hold, Christmas tree branches strewn over fuchsia hedges already flowering. And lawn clippings from a sunny day's mowing, clotting the drains where cow shit from the road is also washed. This congruence of cohabitation. And all running down to the sea, the thin coasts of islands collecting the bits – farmland to edge of island and islands, to look out over the radioactive arms-ordnanced Atlantic Pond (or locally, the Celtic Sea). To look 'across' to a Newer World where so many have gone and still go, to big cities to make the best chance in a migration slot semi-pre-written along older diasporic lines, lines of identity we personally cannot ascribe to, not now in its official deployments of control. But is this because we are of the Australian migrational urge, drift, compulsion, escape, recall, return …?

Moving through the small city of Limerick yesterday and thinking of my great-great-grandmother Margaret, who at the age of twenty-two travelled to Richmond, Melbourne, in the search of a new life, but with little choice as well, famine migrant like so many of my ancestors, a single young woman on the rough boat, and her two marriages with one death and one abandonment (a sailor sailed the sea), and her children removed because she was out working and the 'authorities' split the children up and sent them as far away from Margaret and each other as they could, per policy (one to Ballarat … another to …. and so on), and the consequences of unbelonging. And in Limerick, the horses of Travellers grazing semi-free (untethered in the traffic) on patches of lawn between roads and alongside tenements, and the desire and ability to move on in presence and unfixedness, to unmake and remake the paradoxes of state control. But social and cultural controls exist, and to be shunned by one's own community is easiest and hardest at once – to be accepted here as a blowback, to be of the rural, and yet anathema. And at home, on stolen land watching the theft being rewritten as connection by others wanting to exonerate themselves, to alleviate their consciences, is as painful as it is understandable. Colonialism's many forms defeat the colonised again and again, even when they rise above it and redefine 'possession'.

~

We hear of boobook owls from Mum. Can we call the male and female and three maturing chicks a family? Should we? Well, they are together in a eucalypt planted by my brother below the York house, watched over by the mountain Walwalinj. The boobook owls themselves, young and old, daylight-watch, and they will decide how to share space and work space among themselves. Sometimes one lid is open, the other closed, mostly they stare aware waiting for evening. My cousin Ian, who helped save the noisy scrub-bird down at Two Peoples Bay back in the eighties, is apparently very interested because boobooks usually have a *maximum* of three chicks, and this is not common. Seeing the photos Mum took with a telescopic lens from the back of the house so as not to be intrusive, you get the feeling the boobooks are preparing to disperse, to realign in adjacent areas, make territory. They are working together to separate, but to remain in contact somehow. I send Frieda Mum's photos because she has been writing to me about raising the snowy owl chicks at her house in Wales. It is 38 degrees in York near Walwalinj today, and we hear that the boobooks are keeping still if wide-eyed in daylight, pulling night into focus. We are here, and we are there. The boobooks are emphatically there.

~

The farms around Schull are generally small, but big by non-colonial nineteenth-century standards. But what standard is that? Well, there are residues – how to piece a place together, how to deal with offspring to keep a farm intact. Migration. One hundred and forty-seven acres – 'large farm for sale'. Sixty-nine acres – 'roadside farm'. Most are around 30 acres. The milking shed is next to the town, right as you come into the village, next to new tourist accommodation, the 'Irish cottage experience', a few buildings from the new Centra. And so on it goes. But the cowsheds and the dairy keep working, and the old blokes in their flat caps doggedly drive through town on their tractors – pulling over in the main street to pass a greeting or a word … one arrives at the local doctor's surgery in his tractor, a younger man takes his kid to school. His wife might be a teacher there, she might be an artist, she might work on the farm, she might do 'home duties', she might be anyone at all. She might have answered an advert by a forty-five-year-old man for a wife – they still happen in the local papers. This is not quaint, this is life and residues and consequences and the reach of the church, for all liberations of newer generations. Ireland voted for gay marriage before Australia could manage to come to its collective senses. Change has come here, but change is also pushed back against, and the Church is a monolith, though other religious worship is increasingly finding a presence.

Language reclaiming and language wariness where language was oppressed is innate to so many issues of belonging. I still recoil when people suggest Irish is a second language to English. What is English, that linguistic holdall of so many languages, of expansionism? It too has its cores, and they are a long way from its imperialistic excesses. But it's a mistake to let a new nationalism arise out of any language – a language is a right, but not an exclusion. How does, say, enforced Irish in schools (along with enforced English) work with the reality and the need for transculturality, for refugees to be housed and respected, for new speakings of place? There is conflict but it has to be resolved, and this is known and part of the public discussion. But on the back roads with the mainly male road bowlers, sometimes, but not always (by no means always), different and more retrograde conversations take place. What is tradition what is culture and what is the reality of the 'others' in the twilight from whom the land was taken so many many centuries ago? Why do the spirits of those who came before – the people of the earliest tribes of Ireland, the pre-Celtic peoples, the Tuatha de Danann – distract and lure, drag someone into the twilight, take them into the other world? These are rural questions, like the heroics and land disputes and gender crises of *The Táin* – people and cows and markers. The borders between properties, families, insiders and outsiders, protectors and invaders, oppressed and oppressors, haves and have-nots, educated and uneducated (the demarcations of anti-colonial hedge schools), so many states of being. Ancestrally I am part of this, and not. Alienated. Or not. But I know it's all in flux, and has to be. And then there's the American fetishisation of a past Ireland that sees a vast flow of capital, but also stymies it in so many ways, especially as the market dictates commitment. Computer companies that rode the Celtic Tiger, for instance, cut back drastically with the economic crash.

A slurry wagon – that most pivotal and prized of West Cork farm possessions – is abandoned in a boggy field. Blackbirds and robins buzz around it, skipping across from a rocky-hedge mix, and rooks are perched on top. It doesn't look to be in bad repair, which means something has really gone wrong on this small farm. It was there two years ago, and the fact that it has submerged to the axles means it hasn't just been parked for later use. It has been abandoned. I don't know if it still carries its load of slurry, or not.

As part of the post-peat energy crisis – peat a carbon release of the first order – there's weirdly national talk about generating power from slurry. Brexit heads the news, then slurry.

~

When we arrived back here, there was a hammering sound close by for two days and nights. Then there was the sound of leaf blowers – at least two of them – for another day and a night. I couldn't work it out, and being susceptible to such repetitive noises, I found it hard to concentrate on things (though I don't get bothered by music or 'family' background noise at all), but then it clicked that the nearby wintering cow shed was being prepared (very late), and sure enough, I went and took a look, and there was the farmer and a mate, finishing things off. The cows in, locked away till spring turnout, unless the warmth stays or comes early. The cows we hear distressed at nights when their calves are separated off, separated off then taken to slaughter. There's nothing pretty about it, though the cows are unquestionably beautiful. I have written poems about at least some of those same cows – Charolais, unusual around here, where there are mainly Jersey cows. I have written about the cows of the dairy farm we lived next to in various states of distress, or enjoying their ruminations, at various times of year. It's a brute reality of dwelling in the rural anywhere.

A couple of nights ago I listened for two hours as a vixen screamed out for a mate. She was stationed below the second-storey bedroom window, her call-cry radiating out around fields, hedges, along the fast-moving stream, and even into the village proper, into the main street … the shrieks and howls, the complex linguistics of longing or need or calling or whatever dynamic it has and they have outside my anthropomorphic register. We often used to see and hear foxes between 2013 and 2016, and I hope it was one of those same foxes – its territory. Territory as time and space, as topography and growth, but also loss. So much gorse burning, so much grubbing out, so much poisoning, so much edging in of new buildings, even in these sparse places. And today I saw an entire hillside garden of about an acre dug out and just bare bloody clay – stale blood of history, of the funeral route down through Colla nearby … of stones not touched for decades, maybe centuries, maybe never. Grubbed up with a sign attached to a concrete post saying, 'Japanese knotweed – do not enter these premises, do not disturb ground etc.'

Almost dark at 4.40 p.m. Such short days. Humans haven't managed to mess with the length of days yet – but that's not completely true, is it? Virtually and literally. Chronology and revolution, spin and tilt – all are variables humans will play with. The atomics of the UK and France seep across water from different angles, different directions … traces here, too. A separate story, but not really. And the sun god Belenus will rise, and also the banshee – the female fox's call is described here (and in many places) as 'like a screaming banshee', and the excitement around Halloween and ghoulishness in Schull, a place like Skibbereen and many other towns and locales where people went green from eating dock during the famines, especially the Great Famine, and were buried in their thousands in cemeteries so very very small. Time and space – contradiction/s.

Tim is back from seeing his old schoolmate Rory, son of photographer John D'Alton, with whom I did a book of poetry and photos a few years back. We know the family – Bridie, Grainne and Emmet, as well as John and Rory, who own Newman's pub and coffee shop – from our years here. John and I once did a documentary for Irish television about our work together, and we are now thinking about islands of Roaring Water Bay, the Carberries, and the specifically local. Today, walking the Colla Highlands, I spent much time studying the low islands from different angles, thinking about light and water, reflection and absorption, about their bareness and rurality, about seals and their life outside human habitation. But humans and even the barest smallest island have been intimate for as far back as the bardic schools, and much much further back than that. They are a key to Casaubon's *All Mythologies*, but maybe ones he missed from his English colonial centre, from his desiring for a classical world which reached *here* in ways he couldn't see. Ptolemy, monks, and austerity … colonialisms and colonial resistances. The paradoxes, which do not include the *Star Wars* producers coopting (to the delight of many locals) the Brow Head cliffs near Crookhaven for their mock-up Millennium Falcon, or earlier, the beehive monk cells of the Skelligs protected by their 'wild seas'. The Force is economics.

Church bells still sound, and Christmas in the village was an intense mixture of Santa and Christ. Kids here cling to Santa to a very late age, as Tim will tell you. He wanted to let them know the truth, as it frustrated him, but as we said at the time, truth is relative. And that's a worrying gap to slip through, as different versions of being local and not local slip in and out of Irishness, which is not straightforward as a vehement destructive nationalism, because of the vehement destructive nationalism of a colonialism that can't quite be shaken. British numberplates on Range Rovers appear at regular intervals on the most isolated tracks, potential post-Brexit buyers scoping out the remaining bargains as the local economy lifts. A getaway will mean something different after the racist barriers of physicality and consciousness go up in Britain soon.

When we were down on the Beara Peninsula a couple of weeks ago, below the Daphne du Maurier–reconfigured Hungry Hill which was shrouded in cloud, as we wove our way through road bowling, as we entered Castletownbere and its sailor-inn sense of things, the fishing fleet tied up along the docks, Tracy reminded us all that Bere Island remained in British hands after independence as one of three Treaty Ports, and they didn't let go till 1938. A military island still, and always a rural one, and one of ancient standing stones and tombs. The identification of rural with military goes hand in hand with ambush sites and gaps and passes through the mountain ranges. Where the raddled black-faced sheep cling on to the rugged slopes, working the tufts of grass, their will like sinews wind-torn on the straggled fences which they breach regularly to get onto the roads, so too the psychology of war and resistance, of families, tribes and land.

Not 'valuable' land, but land of presence. That goes deep and is hard to get around.

The vegan billboards are a way through into something more fluid, more generous, and yet also respectful of the past. To liberate the cows from their servitude, to liberate the animals, is a vital step in the polyphonous rurality, in the collective belonging of life to a biosphere being emptied of life. Mostly, I'd like to believe the generational shift to veganism is permanent, as to not eat or use animals is getting to the very threads of existence, and that cultural choice and respect can be in dialogue, and that people's identification with country is a fact but not an exclusion. Complexity of presence is simple coexistence, and if the rural can make food that doesn't unmake life, that feeds without occluding, then we are moving towards wresting the planet back for itself. In seeking to achieve this, we will be moving away from our greed, our advertised mutually assured destruction, which we've allowed by underwriting governance we all try to benefit from, to extract the best for ourselves and our communities that we can, at costs to others, and at massive cost to animal and indeed plant life. Think outside property, outside ownership, and share what's to be shared, and respect what can't be shared. Let things grow in their own way – not all needs to be husbanded and controlled.

Farming is not a right to destroy in the name of feeding. Farming that damages for short-term gain, even within the protection racket of 'traditional farming practice' – short-term might be long-term alteration ranging from the clearing of the Western Australian wheatbelt to the GM corn crops of Ohio and the draining of turloughs in Ireland. The farmer is not a sacred being; the farmer is most often about profit at the expense of other life. The best environmental *argument* deployed by Queensland pastoralists, as they clear tens of thousands of hectares of native vegetation, is that because they 'work in conjunction with nature', they 'naturally' want what's best for the land because they are both in sync with it (yet they live on it because it is stolen … they are false custodians, not true custodians) and their livelihoods rely on its wellbeing – this is untrue. Their aims are short-term, or only generational in the sense of their own families, and are part of a profit-loss gain scenario to increase the material wellbeing of themselves and their own. For the non-Indigenous Australian farmer, there is no inherent totemic speaking of land to person or vice versa beyond the romantic notion of connection – if there were, the fate of non-human animals and plants would be uppermost in their minds. I remind myself of this constantly – it's easy to forget.

~

Tractors. A tractor driven along the main road from a distant town in the Burren to Galway city. A long trailback of traffic behind it on the narrow, winding macadam, potholed and squeezed between stacked karst stone walls (those claimings of space, relevance and authority, which equivocate between the temporary and the permanent … the land itself induces as recuperative ambiguity). Oncoming traffic slows and edges past, for the tractor's wheels occupy a band on the far side of the dividing line. The driver, perched up high, drives against opposition, each revolution of the great rear tyres a statement, a tale adding up to an epic. In summer here down in Schull when the hay is being cut and baled and carted, or cut and piled high in wagons and carted to silage pits for covering, tractors move constantly through the village, down past Rosewood from the high place of the monks into the main street; farms are located field by field across the area. Students home from university are working their vacation for family, and the tractors are being driven at speeds they're not used to – young men and women throwing them around to get the job done as fast as possible, phones to their ears or earphones in, one hand on the wheel in high range dragging a load against the gearing. I am reminded of family at wheatbelt harvests, all coming out to move field bins, deliver food and drink, ensure the water truck is ready. It's practical, dusty, tiring and irritating.

Yes, my uncle taught me to drive a tractor when I was about nine or ten, not that much later than when he taught me to drive the ute. Jam tins over vertical exhaust pipes, hessian wheat sacks on seats, and how to put on and take off duel wheels. And how to use that PTO with a belt to the chaff cutter. These weren't just exercises to keep the kid occupied on weekend and holiday visits – for me they were core to understanding a world outside the city, a world that fed other worlds. It was enthralling and also rebarbative. I was lucky in that I was warmly welcomed in, but also fed practical and critical information. It came with a morality, but I was able to add to that morality and come to my own decisions. The tractor was the symbol of fertility but also control, and I wrestled with it. On the huge farm my father managed for a Perth millionaire, where he looked after the heavy machinery and his wife did the bookkeeping, I confronted and was confronted by tractors so huge they changed my sense of the proportions of the world – what it took to feed the world's population, and the damage that could be done to the surface, the depth to which it could be altered. Tractors were vastness, and those massive Steiger Panthers and huge Cases changed the case itself. They were tautologies. They were all adjectives and nouns designed to put verbs into action. And they are a refrain through this versioning of a world.

The first old tractor I drove, hitting the pedal hard with my small foot on its short leg, almost standing, a double pedal – one pedal for each rear wheel with a bridge across the two – and hitting it hard almost standing up and it hitting the metal … pedal to the metal … and the turning with wheel and turning with brake … turn on a pin in the mud, wheels turning wheels unturning turning turning, making a path to the path, across the furrows cut earlier, reshaping the land. It's all come back to me, I could do the tractor work now, right now, after all these decades – it's visceral, it's imprinted … I can't disregard it. The tractor is an extension of me even if I reject it. Each wheel turning independently, then together, compensating for the ground, the ground worked and altered and colonising and abused and reshaped and nurtured into a bizarre faux fertility. This is me belonging and unbelonging, caught for thirty k's behind an unpassable tractor on the coast road from Kinvarra to Galway city driven by a fellow imprinted stranger who is no stranger to this road nor the country around it in the country my ancestors fled from or were driven from by colonisers to become colonisers. Own up to it, consider the costs of imprinting, the pyrography. I feel it.

Epilogue

It's a polyphonous conversation, but it's one with absolute closure if we're not careful. And with every cell of my being, every abstraction of my psyche, I reject closure. *Carpe diem* should have nothing to do with testosterone, conflict and power – it should have to do with immediacy and obligation. We have an obligation to *everything*. And as I write this, Tim, who turns sixteen tomorrow, comes in to say he's seen the Eurasian oystercatcher in breeding plumage down near the Schull Pier again – a couple of weeks ago he saw oystercatcher chicks! Their breeding season here is March to June, yet these sightings have occurred in December and January. Out of kilter, disturbed, trying to make life happen and function. They are doing all they can against all we throw at them.

And to get 'back home' from this home in Schull, to our displaced and displacing home of Jam Tree Gully, back to the intensity of our unaligned belonging, we add to that disturbance. Imprint. Air travel is a fait accompli for the planet. Cause and effect. Consequences. We need to recognise this and act to thwart the closure, to repair, and yes, to *heal*. To step back in our stepping out. 'Heal' is an easy word, but in reality, an uncomfortable one for so many of us, it would seem. We all have choices to make. Next week, before we arrive home, Guru will deliver a load of fresh drinking water for the top gravity-fed tank. Daytime temps are reaching the forties, even the mid-forties. We will need the water, we need the covered water supply over-arched by York gums, we need the buried pipe that takes the water down the hill to the additional tap Guru inserted over the kitchen sink. Two taps, two qualities of water. We need all the water we can get, and when we have it, to use it sparingly and respectfully. And here, in Schull, it rains soft or hard and regularly. For now.

Poems from central Ohio

Peonies, 105 Brooklyn Street, Gambier

These peonies being like nothing else,
we have only the word itself – or conveyance
of the storm, location, centrifuge of sparklers
wrapped in crinoline, synthetic flowers
my grandmother used to style for shows
of the flourishing;
                                        tossed up in green plumage,
coeval with blood red or eye-white, contesting
the blue covering of carbon and green plastic
black on the edge that keeps the tomato seed
of an earlier season from rejoining the soil,
tossing up a fruit to parody peonies
in lush despoiling, shagged in pile-driving rain,
bereft of prayers of adoration
that make sentience bearable;
                                                            I tug a splash
of colour like a banner across my going,
to forget the mower cutting down
the spears of asparagus until the crowns
are dry while the ground is sodden, these vegetable
contradictions when the village encloses,
refuses to let you out no matter how far from peonies
you leave your calling cards:
                                                        those remembered flowerings
steeped in emblems and perfumes, as blank
as someone else's ribbons won
before you were born, colour fading
tantamount to facilitating sparrows and robins,

as rare as the imprint of iris,
each to his own, hanging about like solar panels
in the filling dark, collecting what's not caught up
in peonies as implosive as murmur.

In expectation of the turkey vulture

There's no bird for comparison:
shrunken head, embalmer of routes
veined by road surfaces, thin-on or rich,
as temporal: the hurting prayer,
narcissus-drop when thermals
lack charisma: how can we think
of anything but war? My summer
birthday in the Avon Valley
is Groundhog Day here,
and a malignant weatherman
tells me it will always
be that way, wherever I go:
                                        once here,
you've been got at.
                                The turkey vulture
only flies over Gambier in summer,
picking at the dead souls
of small birds, drop-ins by movie stars
and rock icons. Rodents
brisk in reactive corn fields.
I can't show connection
no matter the accuracy
of gauge or euphemism,
and increasingly nowhere
where seasons don't meet
along rippled, disturbed edges,
as much carrion laid out for removal
as anywhere in extremis:
a crow hacks at the corpse
of all passers-by, as if
it were yesterday.

Moment in the sun: A georgic …

The long winter
makes its own language:
snow-dump, door-jam,
dirty snow
compacted
on road's edge.
Let me tell you
how they cultivate
spring here: the war
is silenced,
the houses shift
comfortably
from white to pink,
and Edward Scissorhands
comes down from the castle
of American Gothic.
Bright but incredulous
smiles shimmer
momentarily
with a rumour
from elsewhere:
they find it hard to believe,
and if true, then it must be
all for the good.
The bluebirds are out,
raccoons culled by the road,
the groundhog
locked up in repetitions
of shadow that won't go away,
no matter how bright
the sun.

Yellow ribbons

Yellow ribbons
around town trees
in the dying
centre of Mount Vernon,
all trade moving
out to strip malls,
are the end of theory:
the signifier corrupted,
imperial markers
of loss in conquest,
or potential of spontaneous
and simultaneous
daffodils sparking
along the road edge,
bordering our place
without fences,
our place that's owned
by others who let us know
with glances
through the window,
imprints in still
snow-tender grass,
loud smiles
as the oil flows
like Coke,
like Seven-Up.

On the absence of the actual: Four manifestations

1.
Fields without fences
promulgate: hills leaven
crests and lulls, fundamental
to families; tanks crenellate
pressure gauges, pipework, pumps
counterweighting sheets and hollows,
pressure points,
solid, liquid, gas: interchanges.

2.
Beavers pinpointing wetlands
to dam against hunter and farmer,
interiorising Candlemass;
groundhogs
charging shadows,
trashed on roadsides,
making TV appearances.
That youth camp in Mohican Forest –
a detention centre, percussion
capping tension between canopy
of pines and birches, surreptitiously
splitting rocks, as far back
as an ice age.

3.
And here, in Holmes County,
the elongation of an error
backtracks prayer:

without electricity, despair
works salt and rain into highways,
and the atheist
believes diurnally.

4.
Narrowing from base
prospect of fire, lookout
towers over forest,
blind spots of redemption
make loss complex
in ice growth,
so far below, shaped by vertigo
and the forest floor.

Trauma

The snow is devastating; moods
tighten, it bites insoles; it lattices

around dirt rippled by snow plough,
complicates near salt crystals, furnaces,

locales of intensest melts; these patterns
I watch to distract and wonder at; super-

structures, gantries, amphitheatres
glazed thinly over, thinner

than a single water molecule
though lustrous as glass panels,

tiny in church windows, shattered
in the murdered city, bombs

drifting down like flurries – up hill
and out of town, slicing across black ice.

Edge-effect requiem for Tom Bigelow

Pushkin was sparse in his use of metaphor.
Should I talk to you of the dynamics,
the I-You, addressee, addressed?
Build the text by metonym?
Boots, walk, grip, track, map.
I read Thomas Hardy, and he teaches me
to write regardless: connect, disconnect.
It's there like Sensurround,
the island of scrub within the field,
birds edging water. One long walk
about and beyond the property
that held conflicting histories: knowing
it would have to go, be broken up –
small allotments and rich houses
already restricting its breath.
The notes I wrote for you – to react,
remake, transcribe. Field notes
drawn like wire, or splinters, or vapour
over the pond. In images, your own,
tacked together in company. Transparent
leaves of a late winter tree, a tree
stuck – or persisting – in early fall.
Maybe through all seasons, never
growing older. Wild turkeys
on the fringe, heat in the edge
effect. You expected them, and they
were there. It's reassuring, even now.
A kite tangled in undergrowth,
hooked up in the waste of crop.

Untangled, gathered up. We,
the public, and publicly: to celebrate,
witness, recognise, never begrudge.
In this, not simply let it pass, or let it be,
but still and unobtrusively. Confidence.
Denial a trail that is checked by mud,
a fence, a roadway. A brilliant stand of maples.
Was it your brother who could tell us
every variety? To say: we believe,
you make belief in me, like internal rhymes,
caesuras mid-line. Those shorter
unplanned walks – vignettes,
some prosaic. Moments in a cold city.
Don't let it get to you. Don't.
A sympathy where irony wore humour away,
exposed a core. Communications interest
us: no person less military,
and yet the memory of comradeship
mattered: recast, recalled when the thin body
of a squirrel was found in the weeds.
Alone, yes, it is good to have company.
We don't die alone. These are not
reminiscences, nor comforts
in a partial narrative. The death
of those close to you is an absorption
of parallels: how's your situation
vis-à-vis ours? Have things improved?
What fills the veins of the unseen body?
What do you choose not to take with you?
Absences, promised walks that never
eventuate but verbally mapped,

threaded wherever others walk?
Nodal points of cardinal and blue jay,
like schematics of a ghost train's route
lighting up in a control room
some way off – removed but close.
The deer came right up to the porch light,
looked past the reflections. We kept
our blinds drawn, though wanted
to open them. Orientate. Compass
of hooves. A refusal to let the passages
close over with snow. And my
first time there – the past
as forgotten in this animation –
here, now! – no darkness in headlights
as a spotted skunk ambles across
the bitumen. You let it pass –
softly, invisibly respecting, invisibly
announcing. Sighting. Sounds gather
in company – to charge the undulating,
throaty hills with crossing, with voice trails
and recordings of deciduous lines
restrung as images, stories of far away
made elsewhere and resonant,
where edges are verdant
and life-supporting.

Ground cover looms large

Ground cover looms large
inside the humidifier, as Passover
casts shadows and red birds

make lustre a fallacy:
lost in green definition.
The wood's uprights

seem busier, and the glass-mad
woodpecker surges: mnemonic
daylight, activity of sunspots.

It began before this,
but intensity is four days'
absence when it all turns:

no eyes anchored by clasps
or optic nerves, just free:
roaming, unhinged

in the picturesque.
All this activity
needs constant input,

there's no stopping,
no hesitation. Humidity
alone can't carry

between charge and contact,
and prayers get caught up,
deflected elsewhere:

encryption lost
when heard in public,
retold as something else.

Insomniac revelations of the elusive subject

1.
I take nothing new to this subject,
as snow builds, a meniscus at the base
of black walnuts and headstones.
The ladder-backed woodpecker is louder
now, after the flu. At night,
everything so colourful in the dark, so loud.

2.
Anachronous, these narratives
we subject ourselves to thorns and welters
of bird spores: sounds in chromes of branches,
incoming maps and photos. Other than myself,
I travel. Noticed out a window, or in someone else's
sense of culinary, as if harvested locally.

3.
No primary names catalogue the ships
that pass as cars through the Cut; papyrus
worked like nicotine patches marshalled
on ceilings, along field edges, cosmopolitan
clearings. Why declare this fit for consumption?
Behest of termites in woody houses?

4.
I forgo my tendency to description:
the streaked bird that is burnt quickly –
stubble quail – whistling 'chu-chi-wit';
as real as this is, as real to shot or parsimony
when thin in summer, this caught wide-lidded,
or caught on a bridge when water strains.

Skunk stigma

It's gunshot we know in the demystifying haze
of morning, the concentrating light,
whether overcast or not; the chemical is: N-
                                        butyl mercaptan,
touched in the woods, go there in sickness
or not at all, the fused shadows of layered birds,
the blue jay and cardinal just grey and ill-shaped
rapid on the undulations of a grassy surface:
afternoon storms intensify growth, the ponderous
carrion-driven searching of the skunk, in the headlights
that's night or a reconfiguring. Without rhythm
memory seems not to fall into place:
the tail where the head should be,
scent and inhalation: perpetual mobility,
the car, creating desolation and invulnerability?
We make with our own hands the man with peak-hat,
sit-on-lawnmower – garage-seller of guns
and bows, owner of that secret golf habit. He read that 'things
were moving'. The stamping of paws,
clicking of teeth, preference to avoid
confrontation. He read in the collusion
of m-sounds, the intention: modular,
modality, molecular, meretricious, mortuary,
manic, mantra, mesmeric, mimetic:
                                        here, our fears,
skunk killer out there
in the morning, aggressive dogs, his frustration
with the educated, the middle classes: projectivist
verse, Frankenthaler paintings. Skunk blood

on log, in bower, the openings
beneath houses, marks in the brain. The shooter warns us:
after dogs, fear skunks most
when it comes to rabies, fear
stigma.

Sludge

Driving somewhere, anywhere
there's little or no sludge: to wheel the pram,
and take our daughter skating. Winter's
getting to all of us, and the town
is not municipally minded;
                                                  out at Apple Valley
there's probably a private covered
walk trail for kids who want to skate
                                                                  and prams
that need to be pushed so the baby
can take in what's fresh of the air.
Enclosed, the gated community
knows no wars though pays
for the purchase of military equipment,
some sons enlist, but as officers;
the snow sludge runs and lifts
the asphalt from road surfaces
in all neighbourhoods. Dead animals
and attendant crows are making appearances,
a bird of prey flies overhead
with a grey corn stalk
for a nest high above
the madding crowd.

A maple tree

1. Fall
Planted memorandum,
this beginning for me –
here, then – the leaves
frothing – vatic –
lifeblood: used
so much here, a flavouring
of local distinction.

2. Winter
Negated, rough lawn
cuts through snow, evening
lightless; but bright
this stark signal, prayer
deeply scored, figurative
stray leaf falling
in perfect impression.

3. Spring (Now)
Offensive, lush sun
coaxing nightgrowth
at three in the afternoon:
seven days of rain,
diminishing warmth
though the tree inclines
towards a temperate
season; side effect
of commemoration.

4. Summer
Interlude as inset
or insert in the commonplace
book chipped out of bark
by a ladderback, lured
by insects or aspects
of childhood we turn over
quietly, when and where
our companions weren't there,
in the kind of light
only detectable
by warmth, then heat.

Red Barn Truisms

1.
I read in a town a couple of hours away
and am told of a rash of barn burnings.
The barns are red, are built by many.
The barns are red, fall to a single flame.

2.
We hear of arms caches among hay
and animals, and grey snow mutes
the response of hardy winter birds –
chickadees, nuthatches, snow buntings.
A grackle and a merlin, a rumour
and someone or something running
through the cornstalks in endless
night, snowdrifts disturbed on hills.
Home, home soon – past Big Bear
closed down car park parody of space,
emptiness. Can you tell maples,
red dogwoods and black walnuts in this?

3.
To say I did, we did, is to say it's memory.
But the great blast that killed the house,
that drove us under heaps of blankets,
baby at your breast, the river and ice
warm in his blood, your milk,
to retreat to the Inn and hole up,
to see icicles conduct epiphanies.
To see all that, to have reached out

to those who held the power.
Never to fall asleep as the body
loses hold of its temperature.

4.
Black ice slide coming home
the back way – past the house
of a thousand planted pines,
into the T-junction, a cosmopolitan
moment of mortality.

5.
As war is made to happen I am in St Louis
and you're in Gambier with the children –
silent vigil on Middle Path, newborn
in the pram already knowing trees
will bloom, the peaceful gathering
of strength. I give a lecture on pacifism
and talk with a woman who has lost
her son before elegies of war are written.

6.
I walk along the Kokosing from Mount Vernon to Gambier
and back again with our daughter. Across the bridge, the river
lightly and gently whitewaters a bend, flatly foaming.
Splintered trees are portals. People pass and we know them
slightly.

How we fit in the silence is a puzzle we won't solve.
We talk like that, walking, difficult walking. Listening
more than talking, the sun low to the horizon, lighting
the woods. At school, a teacher brands a student
on the arm in the name of God. There's that, too.

7.
Head of a deer lolling
off the backless pick-up,
less blood than you'd think.
And killing with rules
and all the rules
broken, you'd think.

8.
'I have a son in the military.'
And that's that. Whatever your politics.

9.
Painted ladies munition wealth
houses where the underground railroad
ran on through – the duality or contradiction
or logical history of the 'most Republican
town in America'? On the edge of the corporation,
slow down past the bar where things are sorted out.
Or, better still, to the health-food store across from the tyre store
where the Mennonite woman discusses life as if it matters.

10.
Daniel Decatur Emmett.
'Dixie'.
Blackface.
Minstrel.
There's a sign.
Students talk about it,
So do I.

11.
A neighbour, a poet who can write
lines of American like a Roman poet,
could only have written the groundhog
climbing a tree and going out on a limb
to fall and break it. Seasonal change
was part of its prosody, I think.

12.
Who was it offered me a red barn to write in?
I am not sure if I've got it right, but there's a vague
memory I am trying to reconstruct. A red barn
in a field of snow, of cornstalks, of edges.
There's a photo, but it might be of a different
red barn. It had lightning conductors on top
and dropped snow quickly. Once, so far far away,
I was struck by lightning twice. There were
more than two conductors to earth truth.

Acknowledgements

Thanks to all those herein who have given permissions for their names to be used, and special thanks to Tracy Ryan, Tim Kinsella, Wendy Kinsella, John 'Guru' Askham, Stephen Kinsella, Dzu, Lorraine Wheeler, and Gerry Wheeler. Also thanks to special Jill Bialosky who engendered the idea of this memoir, and gave much early feedback, to Rachel Bin Salleh for reading an early draft, to Barry Scott for believing and fully supporting and seeing it through, and intense thanks to Penelope Goodes, my editor on this volume, who has given so much and been so rigorous in her care for its final version. Thanks to Curtin University, where I am Professor of Literature and Environment, and for a Curtin Research Fellowship, and to Churchill College, Cambridge University, where I am a Fellow of many years now. I thank Kenyon College, especially the English Department for our many years there, and the community of Schull, West Cork, Ireland. I thank many in the Cambridge community for ongoing dialogue and support. I acknowledge in total respect and admiration and gratitude, the Ballardong Noongar people, from whose land I write, and Yamaji people on whose land I have also lived and written. I apologise for the displacements my rural living has been part of, and hope for fairness and justice in all things. Some of the poems included have been published in earlier books of mine.

John Kinsella is the author of over thirty books. His many awards include the Australian Prime Minister's Literary Award for Poetry, the Victorian premier's Award for Poetry, the John Bray Award for Poetry, the Judith Wright Calanthe Award for Poetry and the Western Australian Premier's Award for Poetry (three times). His most recent works include the poetry volumes *Drowning in Wheat: Selected Poems* (Picador, 2016), and *On the Outskirts* (UQP, 2017), Story collections include *Crow's Breath* (Transit Lounge 2015) and *Old Growth* (Transit Lounge, 2017) and a recent critical volume is *Polysituatedness* (Manchester University Press, 2017). Recent novels are *Lucida Intervalla* (UWAP, 2018) and *Hollow Earth* (Transit Lounge, 2019). He often works in collaboration with other poets, artists, musicians, and activists. With Tracy Ryan he is the co-editor of *The Fremantle Press Anthology of The Western Australian Poetry* (2017). He is a Fellow of Churchill College, Cambridge University, and Professor of Literature and Environment at Curtin University, Western Australia. He lives on Ballardong Noongar land at Jam Tree Gully in the Western Australian wheatbelt, and went to high school on Yamaji land in Geraldton, and has also lived in USA, UK, Ireland and other zones.